CASENOTE LEGAL BRIEFS

CIVIL PROCEDURE

Adaptable to courses utilizing **Yeazell's** casebook
on Civil Procedure

NORMAN S. GOLDENBERG, SENIOR EDITOR
PETER TENEN, MANAGING EDITOR

STAFF WRITERS

JEAN CHRISTINE YOUKER
BILL CARERO
RICHARD BRODY
JAN JONES
STEPHEN BENARDO
TINA ESSER
DAVID GYEPES
DIANE JONES
KEMP RICHARDSON

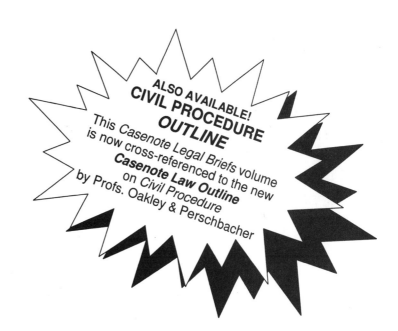

ALSO AVAILABLE!
CIVIL PROCEDURE
OUTLINE
This Casenote Legal Briefs volume
is now cross-referenced to the new
Casenote Law Outline
on Civil Procedure
by Profs. Oakley & Perschbacher

PUBLISHED BY   CASENOTES PUBLISHING CO., INC. 1640 5th ST., SUITE 208 SANTA MONICA, CA 90401

ISBN 0-87457-016-6

FORMAT FOR THE CASENOTE LEGAL BRIEF

PALSGRAF v. LONG ISLAND R.R. CO.
Injured bystander (P) v. Railroad company (D)
N.Y. Ct. App., 248 N.Y. 339, 162 N.E. 99 (1928).

PARTY ID: Quick identification of the relationship between the parties. ◄——

NATURE OF CASE: This section identifies the form of action (e.g., breach of contract, negligence, battery), the type of proceeding (e.g., demurrer, appeal from trial court's jury instructions) or the relief sought (e.g., damages, injunction, criminal sanctions).

NATURE OF CASE: Appeal from judgment affirming verdict for plaintiff seeking damages for personal injury.

FACT SUMMARY: This is included to refresh the student's memory and can be used as a quick reminder of the facts.

FACT SUMMARY: Helen Palsgraf (P) was injured on R.R.'s (D) train platform when R.R.'s (D) guard helped a passenger aboard a moving train, causing his package to fall on the tracks. The package contained fireworks which exploded, creating a shock that tipped a scale onto Palsgraf (P).

CONCISE RULE OF LAW: Summarizes the general principle of law that the case illustrates. It may be used for instant recall of the court's holding and for classroom discussion or home review.

CONCISE RULE OF LAW: The risk reasonably to be perceived defines the duty to be obeyed.

FACTS: This section contains all relevant facts of the case, including the contentions of the parties and the lower court holdings. It is written in a logical order to give the student a clear understanding of the case. The plaintiff and defendant are identified by their proper names throughout and are always labeled with a (P) or (D).

FACTS: Helen Palsgraf (P) purchased a ticket to Rockaway Beach from R.R. (D) and was waiting on the train platform. As she waited, two men ran to catch a train that was pulling out from the platform. The first man jumped aboard, but the second man, who appeared as if he might fall, was helped aboard by the guard on the train who had kept the door open so they could jump aboard. A guard on the platform also helped by pushing him onto the train. The man was carrying a package wrapped in newspaper. In the process, the man dropped his package, which fell on the tracks. The package contained fireworks and exploded. The shock of the explosion was apparently of great enough strength to tip over some scales at the other end of the platform, which fell on Palsgraf (P) and injured her. A jury awarded her damages, and R.R. (D) appealed.

ISSUE: The issue is a concise question that brings out the essence of the opinion as it relates to the section of the casebook in which the case appears. Both substantive and procedural issues are included if relevant to the decision.

ISSUE: Does the risk reasonably to be perceived define the duty to be obeyed?

HOLDING AND DECISION: This section offers a clear and in-depth discussion of the rule of the case and the court's rationale. It is written in easy-to-understand language and answers the issue(s) presented by applying the law to the facts of the case. When relevant, it includes a thorough discussion of the exceptions to the case as listed by the court, any major cites to other cases on point, and the names of the judges who wrote the decisions.

HOLDING AND DECISION: (Cardozo, C.J.) Yes. The risk reasonably to be perceived defines the duty to be obeyed. If there is no foreseeable hazard to the injured party as the result of a seemingly innocent act, the act does not become a tort because it happened to be a wrong as to another. If the wrong was not willful, the plaintiff must show that the act as to her had such great and apparent possibilities of danger as to entitle her to protection. Negligence in the abstract is not enough upon which to base liability. Negligence is a relative concept, evolving out of the common law doctrine of trespass on the case. To establish liability, the defendant must owe a legal duty of reasonable care to the injured party. A cause of action in tort will lie where harm, though unintended, could have been averted or avoided by observance of such a duty. The scope of the duty is limited by the range of danger that a reasonable person could foresee. In this case, there was nothing to suggest from the appearance of the parcel or otherwise that the parcel contained fireworks. The guard could not reasonably have had any warning of a threat to Palsgraf (P), and R.R. (D) therefore cannot be held liable. Judgment is reversed in favor of R.R. (D).

CONCURRENCE / DISSENT: All concurrences and dissents are briefed whenever they are included by the casebook editor.

DISSENT: (Andrews, J.) The concept that there is no negligence unless R.R. (D) owes a legal duty to take care as to Palsgraf (P) herself is too narrow. Everyone owes to the world at large the duty of refraining from those acts that may unreasonably threaten the safety of others. If the guard's action was negligent as to those nearby, it was also negligent as to those outside what might be termed the "danger zone." For Palsgraf (P) to recover, R.R.'s (D) negligence must have been the proximate cause of her injury, a question of fact for the jury.

EDITOR'S ANALYSIS: This last paragraph gives the student a broad understanding of where the case "fits in" with other cases in the section of the book and with the entire course. It is a hornbook-style discussion indicating whether the case is a majority or minority opinion and comparing the principal case with other cases in the casebook. It may also provide analysis from restatements, uniform codes, and law review articles. The editor's analysis will prove to be invaluable to classroom discussion.

EDITOR'S ANALYSIS: The majority defined the limit of the defendant's liability in terms of the danger that a reasonable person in defendant's situation would have perceived. The dissent argued that the limitation should not be placed on liability, but rather on damages. Judge Andrews suggested that only injuries that would not have happened but for R.R.'s (D) negligence should be compensable. Both the majority and dissent recognized the policy-driven need to limit liability for negligent acts, seeking, in the words of Judge Andrews, to define a framework "that will be practical and in keeping with the general understanding of mankind." The Restatement (Second) of Torts has accepted Judge Cardozo's view..

CROSS-REFERENCE TO OUTLINE: Wherever possible, following each case is a cross-reference linking the subject matter of the issue to the appropriate place in the *Casenote Law Outline*, which provides further information on the subject.

[For more information on foreseeability, see Casenote Law Outline on Torts, Chapter 8, § II. 2., Proximate Cause.]

QUICKNOTES: Conveniently defines legal terms found in the case and summarizes the nature of any statutes, codes, or rules referred to in the text.

QUICKNOTES

FORESEEABILITY - The reasonable anticipation that damage is a likely result from certain acts or omissions.

NEGLIGENCE - Failure to exercise that degree of care which a person of ordinary prudence would exercise under similiar circumstances.

PROXIMATE CAUSE - Something which in natural and continuous sequence, unbroken by any new intervening cause, produces an event, and without which the injury would not have occurred.

NOTE TO STUDENT

OUR GOAL. It is the goal of Casenotes Publishing Company, Inc. to create and distribute the finest, clearest and most accurate legal briefs available. To this end, we are constantly seeking new ideas, comments and constructive criticism. As a user of *Casenote Legal Briefs,* your suggestions will be highly valued. With all correspondence, please include your complete name, address, and telephone number, including area code and zip code.

THE TOTAL STUDY SYSTEM. Casenote Legal Briefs are just one part of the Casenotes TOTAL STUDY SYSTEM. Most briefs are (wherever possible) cross-referenced to the appropriate *Casenote Law Outline,* which will elaborate on the issue at hand. By purchasing a Law Outline together with your Legal Brief, you will have both parts of the Casenotes TOTAL STUDY SYSTEM. (See the advertising in the front of this book for a list of Law Outlines currently available.)

A NOTE ABOUT LANGUAGE. Please note that the language used in *Casenote Legal Briefs* in reference to minority groups and women reflects terminology used within the historical context of the time in which the respective courts wrote the opinions. We at Casenotes Publishing Co., Inc. are well aware of and very sensitive to the desires of all people to be treated with dignity and to be referred to as they prefer. Because such preferences change from time to time, and because the language of the courts reflects the time period in which opinions were written, our case briefs will not necessarily reflect contemporary references. We appreciate your understanding and invite your comments.

A NOTE REGARDING NEW EDITIONS. As of our press date, this Casenote Legal Brief is current and includes briefs of all cases in the current version of the casebook, divided into chapters that correspond to that edition of the casebook. However, occasionally a new edition of the casebook comes out in the interim, and sometimes the casebook author will make changes in the sequence of the cases in the chapters, add or delete cases, or change the chapter titles. Should you be using this Legal Brief in conjuction with a casebook that was issued later than this book, you can receive all of the newer cases, which are available free from us, by sending in the "Supplement Request Form" in this section of the book (please follow all instructions on that form). The Supplement(s) will contain all the missing cases, and will bring your Casenote Legal Brief up to date.

EDITOR'S NOTE. Casenote Legal Briefs are intended to supplement the student's casebook, not replace it. There is no substitute for the student's own mastery of this important learning and study technique. If used properly, *Casenote Legal Briefs* are an effective law study aid that will serve to reinforce the student's understanding of the cases.

REF. #1046-96-899

SUPPLEMENT REQUEST FORM

At the time this book was printed, a brief was included for every major case in the casebook and for every existing supplement to the casebook. However, if a new supplement to the casebook (or a new edition of the casebook) has been published since this publication was printed and if that casebook supplement (or new edition of the casebook) was available for sale at the time you purchased this Casenote Legal Briefs book, we will be pleased to provide you the new cases contained therein AT NO CHARGE when you send us a stamped, self-addressed envelope.

TO OBTAIN YOUR FREE SUPPLEMENT MATERIAL, **YOU MUST FOLLOW THE INSTRUCTIONS BELOW PRECISELY** OR YOUR REQUEST WILL NOT BE ACKNOWLEDGED!

1. Please check if there is in fact an existing supplement and, if so, that the cases are not already included in your Casenote Legal Briefs. Check the main table of cases as well as the supplement table of cases, if any.

2. **REMOVE THIS ENTIRE PAGE FROM THE BOOK.** You MUST send this ORIGINAL page to receive your supplement. This page acts as your proof of purchase and contains the reference number necessary to fill your supplement request properly. No photocopy of this page or written request will be honored or answered. Any request from which the reference number has been removed, altered or obliterated will not be honored.

3. Prepare a STAMPED self-addressed envelope for return mailing. Be sure to use a FULL SIZE (9 X 12) ENVELOPE (MANILA TYPE) so that the supplement will fit and AFFIX ENOUGH POSTAGE TO COVER 3 OZ. **ANY SUPPLEMENT REQUEST NOT ACCOMPANIED BY A STAMPED SELF-ADDRESSED ENVELOPE WILL ABSOLUTELY NOT BE FILLED OR ACKNOWLEDGED.**

4. MULTIPLE SUPPLEMENT REQUESTS: If you are ordering more than one supplement, we suggest that you enclose a stamped, self-addressed envelope for each supplement requested. If you enclose only one envelope for a multiple request, your order may not be filled immediately should any supplement which you requested still be in production. In other words, your order will be held by us until it can be filled completely.

5. Casenotes prints two kinds of supplements. A "New Edition" supplement is issued when a new edition of your casebook is published. A "New Edition" supplement gives you all major cases found in the new edition of the casebook which did not appear in the previous edition. A regular "supplement" is issued when a paperback supplement to your casebook is published. If the box at the lower right is stamped, then the "New Edition" supplement was provided to your bookstore and is *not* available from Casenotes; however, Casenotes will still send you any regular "supplements" which have been printed either before or after the new edition of your casebook appeared and which, according to the reference number at the top of this page, have not been included in this book. If the box is not stamped, Casenotes will send you any supplements, "New Edition" and/or regular, needed to completely update your Casenote Legal Briefs.

 NOTE: **REQUESTS FOR SUPPLEMENTS WILL NOT BE FILLED UNLESS THESE INSTRUCTIONS ARE COMPLIED WITH!**

6. Fill in the following information:

Full title of CASEBOOK _____ **CIVIL PROCEDURE**

CASEBOOK author's name _____ **Yeazell**

Copyright year of new edition or new paperback supplement _____

Name and location of bookstore where this Casenote Legal Brief was purchased _____

Name and location of law school you attend _____

Any comments regarding Casenote Legal Briefs _____

NOTE: IF THIS BOX IS STAMPED, NO NEW EDITION SUPPLEMENT CAN BE OBTAINED BY MAIL.

PUBLISHED BY CASENOTES PUBLISHING CO., INC. 1640 5th ST, SUITE 208 SANTA MONICA, CA 90401

PLEASE PRINT

NAME _____ PHONE _____ DATE _____

ADDRESS/CITY/STATE/ZIP _____

Announcing the First *Totally Integrated* Law Study System

CASENOTE LEGAL BRIEFS

CLASSROOM PREPARATION ▼

▼ **EXAM PREPARATION**

Legal Briefs
summarize cases
in your casebook
to improve
comprehension
and recall.

Case briefs
cross-referenced
to *Outline* for
further discussion
of cases & law.

CASEBOOK

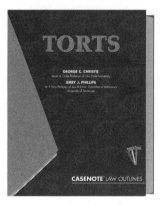

CASENOTE LAW OUTLINES

Outline cross-referenced to most
casebooks to help prepare for class & exams.

▼ **PERIODIC REVIEWS** ▼

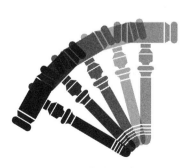

CASENOTES PUBLISHING COMPANY INC.
"Preparation is nine-tenths of the law. . ."

the *Ultimate Outline*

➤ **RENOWNED AUTHORS:** Every **Casenote Law Outline** is written by highly respected, nationally recognized professors.

➤ **KEYED TO CASENOTE LEGAL BRIEF BOOKS:** In most cases, **Casenote Law Outlines** work in conjunction with the **Casenote Legal Briefs** so that you can see how each case in your textbook relates to the entire subject area. In addition, **Casenote Law Outlines** are cross-referenced to most major casebooks.

➤ **FREE SUPPLEMENT SERVICE:** As part of being the most up-to-date legal outline on the market, whenever a new supplement is published, the corresponding outline can be updated for free using the supplement request form found in this book.

ADMINISTRATIVE LAW (1996) $21.95
    Charles H. Koch, Jr., Dudley W. Woodbridge Professor of Law, College of William and Mary
    Sidney A. Shapiro, John M. Rounds Professor of Law, University of Kansas

CIVIL PROCEDURE (1996) $22.95
    John B. Oakley, Professor of Law, University of California, Davis School of Law
    Rex R. Perschbacher, Dean of University of California, Davis School of Law

COMMERCIAL LAW (see SALES ● SECURED TRANSACTIONS ● NEGOTIABLE INSTRUMENTS & PAYMENT SYSTEMS)

CONFLICT OF LAWS (1996) $21.95
    Luther L. McDougal, III, W.R. Irby Professor of Law, Tulane University
    Robert L. Felix, James P. Mozingo, III, Professor of Law, University of South Carolina

CONSTITUTIONAL LAW (1997) $24.95
    Gary Goodpaster, Professor of Law, University of California, Davis School of Law

CONTRACTS (1996) $21.95
    Daniel Wm. Fessler, Professor of Law, University of California, Davis School of Law

CORPORATIONS (1997) $24.95
    Lewis D. Solomon, Arthur Selwin Miller Research Professor of Law, George Washington University
    Daniel Wm. Fessler, Professor of Law, University of California, Davis School of Law
    Arthur E. Wilmarth, Jr., Associate Professor of Law, George Washington University

CRIMINAL LAW (1996) $21.95
    Joshua Dressler, Professor of Law, McGeorge School of Law

CRIMINAL PROCEDURE (1997) $20.95
    Joshua Dressler, Professor of Law, McGeorge School of Law

ESTATE & GIFT TAX $21.95
    Joseph M. Dodge, W.H. Francis Professor of Law, University of Texas at Austin

EVIDENCE (1996) $23.95
    Kenneth Graham, Jr., Professor of Law, University of California, Los Angeles

FEDERAL COURTS (1997) $22.95
    Howard P. Fink, Isadore and Ida Topper Professor of Law, Ohio State University
    Linda S. Mullenix, Bernard J. Ward Centennial Professor of Law, University of Texas

FEDERAL INCOME TAXATION (1998) $22.95
    Joseph M. Dodge, W.H. Francis Professor of Law, University of Texas at Austin

LEGAL RESEARCH (1996) $21.95
    Nancy L. Schultz, Professor of Law, Chapman University
    Louis J. Sirico, Jr., Professor of Law, Villanova University

NEGOTIABLE INSTRUMENTS & PAYMENT SYSTEMS (1995) $22.95
    Donald B. King, Professor of Law, Saint Louis University
    Peter Winship, James Cleo Thompson, Sr. Trustee Professor, SMU

PROPERTY (1997) $22.95
    Sheldon F. Kurtz, Percy Bordwell Professor of Law, University of Iowa
    Patricia Cain, Professor of Law, University of Iowa

SALES $21.95
    Robert E. Scott, Dean and Lewis F. Powell, Jr. Professor of Law, University of Virginia
    Donald B. King, Professor of Law, Saint Louis University

SECURED TRANSACTIONS (1995 w/ '96 supp.) $20.95
    Donald B. King, Professor of Law, Saint Louis University

TORTS (1996) $22.95
    George C. Christie, James B. Duke Professor of Law, Duke University
    Jerry J. Phillips, W.P. Toms Professor of Law, University of Tennessee

WILLS, TRUSTS, & ESTATES (1996) $22.95
    William M. McGovern, Professor of Law, University of California, Los Angeles

CASENOTE LEGAL BRIEFS™

PRICE LIST EFFECTIVE JULY 1, 1999 ● PRICES SUBJECT TO CHANGE WITHOUT NOTICE

Ref. No.	Course	Adaptable to Courses Utilizing	Retail Price
1265	ADMINISTRATIVE LAW	ASIMOW, BONFIELD & LAVIN	20.00
1263	ADMINISTRATIVE LAW	BREYER, STEWART & SUNSTEIN	21.00
1266	ADMINISTRATIVE LAW	CASS, DIVER & BEERMAN	19.00
1260	ADMINISTRATIVE LAW	GELLHORN, B., S., R. & F.	19.00
1264	ADMINISTRATIVE LAW	MASHAW, MERRILL & SHANE	20.50
1267	ADMINISTRATIVE LAW	REESE	19.00
1262	ADMINISTRATIVE LAW	SCHWARTZ	20.00
1350	AGENCY & PARTNERSHIP (ENT.ORG)	CONARD, KNAUSS & SIEGEL	23.00
1351	AGENCY & PARTNERSHIP	HYNES	23.00
1281	ANTITRUST (TRADE REGULATION)	HANDLER, P., G. & W.	19.50
1283	ANTITRUST	SULLIVAN & HOVENKAMP	20.00
1611	BANKING LAW	MACEY & MILLER	19.00
1305	BANKRUPTCY	JORDAN, WARREN & BUSSELL	19.00
1058	BUSINESS ASSOCIATIONS (CORPORATIONS)	KLEIN & RAMSEYER	21.00
1059	BUSINESS ORGANIZATIONS (CORPORATIONS)	SODERQUIST, S., C., & S.	23.00
1040	CIVIL PROCEDURE	COUND, F., M. & S	21.00
1043	CIVIL PROCEDURE	FIELD, KAPLAN & CLERMONT	22.00
1049	CIVIL PROCEDURE	FREER & PERDUE	18.00
1041	CIVIL PROCEDURE	HAZARD, TAIT & FLETCHER	21.00
1047	CIVIL PROCEDURE	MARCUS, REDISH & SHERMAN	21.00
1044	CIVIL PROCEDURE	ROSENBERG, S. & D.	22.00
1046	CIVIL PROCEDURE	YEAZELL	19.00
1311	COMM'L LAW	FARNSWORTH, H., R., H. & M.	21.00
1312	COMM'L LAW	JORDAN & WARREN	21.00
1310	COMM'L LAW (SALES/SEC.TR./PAY.LAW [Sys.])	SPEIDEL, SUMMERS & WHITE	24.00
1313	COMM'L LAW (SALES/SEC.TR./PAY.LAW)	WHALEY	22.00
1314	COMMERCIAL TRANSACTIONS	LOPUKI, W., K. & M.	21.00
1320	COMMUNITY PROPERTY	BIRD	19.50
1630	COMPARATIVE LAW	SCHLESINGER, B., D., H & W.	18.00
1048	COMPLEX LITIGATION	MARCUS & SHERMAN	19.00
1072	CONFLICTS	BRILMAYER	19.00
1071	CONFLICTS	CRAMTON, C. K., & K.	19.00
1070	CONFLICTS	ROSENBERG, HAY & W.	22.00
1073	CONFLICTS	SYMEONIDES, P., & M.	22.00
1086	CONSTITUTIONAL LAW	BREST & LEVINSON	20.00
1082	CONSTITUTIONAL LAW	COHEN & VARAT	23.00
1088	CONSTITUTIONAL LAW	FARBER, ESKRIDGE & FRICKEY	20.00
1080	CONSTITUTIONAL LAW	GUNTHER & SULLIVAN	21.00
1081	CONSTITUTIONAL LAW	LOCKHART, K., C., S. & F.	20.00
1085	CONSTITUTIONAL LAW	ROTUNDA	21.00
1089	CONSTITUTIONAL LAW (FIRST AMENDMENT)	SHIFFRIN & CHOPER	17.00
1087	CONSTITUTIONAL LAW	STONE, S., S. & T.	21.00
1103	CONTRACTS	BARNETT	23.00
1102	CONTRACTS	BURTON	22.00
1017	CONTRACTS	CALAMARI, PERILLO & BENDER	25.00
1101	CONTRACTS	CRANDALL & WHALEY	22.00
1014	CONTRACTS	DAWSON, HARVEY & H.	21.00
1010	CONTRACTS	FARNSWORTH & YOUNG	20.00
1011	CONTRACTS	FULLER & EISENBERG	23.00
1013	CONTRACTS	KESSLER, GILMORE & KRONMAN	25.00
1016	CONTRACTS	KNAPP & CRYSTAL	22.50
1012	CONTRACTS	MURPHY & SPEIDEL	24.00
1015	CONTRACTS	ROSETT	23.00
1019	CONTRACTS	VERNON	22.00
1502	COPYRIGHT	GOLDSTEIN	20.00
1501	COPYRIGHT	NIMMER, M., M. & N.	21.50
1218	CORPORATE TAXATION	LIND, S. L. & R.	16.00
1050	CORPORATIONS	CARY & EISENBERG	23.00
1054	CORPORATIONS	CHOPER, COFFEE, & GILSON	23.50
1350	CORPORATIONS (ENTERPRISE ORG.)	CONARD, KNAUSS & SIEGEL	23.00
1053	CORPORATIONS	HAMILTON	21.00
1058	CORPORATIONS (BUSINESS ASSOCIATIONS	KLEIN & RAMSEYER	21.00
1057	CORPORATIONS	O'KELLEY & THOMPSON	23.00
1059	CORPORATIONS (BUSINESS ORG.)	SODERQUIST, S., C. & S.	23.00
1056	CORPORATIONS	SOLOMON, S., B. & W.	21.00
1052	CORPORATIONS	VAGTS	20.00
1300	CREDITOR'S RIGHTS (DEBTOR-CREDITOR)	RIESENFELD	23.00
1550	CRIMINAL JUSTICE	WEINREB	20.00
1029	CRIMINAL LAW	BONNIE, C., J. & L.	19.00
1020	CRIMINAL LAW	BOYCE & PERKINS	24.00
1028	CRIMINAL LAW	DRESSLER	23.00
1027	CRIMINAL LAW	JOHNSON	22.00
1021	CRIMINAL LAW	KADISH & SCHULHOFER	21.00
1026	CRIMINAL LAW	KAPLAN, WEISBERG & BINDER	22.00
1205	CRIMINAL PROCEDURE	ALLEN, KUHNS & STUNTZ	19.00
1206	CRIMINAL PROCEDURE	DRESSLER & THOMAS	24.00
1202	CRIMINAL PROCEDURE	HADDAD, Z., S. & B.	22.00
1200	CRIMINAL PROCEDURE	KAMISAR, LAFAVE & ISRAEL	21.00
1204	CRIMINAL PROCEDURE	SALTZBURG & CAPRA	19.00
1300	DEBTOR-CREDITOR (CREDITORS RIGHTS)	RIESENFELD	23.00
1304	DEBTOR-CREDITOR	WARREN & WESTBROOK	23.00
1224	DECEDENTS ESTATES (TRUSTS)	RITCHIE, A, & E.(DOBRIS & STERK).	23.00
1222	DECEDENTS ESTATES	SCOLES & HALBACH	23.50
	DOMESTIC RELATIONS (see FAMILY LAW)		
3000	EDUCATION LAW (COURSE OUTLINE)	AQUILA & PETZKE	27.50
1670	EMPLOYMENT DISCRIMINATION	FRIEDMAN & STRICKLER	19.00
1671	EMPLOYMENT DISCRIMINATION	ZIMMER, SULLIVAN, R. & C.	20.00
1660	EMPLOYMENT LAW	ROTHSTEIN, KNAPP & LIEBMAN	21.50
1350	ENTERPRISE ORGANIZATION	CONARD, KNAUSS & SIEGEL	23.00
1342	ENVIRONMENTAL LAW	ANDERSON, MANDELKER & T.	18.00
1341	ENVIRONMENTAL LAW	FINDLEY & FARBER	20.00
1345	ENVIRONMENTAL LAW	MENELL & STEWART	19.00
1344	ENVIRONMENTAL LAW	PERCIVAL, MILLER, S. & L.	20.00
1343	ENVIRONMENTAL LAW	PLATER, A., G. & G.	19.00
1217	ESTATE & GIFT TAXATION	BITTKER, CLARK & McCOUCH	17.00
	ETHICS (see PROFESSIONAL RESPONSIBILITY)		
1065	EVIDENCE	GREEN & NESSON	22.00
1066	EVIDENCE	MUELLER & KIRKPATRICK	19.00
1064	EVIDENCE	STRONG, BROUN & M..	24.50
1062	EVIDENCE	SUTTON & WELLBORN	24.00
1061	EVIDENCE	WALTZ & PARK	21.00
1060	EVIDENCE	WEINSTEIN, M., A. & B.	24.50
1244	FAMILY LAW (DOMESTIC RELATIONS)	AREEN	24.00
1242	FAMILY LAW (DOMESTIC RELATIONS)	CLARK & GLOWINSKY	21.00
1245	FAMILY LAW (DOMESTIC RELATIONS)	ELLMAN, KURTZ & BARTLETT	22.00
1246	FAMILY LAW (DOMESTIC RELATIONS)	HARRIS, T. & W.	21.00
1243	FAMILY LAW (DOMESTIC RELATIONS)	KRAUSE, O., E. & G.	26.00
1240	FAMILY LAW (DOMESTIC RELATIONS)	WADLINGTON	22.00
1231	FAMILY PROPERTY LAW (WILLS/TRUSTS)	WAGGONER, A. & F.	22.00
1360	FEDERAL COURTS	FALLON, M. & S. (HART & W.)	21.00
1360	FEDERAL COURTS	HART & WECHSLER (FALLON)	21.00
1363	FEDERAL COURTS	LOW & JEFFRIES	18.00
1361	FEDERAL COURTS	McCORMICK, C. & W.	22.00
1364	FEDERAL COURTS	REDISH & SHERRY	19.00
1690	FEDERAL INDIAN LAW	GETCHES, W. & W.	22.00
1089	FIRST AMENDMENT (CONSTITUTIONAL LAW)	SHIFFRIN & CHOPER	17.00
1700	GENDER AND LAW (SEX DISCRIMINATION)	BARTLETT & HARRIS	21.00
1510	GRATUITOUS TRANSFERS	CLARK, L., M., A., & M.	20.00
1651	HEALTH CARE LAW	CURRAN, H., B. & O.	23.00
1650	HEALTH LAW	FURROW, J., J. & S.	19.50
1640	IMMIGRATION LAW	ALEINIKOFF, MARTIN & M.	18.00
1641	IMMIGRATION LAW	LEGOMSKY	21.00
1690	INDIAN LAW	GETCHES, W. & W.	22.00
1371	INSURANCE LAW	KEETON	23.00
1370	INSURANCE LAW	YOUNG & HOLMES	19.00
1503	INTELLECTUAL PROPERTY	MERGES, M., L. & J.	21.00
1394	INTERNATIONAL BUSINESS TRANSACTIONS	FOLSOM, GORDON & SPANOGLE	17.00
1393	INTERNATIONAL LAW	CARTER & TRIMBLE	18.00
1392	INTERNATIONAL LAW	HENKIN, P., S. & S.	19.00
1390	INTERNATIONAL LAW	OLIVER, F., B., S. & W.	24.00
1331	LABOR LAW	COX, BOK, GORMAN & FINKIN	21.00
1471	LAND FINANCE (REAL ESTATE TRANS.)	BERGER & JOHNSTONE	20.00
1620	LAND FINANCE (REAL ESTATE TRANS.)	NELSON & WHITMAN	21.00
1452	LAND USE	CALLIES, FREILICH & ROBERTS	19.00
1421	LEGISLATION	ESKRIDGE & FRICKEY	17.00
1480	MASS MEDIA	FRANKLIN & ANDERSON	17.00
1312	NEGOTIABLE INSTRUMENTS (COMM. LAW)	JORDAN & WARREN	21.00
1541	OIL & GAS	KUNTZ, L., A., S. & P..	20.00
1540	OIL & GAS	MAXWELL, WILLIAMS, M. & K.	20.00
1561	PATENT LAW	ADELMAN, R., T. & W.	24.00
1560	PATENT LAW	FRANCIS & COLLINS	25.00
1310	PAYMENT LAW [SYST.][COMM. LAW]	SPEIDEL, SUMMERS & WHITE	24.00
1313	PAYMENT LAW (COMM.LAW / NEG. INST.)	WHALEY	22.00
1431	PRODUCTS LIABILITY	OWEN, MONTGOMERY & K.	24.00
1091	PROF. RESPONSIBILITY (ETHICS)	GILLERS	15.00
1093	PROF. RESPONSIBILITY (ETHICS)	HAZARD, KONIAK & CRAMTON	20.00
1092	PROF. RESPONSIBILITY (ETHICS)	MORGAN & ROTUNDA	15.00
1030	PROPERTY	CASNER & LEACH	23.00
1031	PROPERTY	CRIBBET, J., F. & S.	23.50
1037	PROPERTY	DONAHUE, KAUPER & MARTIN	20.00
1035	PROPERTY	DUKEMINIER & KRIER	22.00
1034	PROPERTY	HAAR & LIEBMAN	22.50
1036	PROPERTY	KURTZ & HOVENKAMP	21.00
1033	PROPERTY	NELSON, STOEBUCK, & W.	22.50
1032	PROPERTY	RABIN & KWALL	22.00
1038	PROPERTY	SINGER	20.50
1621	REAL ESTATE TRANSACTIONS	GOLDSTEIN & KORNGOLD	20.00
1471	REAL ESTATE TRANS. & FIN. (LAND FINANCE)	BERGER & JOHNSTONE	20.00
1620	REAL ESTATE TRANSFER & FINANCE	NELSON & WHITMAN	20.00
1254	REMEDIES (EQUITY)	LAYCOCK	22.00
1253	REMEDIES (EQUITY)	LEAVELL, L., N. & K-F.	23.00
1252	REMEDIES (EQUITY)	RE & RE	25.00
1255	REMEDIES (EQUITY)	SHOBEN & TABB	24.50
1250	REMEDIES (EQUITY)	RENDLEMAN	27.00
1310	SALES (COMM. LAW)	SPEIDEL, SUMMERS & WHITE	24.00
1313	SALES (COMM. LAW)	WHALEY	22.00
1312	SECURED TRANS. (COMMERICAL LAW)	JORDAN & WARREN	21.00
1310	SECURED TRANS.	SPEIDEL, SUMMERS & WHITE	24.00
1313	SECURED TRANS. (COMMERCIAL LAW)	WHALEY	22.00
1272	SECURITIES REGULATION	COX, HILLMAN, LANGEVOORT	20.00
1270	SECURITIES REGULATION	JENNINGS, M., C. & S.	20.00
1680	SPORTS LAW	WEILER & ROBERTS	19.50
1217	TAXATION (ESTATE & GIFT)	BITTKER, CLARK & McCOUCH	17.00
1219	TAXATION (INDIV. INCOME)	BURKE & FRIEL	21.00
1212	TAXATION (FEDERAL INCOME)	FREELAND, LIND & STEPHENS	20.00
1211	TAXATION (FEDERAL INCOME)	GRAETZ & SCHENK	19.00
1210	TAXATION (FEDERAL INCOME)	KLEIN & BANKMAN	20.00
1218	TAXATION (CORPORATE)	LIND, S., L. & R.	16.00
1006	TORTS	DOBBS	21.00
1003	TORTS	EPSTEIN	22.50
1004	TORTS	FRANKLIN & RABIN	19.50
1001	TORTS	HENDERSON, P. & S.	22.50
1000	TORTS	PROSSER, W., S., K. & P.	25.00
1005	TORTS	SHULMAN, JAMES & GRAY	24.00
1281	TRADE REGULATION (ANTITRUST)	HANDLER, P., G. & W.	19.50
1410	U.C.C.	EPSTEIN, MARTIN, H. & N.	17.00
1510	WILLS/TRUSTS (GRATUITOUS TRANSFER)	CLARK, L., M., A., & M.	20.00
1223	WILLS, TRUSTS & ESTATES	DUKEMINIER & JOHANSON	21.00
1220	WILLS	MECHEM & ATKINSON	22.00
1231	WILLS/TRUSTS (FAMILY PROPERTY LAW)	WAGGONER, A. & F.	22.00

CASENOTES PUBLISHING CO., INC. ● **1640 FIFTH STREET, SUITE 208** ● **SANTA MONICA, CA 90401** ● **(310) 395-6500**

E-Mail Address- casenote@westworld.com ● Website- www: http://www.casenotes.com

HOW TO BRIEF A CASE

A. DECIDE ON A FORMAT AND STICK TO IT

Structure is essential to a good brief. It enables you to arrange systematically the related parts that are scattered throughout most cases, thus making manageable and understandable what might otherwise seem to be an endless and unfathomable sea of information. There are, of course, an unlimited number of formats that can be utilized. However, it is best to find one that suits your needs and stick to it. Consistency breeds both efficiency and the security that when called upon you will know where to look in your brief for the information you are asked to give.

Any format, as long as it presents the essential elements of a case in an organized fashion, can be used. Experience, however, has led *Casenotes* to develop and utilize the following format because of its logical flow and universal applicability.

NATURE OF CASE: This is a brief statement of the legal character and procedural status of the case (e.g., "Appeal of a burglary conviction").

There are many different alternatives open to a litigant dissatisfied with a court ruling. The key to determining which one has been used is to discover *who is asking this court for what.*

This first entry in the brief should be kept as *short as possible.* The student should use the court's terminology if the student understands it. But since jurisdictions vary as to the titles of pleadings, the best entry is the one that apprises the student of who wants what in this proceeding, not the one that sounds most like the court's language.

CONCISE RULE OF LAW: A statement of the general principle of law that the case illustrates (e.g., "An acceptance that varies any term of the offer is considered a rejection and counteroffer").

Determining the rule of law of a case is a procedure similar to determining the issue of the case. Avoid being fooled by red herrings; there may be a few rules of law mentioned in the case excerpt, but usually only one is *the* rule with which the casebook editor is concerned. The techniques used to locate the issue, described below, may also be utilized to find the rule of law. Generally, your best guide is simply the chapter heading. It is a clue to the point the casebook editor seeks to make and should be kept in mind when reading every case in the respective section.

FACTS: A synopsis of only the essential facts of the case, i.e., those bearing upon or leading up to the issue.

The facts entry should be a short statement of the events and transactions that led one party to initiate legal proceedings against another in the first place. While some cases conveniently state the salient facts at the beginning of the decision, in other instances they will have to be culled from hiding places throughout the text, even from concurring and dissenting opinions. Some of the "facts" will often be in dispute and should be so noted. Conflicting evidence may be briefly pointed up. "Hard" facts must be included. Both must be *relevant* in order to be listed in the facts entry. It is impossible to tell what is relevant until the entire case is read, as the ultimate determination of the rights and liabilities of the parties may turn on something buried deep in the opinion.

The facts entry should never be longer than one to three *short* sentences.

It is often helpful to identify the role played by a party in a given context. For example, in a construction contract case the identification of a party as the "contractor" or "builder" alleviates the need to tell that that party was the one who was supposed to have built the house.

It is always helpful, and a good general practice, to identify the "plaintiff" and the "defendant." This may seem elementary and uncomplicated, but, especially in view of the creative editing practiced by some casebook editors, it is sometimes a difficult or even impossible task. Bear in mind that the *party presently* seeking something from this court may not be the plaintiff, and that sometimes only the cross-claim of a defendant is treated in the excerpt. Confusing or misaligning the parties can ruin your analysis and understanding of the case.

ISSUE: A statement of the general legal question answered by or illustrated in the case. For clarity, the issue is best put in the form of a question capable of a "yes" or "no" answer. In reality, the issue is simply the Concise Rule of Law put in the form of a question (e.g., "May an offer be accepted by performance?").

The major problem presented in discerning what is *the* issue in the case is that an opinion usually purports to raise and answer several questions. However, except for rare cases, only one such question is really the issue in the case. Collateral issues not necessary to the resolution of the matter in controversy are handled by the court by language known as *"obiter dictum"* or merely *"dictum."* While dicta may be included later in the brief, it has no place under the issue heading.

To find the issue, the student again asks *who wants what* and then goes on to ask *why did that party succeed or fail in getting it.* Once this is determined, the "why" should be turned into a question.

The complexity of the issues in the cases will vary, but in all cases a single-sentence question should sum up the issue. *In a few cases,* there will be two, or even more rarely, three issues of equal importance to the resolution of the case. Each should be expressed in a single-sentence question.

Since many issues are resolved by a court in coming to a final disposition of a case, the casebook editor will reproduce the portion of the opinion containing the issue or issues most relevant to the area of law under scrutiny. A noted law professor gave this advice: "Close the book; look at the title on the cover." Chances are, if it is Property, the student need not concern himself with whether, for example, the federal government's treatment of the plaintiff's land really raises a federal question sufficient to support jurisdiction on this ground in federal court.

The same rule applies to chapter headings designating sub-areas within the subjects. They tip the student off as to what the text is designed to teach. The cases are arranged in a casebook to show a progression or development of the law, so that the preceding cases may also help.

It is also most important to remember to *read the notes and questions* at the end of a case to determine what the editors wanted the student to have gleaned from it.

HOLDING AND DECISION: This section should succinctly explain the rationale of the court in arriving at its decision. In capsulizing the "reasoning" of the court, it should always include an application of the general rule or rules of law to the specific facts of the case. Hidden justifications come to light in this entry; the reasons for the state of the law, the public policies, the biases and prejudices, those considerations that influence the justices' thinking and, ultimately, the outcome of the case. At the end, there should be a short indication of the disposition or procedural resolution of the case (e.g., "Decision of the trial court for Mr. Smith (P) reversed").

The foregoing format is designed to help you "digest" the reams of case material with which you will be faced in your law school career. Once mastered by practice, it will place at your fingertips the information the authors of your casebooks have sought to impart to you in case-by-case illustration and analysis.

B. BE AS ECONOMICAL AS POSSIBLE IN BRIEFING CASES

Once armed with a format that encourages succinctness, it is as important to be economical with regard to the time spent on the actual reading of the case as it is to be economical in the writing of the brief itself. This does not mean "skimming" a case. Rather, it means reading the case with an "eye" trained to recognize into which "section" of your brief a particular passage or line fits and having a system for quickly and precisely marking the case so that the passages fitting any one particular part of the brief can be easily identified and brought together in a concise and accurate manner when the brief is actually written.

It is of no use to simply repeat everything in the opinion of the court; the student should only record enough information to trigger his or her recollection of what the court said. Nevertheless, an accurate statement of the "law of the case," i.e., the legal principle applied to the facts, is absolutely essential to class preparation and to learning the law under the case method.

To that end, it is important to develop a "shorthand" that you can use to make margin notations. These notations will tell you at a glance in which section of the brief you will be placing that particular passage or portion of the opinion.

Some students prefer to underline all the salient portions of the opinion (with a pencil or colored underliner marker), making marginal notations as they go along. Others prefer the color-coded method of underlining, utilizing different colors of markers to underline the salient portions of the case, each separate color being used to represent a different section of the brief. For example, blue underlining could be used for passages relating to the concise rule of law, yellow for those relating to the issue, and green for those relating to the holding and decision, etc. While it has its advocates, the color-coded method can be confusing and time-consuming (all that time spent on changing colored markers). Furthermore, it can interfere with the continuity and concentration many students deem essential to the reading of a case for maximum comprehension. In the end, however, it is a matter of personal preference and style. Just remember, whatever method you use, underlining must be used sparingly or its value is lost.

For those who take the marginal notation route, an efficient and easy method is to go along underlining the key portions of the case and placing in the margin alongside them the following "markers" to indicate where a particular passage or line "belongs" in the brief you will write:

N	(NATURE OF CASE)
CR	(CONCISE RULE OF LAW)
I	(ISSUE)
HC	(HOLDING AND DECISION, relates to the CONCISE RULE OF LAW behind the decision)
HR	(HOLDING AND DECISION, gives the RATIONALE or reasoning behind the decision)
HA	(HOLDING AND DECISION, APPLIES the general principle(s) of law to the facts of the case to arrive at the decision)

Remember that a particular passage may well contain information necessary to more than one part of your brief, in which case you simply note that in the margin. If you are using the color-coded underlining method instead of margin notation, simply make asterisks or checks in the margin next to the passage in question in the colors that indicate the additional sections of the brief where it might be utilized.

The economy of utilizing "shorthand" in marking cases for briefing can be maintained in the actual brief writing process itself by utilizing "law student shorthand" within the brief. There are many commonly used words and phrases for which abbreviations can be substituted in your briefs (and in your class notes also). You can develop abbreviations that are personal to you and which will save you a lot of time. A reference list of briefing abbreviations will be found elsewhere in this book.

C. USE BOTH THE BRIEFING PROCESS AND THE BRIEF AS A LEARNING TOOL

Now that you have a format and the tools for briefing cases efficiently, the most important thing is to make the time spent in briefing profitable to you and to make the most advantageous use of the briefs you create. Of course, the briefs are invaluable for classroom reference when you are called upon to explain or analyze a particular case. However, they are also useful in reviewing for exams. A quick glance at the fact summary should bring the case to mind, and a rereading of the concise rule of law should enable you to go over the underlying legal concept in your mind, how it was applied in that particular case, and how it might apply in other factual settings.

As to the value to be derived from engaging in the briefing process itself, there is an immediate benefit that arises from being forced to sift through the essential facts and reasoning from the court's opinion and to succinctly express them in your own words in your brief. The process ensures that you understand the case and the point that it illustrates, and that means you will be ready to absorb further analysis and information brought forth in class. It also ensures you will have something to say when called upon in class. The briefing process helps develop a mental agility for getting to the *gist* of a case and for identifying, expounding on, and applying the legal concepts and issues found there. Of most immediate concern, that is the mental process on which you must rely in taking law school examinations. Of more lasting concern, it is also the mental process upon which a lawyer relies in serving his clients and in making his living.

GLOSSARY

COMMON LATIN WORDS AND PHRASES ENCOUNTERED IN LAW

A FORTIORI: Because one fact exists or has been proven, therefore a second fact that is related to the first fact must also exist.

A PRIORI: From the cause to the effect. A term of logic used to denote that when one generally accepted truth is shown to be a cause, another particular effect must necessarily follow.

AB INITIO: From the beginning; a condition which has existed throughout, as in a marriage which was void ab initio.

ACTUS REUS: The wrongful act; in criminal law, such action sufficient to trigger criminal liability.

AD VALOREM: According to value; an ad valorem tax is imposed upon an item located within the taxing jurisdiction calculated by the value of such item.

AMICUS CURIAE: Friend of the court. Its most common usage takes the form of an amicus curiae brief, filed by a person who is not a party to an action but is nonetheless allowed to offer an argument supporting his legal interests.

ARGUENDO: In arguing. A statement, possibly hypothetical, made for the purpose of argument, is one made arguendo.

BILL QUIA TIMET: A bill to quiet title (establish ownership) to real property.

BONA FIDE: True, honest, or genuine. May refer to a person's legal position based on good faith or lacking notice of fraud (such as a bona fide purchaser for value) or to the authenticity of a particular document (such as a bona fide last will and testament).

CAUSA MORTIS: With approaching death in mind. A gift causa mortis is a gift given by a party who feels certain that death is imminent.

CAVEAT EMPTOR: Let the buyer beware. This maxim is reflected in the rule of law that a buyer purchases at his own risk because it is his responsibility to examine, judge, test, and otherwise inspect what he is buying.

CERTIORARI: A writ of review. Petitions for review of a case by the United States Supreme Court are most often done by means of a writ of certiorari.

CONTRA: On the other hand. Opposite. Contrary to.

CORAM NOBIS: Before us; writs of error directed to the court that originally rendered the judgment.

CORAM VOBIS: Before you; writs of error directed by an appellate court to a lower court to correct a factual error.

CORPUS DELICTI: The body of the crime; the requisite elements of a crime amounting to objective proof that a crime has been committed.

CUM TESTAMENTO ANNEXO, ADMINISTRATOR (ADMINISTRATOR C.T.A.): With will annexed; an administrator c.t.a. settles an estate pursuant to a will in which he is not appointed.

DE BONIS NON, ADMINISTRATOR (ADMINISTRATOR D.B.N.): Of goods not administered; an administrator d.b.n. settles a partially settled estate.

DE FACTO: In fact; in reality; actually. Existing in fact but not officially approved or engendered.

DE JURE: By right; lawful. Describes a condition that is legitimate "as a matter of law," in contrast to the term "de facto," which connotes something existing in fact but not legally sanctioned or authorized. For example, de facto segregation refers to segregation brought about by housing patterns, etc., whereas de jure segregation refers to segregation created by law.

DE MINIMUS: Of minimal importance; insignificant; a trifle; not worth bothering about.

DE NOVO: Anew; a second time; afresh. A trial de novo is a new trial held at the appellate level as if the case originated there and the trial at a lower level had not taken place.

DICTA: Generally used as an abbreviated form of obiter dicta, a term describing those portions of a judicial opinion incidental or not necessary to resolution of the specific question before the court. Such nonessential statements and remarks are not considered to be binding precedent.

DUCES TECUM: Refers to a particular type of writ or subpoena requesting a party or organization to produce certain documents in their possession.

EN BANC: Full bench. Where a court sits with all justices present rather than the usual quorum.

EX PARTE: For one side or one party only. An ex parte proceeding is one undertaken for the benefit of only one party, without notice to, or an appearance by, an adverse party.

EX POST FACTO: After the fact. An ex post facto law is a law that retroactively changes the consequences of a prior act.

EX REL.: Abbreviated form of the term ex relatione, meaning, upon relation or information. When the state brings an action in which it has no interest against an individual at the instigation of one who has a private interest in the matter.

FORUM NON CONVENIENS: Inconvenient forum. Although a court may have jurisdiction over the case, the action should be tried in a more conveniently located court, one to which parties and witnesses may more easily travel, for example.

GUARDIAN AD LITEM: A guardian of an infant as to litigation, appointed to represent the infant and pursue his/her rights.

HABEAS CORPUS: You have the body. The modern writ of habeas corpus is a writ directing that a person (body) being detained (such as a prisoner) be brought before the court so that the legality of his detention can be judicially ascertained.

IN CAMERA: In private, in chambers. When a hearing is held before a judge in his chambers or when all spectators are excluded from the courtroom.

IN FORMA PAUPERIS: In the manner of a pauper. A party who proceeds in forma pauperis because of his poverty is one who is allowed to bring suit without liability for costs.

INFRA: Below, under. A word referring the reader to a later part of a book. (The opposite of supra.)

IN LOCO PARENTIS: In the place of a parent.

IN PARI DELICTO: Equally wrong; a court of equity will not grant requested relief to an applicant who is in pari delicto, or as much at fault in the transactions giving rise to the controversy as is the opponent of the applicant.

IN PARI MATERIA: On like subject matter or upon the same matter. Statutes relating to the same person or things are said to be in pari materia. It is a general rule of statutory construction that such statutes should be construed together, i.e., looked at as if they together constituted one law.

IN PERSONAM: Against the person. Jurisdiction over the person of an individual.

IN RE: In the matter of. Used to designate a proceeding involving an estate or other property.

IN REM: A term that signifies an action against the res, or thing. An action in rem is basically one that is taken directly against property, as distinguished from an action in personam, i.e., against the person.

INTER ALIA: Among other things. Used to show that the whole of a statement, pleading, list, statute, etc., has not been set forth in its entirety.

INTER PARTES: Between the parties. May refer to contracts, conveyances or other transactions having legal significance.

INTER VIVOS: Between the living. An inter vivos gift is a gift made by a living grantor, as distinguished from bequests contained in a will, which pass upon the death of the testator.

i

IPSO FACTO: By the mere fact itself.

JUS: Law or the entire body of law.

LEX LOCI: The law of the place; the notion that the rights of parties to a legal proceeding are governed by the law of the place where those rights arose.

MALUM IN SE: Evil or wrong in and of itself; inherently wrong. This term describes an act that is wrong by its very nature, as opposed to one which would not be wrong but for the fact that there is a specific legal prohibition against it (malum prohibitum).

MALUM PROHIBITUM: Wrong because prohibited, but not inherently evil. Used to describe something that is wrong because it is expressly forbidden by law but that is not in and of itself evil, e.g., speeding.

MANDAMUS: We command. A writ directing an official to take a certain action.

MENS REA: A guilty mind; a criminal intent. A term used to signify the mental state that accompanies a crime or other prohibited act. Some crimes require only a general mens rea (general intent to do the prohibited act), but others, like assault with intent to murder, require the existence of a specific mens rea.

MODUS OPERANDI: Method of operating; generally refers to the manner or style of a criminal in committing crimes, admissible in appropriate cases as evidence of the identity of a defendant.

NEXUS: A connection to.

NISI PRIUS: A court of first impression. A nisi prius court is one where issues of fact are tried before a judge or jury.

N.O.V. (NON OBSTANTE VEREDICTO): Notwithstanding the verdict. A judgment n.o.v. is a judgment given in favor of one party despite the fact that a verdict was returned in favor of the other party, the justification being that the verdict either had no reasonable support in fact or was contrary to law.

NUNC PRO TUNC: Now for then. This phrase refers to actions that may be taken and will then have full retroactive effect.

PENDENTE LITE: Pending the suit; pending litigation underway.

PER CAPITA: By head; beneficiaries of an estate, if they take in equal shares, take per capita.

PER CURIAM: By the court; signifies an opinion ostensibly written "by the whole court" and with no identified author.

PER SE: By itself, in itself; inherently.

PER STIRPES: By representation. Used primarily in the law of wills to describe the method of distribution where a person, generally because of death, is unable to take that which is left to him by the will of another, and therefore his heirs divide such property between them rather than take under the will individually.

PRIMA FACIE: On its face, at first sight. A prima facie case is one that is sufficient on its face, meaning that the evidence supporting it is adequate to establish the case until contradicted or overcome by other evidence.

PRO TANTO: For so much; as far as it goes. Often used in eminent domain cases when a property owner receives partial payment for his land without prejudice to his right to bring suit for the full amount he claims his land to be worth.

QUANTUM MERUIT: As much as he deserves. Refers to recovery based on the doctrine of unjust enrichment in those cases in which a party has rendered valuable services or furnished materials that were accepted and enjoyed by another under circumstances that would reasonably notify the recipient that the rendering party expected to be paid. In essence, the law implies a contract to pay the reasonable value of the services or materials furnished.

QUASI: Almost like; as if; nearly. This term is essentially used to signify that one subject or thing is almost analogous to another but that material differences between them do exist. For example, a quasi-criminal proceeding is one that is not strictly criminal but shares enough of the same characteristics to require some of the same safeguards (e.g., procedural due process must be followed in a parol hearing).

QUID PRO QUO: Something for something. In contract law, the consideration, something of value, passed between the parties to render the contract binding.

RES GESTAE: Things done; in evidence law, this principle justifies the admission of a statement that would otherwise be hearsay when it is made so closely to the event in question as to be said to be a part of it, or with such spontaneity as not to have the possibility of falsehood.

RES IPSA LOQUITUR: The thing speaks for itself. This doctrine gives rise to a rebuttable presumption of negligence when the instrumentality causing the injury was within the exclusive control of the defendant, and the injury was one that does not normally occur unless a person has been negligent.

RES JUDICATA: A matter adjudged. Doctrine which provides that once a court of competent jurisdiction has rendered a final judgment or decree on the merits, that judgment or decree is conclusive upon the parties to the case and prevents them from engaging in any other litigation on the points and issues determined therein.

RESPONDEAT SUPERIOR: Let the master reply. This doctrine holds the master liable for the wrongful acts of his servant (or the principal for his agent) in those cases in which the servant (or agent) was acting within the scope of his authority at the time of the injury.

STARE DECISIS: To stand by or adhere to that which has been decided. The common law doctrine of stare decisis attempts to give security and certainty to the law by following the policy that once a principle of law as applicable to a certain set of facts has been set forth in a decision, it forms a precedent which will subsequently be followed, even though a different decision might be made were it the first time the question had arisen. Of course, stare decisis is not an inviolable principle and is departed from in instances where there is good cause (e.g., considerations of public policy led the Supreme Court to disregard prior decisions sanctioning segregation).

SUPRA: Above. A word referring a reader to an earlier part of a book.

ULTRA VIRES: Beyond the power. This phrase is most commonly used to refer to actions taken by a corporation that are beyond the power or legal authority of the corporation.

ADDENDUM OF FRENCH DERIVATIVES

IN PAIS: Not pursuant to legal proceedings.

CHATTEL: Tangible personal property.

CY PRES: Doctrine permitting courts to apply trust funds to purposes not expressed in the trust but necessary to carry out the settlor's intent.

PER AUTRE VIE: For another's life; in property law, an estate may be granted that will terminate upon the death of someone other than the grantee.

PROFIT A PRENDRE: A license to remove minerals or other produce from land.

VOIR DIRE: Process of questioning jurors as to their predispositions about the case or parties to a proceeding in order to identify those jurors displaying bias or prejudice.

NOTES

Don't Forget!

The *Casenote Civil Proceedure Law Outline* is specifically designed to work with this book.

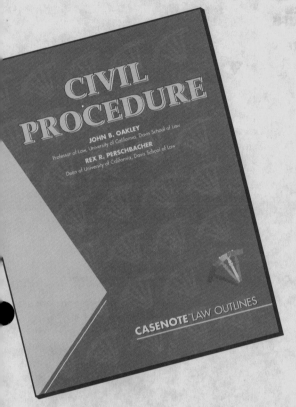

RENOWNED AUTHORS: Every *Casenote Law Outline* is written by highly respected, nationally recognized professors.

KEYED TO BRIEF BOOKS: In most cases, *Casenote Law Outlines* work in conjunction with the *Casenote Legal Briefs* so that you can see how each case in your textbook relates to the entire subject area. In addition, you can use the *Casenote Legal Brief* book to focus in on all the sections of your *Casenote Law Outline* covered by your textbook.

ORGANIZED AND EASILY ACCESSIBLE: Not only have the authors done the work of distilling all the subject information into organized sections, all this information is easily accessible through the Index, Cross-Reference Chart, and Tables of Contents, Cases, and Code Sections.

HONE YOUR EXAM SKILLS: The Exam Preparation section allows you to practice on sample multiple choice questions and/or short essay problems.

FREE SUPPLEMENT SERVICE: As part of being the most up-to-date legal outline on the market, whenever a new supplement is published, the corresponding outline can be updated for free using the supplement request form found in this book.

About the authors:

John B. Oakley is a professor at UC Davis School of Law, where he has taught since 1975. He is the Reporter for the American Law Institute's Federal Judicial Code Revision Project, has twice served as chairperson of the Association of American Law Schools' Section on Civil Procedure, and, with Charles Alan Wright, is the author of Federal Courts-Cases and Materials: Tenth Edition.

Rex R. Perschbacher is Dean of UC Davis School of Law and has been on its faculty since 1972. He is co-author of California Trial Techniques, Cases and Materials on Civil Procedure (3rd ed.), California Civil Procedure, Problems in Legal Ethics (4th ed.), and California Legal Ethics (2nd ed.).

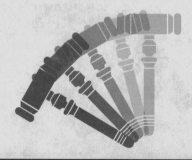

Preparation is nine-tenths of the law.

REF. # 5040

Announcing the First *Totally Integrated* Law Study System

CASENOTE LEGAL BRIEFS

CLASSROOM PREPARATION

EXAM PREPARATION

Legal Briefs summarize cases in your casebook to improve comprehension and recall.

Case briefs cross-referenced to *Outline* for further discussion of cases & law.

CASEBOOK

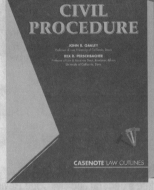

CASENOTE LAW OUTLINES

Outline cross-referenced to most casebooks to help prepare for class & exams.

▼ PERIODIC REVIEWS ▼

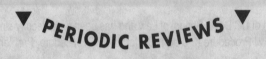

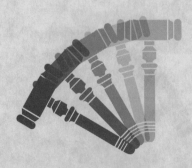

CASENOTES PUBLISHING COMPANY INC.

"Preparation is nine-tenths of the law. . ."

TABLE OF CASES

Continued on next page.

TABLE OF CASES (Continued)

CHAPTER 1
AN OVERVIEW OF PROCEDURE

QUICK REFERENCE RULES OF LAW

1. **Subject Matter Jurisdiction.** A student who resides in a state maintaining a home there and having the intention to remain indefinitely is a citizen of that state for diversity purposes. (Gordon v. Steele)

   [For more information on diversity as a function of domicile, see Casenote Law Outline on Civil Procedure, Chapter 4, Federal Subject-Matter Jurisdiction and Related Doctrines Affecting Choice of a Federal Forum, § IV, The Diversity Jurisdiction of the District Courts.]

2. **The Lawyer's Responsibility.** Federal Rule of Civil Procedure 11 imposes an obligation on counsel and client to stop, think, investigate and research before filing papers either to initiate the suit or to conduct the litigation. (Bridges v. Diesel Service, Inc.)

3. **The Complaint.** A complaint which alleges only that a defendant negligently drove a motor vehicle and thereby injured the plaintiff is sufficient under F.R.C.P. 8. (Bell v. Novick Transfer Co.)

   [For more information on pleadings, see Casenote Law Outline on Civil Procedure, Chapter 5, Pleading, § IV, Special Pleading Requirements.]

4. **Compulsory Joinder.** Joint tortfeasors are not necessary parties under Fed. R. Civ. P. 19. (Temple v. Synthes Corp.)

   [For more information on compulsory joinder, see Casenote Law Outline on Civil Procedure, Chapter 6, Joinder of Claims and Parties, § I, Joinder of Claims.]

5. **Factual Development.** The reasons for changes in a contract form made as a result of confidential communication between a party and his attorney are protected from discovery by the attorney-client privilege. (Goldinger v. Boron Oil Co.)

   [For more information on scope of discovery, see Casenote Law Outline on Civil Procedure, Chapter 7, Discovery, § III, Outline of the Scope of Discovery Under Federal Rules.]

6. **Pretrial Disposition.** Under Fed. R. Civ. P. 56, a federal court must enter summary judgment if after complete discovery a party fails to show that the evidence, viewed in the light most favorable to that party, is sufficient to establish the existence of an essential element on which that party has the burden of proof. (Houchens v. American Home Assurance Co.)

   [For more information on summary judgments, see Casenote Law Outline on Civil Procedure, Chapter 8, Pre-Trial Procedure and Dispositions—Alternatives to Trial, Pre-Trial Conferences, Dismissal, Default Judgment, and Summary Judgment, § IV, Summary judgments.]

7. **Trial.** A judgment notwithstanding the verdict should only be granted where the evidence so strongly points in favor of a moving party that reasonable people could not arrive at a contrary verdict. (Norton v. Snapper Power Equipment)

   [For more information on judgments notwithstanding the evidence, see Casenote Law Outline on Civil Procedure, Chapter 9, Trial and Post-Trial Motions, § VI, Post-Verdict Motions.]

8. **Former Adjudication.** Where a person suffers both personal injuries and property damage as a result of the same wrongful act, only a single cause for action arises, the different injuries occasioned thereby being separate items of damages from such act. (Rush v. City of Maple Heights)

   [For more information on scope of claim or cause of action, see Casenote Law Outline on Civil Procedure, Chapter 12, Preclusion Doctrines—Res Judicata and Collateral Estoppel, § I, Res Judicata Defined.]

9. **Appeals.** An order of the court made under Federal Rule of Civil Procedure 34 for discovery and production of documents is interlocutory and therefore not appealable. (Apex Hosiery Co. v. Leader)

   [For more information on appeal, see Casenote Law Outline on Civil Procedure, Chapter 10, § III, The Federal Courts and the Model of Finality.]

GORDON v. STEELE

Injured student (P) v. Physician (D)

376 F. Supp. 575 (W.D. Pa. 1974).

NATURE OF CASE: Motion to dismiss for lack of diversity.

FACT SUMMARY: Gordon (P) brought a diversity malpractice action against Steele (D), a Pennsylvania resident, for negligent medical treatment to her wrist and Steele (D) contested diversity claiming that Gordon (P), though a student In Idaho, was really a citizen of Pennsylvania where her parents lived before she began college.

CONCISE RULE OF LAW: A student who resides in a state maintaining a home there and having the intention to remain indefinitely is a citizen of that state for diversity purposes.

FACTS: Steele (D) treated Gordon's (P) wrist and diagnosed that there was no fracture. Continued pain and disability led to further treatment which revealed that there was a fracture. Gordon (P) brought this suit for malpractice for the negligent diagnosis in federal court, asserting jurisdiction by reason of diversity of citizenship. After the diagnosis, but before the suit was brought, Gordon (P) moved to Idaho to attend college, renting an apartment there which she retained ever since. She returned to Pennsylvania on a few occasions to visit her parents and to see Dr. Steele (D), but intended to live in Idaho permanently to retain her ties to the Mormon Church. Steele (D) contested diversity of citizenship on the ground that Gordon (P) was in reality a Pennsylvania resident in a motion to dismiss for lack of diversity.

ISSUE: Is a student who resides in a state maintaining a home there and having the intention to remain indefinitely a citizen of that state for diversity purposes?

HOLDING AND DECISION: (Knox, J.) Yes. The subjective intentions of a person to remain in a state is relevant to a determination of citizenship or domicile. If the intention is to remain for an indefinite period of time and the person is present in the state, he has acquired a new domicile there. A future intention to possibly move one day as the inevitable changes in life take place is not sufficient to defeat a present intention to remain. Here, Gordon (P) intended to remain in Idaho and no intention to return to Pennsylvania has been shown. A student who resides in a state maintaining a home there and having the intention of remaining indefinitely is a citizen of that state for diversity purposes. Motion denied.

EDITOR'S ANALYSIS: Domicile is a concept which has plagued the courts and scholars. While not dispositive, the subjective intent to remain indefinitely is a key element of determining domicile. A person has only one domicile regardless of the number of states in which he is a citizen.

[For more information on diversity as a function of domicile, see Casenote Law Outline on Civil Procedure, Chapter 4, Federal Subject-Matter Jurisdiction and Related Doctrines Affecting Choice of a Federal Forum, § IV, The Diversity Jurisdiction of the District Courts.]

QUICKNOTES

DIVERSITY OF CITIZENSHIP - The authority of a federal court to hear and determine cases involving $10,000 or more and in which the parties are citizens of different states, or in which one party is an alien.

DOMICILE - A person's permanent home or principal establishment to which he has an intention of returning when he is absent therefrom.

NOTES:

BRIDGES v. DIESEL SERVICE INC.
Disabled employee (P) v. Employer (D)
1994 U.S. Dist. LEXIS 9429 (E.D. Pa. 1994).

NATURE OF CASE: Motion for sanctions pursuant to Federal Rule of Civil Procedure 11.

FACT SUMMARY: Bridges (P) commenced this action against Diesel Service Inc. (D) under the Americans with Disabilities Act (ADA) alleging that his employer dismissed him from his job as a result of a disability.

CONCISE RULE OF LAW: Federal Rule of Civil Procedure 11 imposes an obligation on counsel and client to stop, think, investigate and research before filing papers either to initiate the suit or to conduct the litigation.

FACTS: Bridges (P) commenced this action against Diesel Service Inc. (D) under the Americans with Disabilities Act (ADA) alleging that his employer dismissed him from his job as a result of a disability. By Order dated June 29, 1994, the Court dismissed Bridges' (P) complaint without prejudice for failure to exhaust administrative remedies. In particular, Bridges (P) did not file a charge with the Equal Employment Opportunity Commission (EEOC) until after commencement of this action. Diesel Service, Inc. (D) then moved for sanctions pursuant to Federal Rule of Civil Procedure 11.

ISSUE: Does Federal Rule of Civil Procedure 11 impose an obligation on counsel and client to stop, think, investigate and research before filing papers either to initiate the suit or to conduct the litigation?

HOLDING AND DECISION: (Huyett, J.) Yes. Federal Rule of Civil Procedure 11 imposes an obligation on counsel and client to stop, think, investigate and research before filing papers either to initiate the suit or to conduct the litigation. The Court is not convinced that Plaintiff's lawyer displayed a competent level of legal research. A brief review of case law would have revealed the EEOC filing requirement. Further, an award of sanctions for failure to exhaust administrative remedies is not unprecedented. However, the court will not grant sanctions. The prime goal of Rule 11 sanctions is deterrence of improper conduct. In this case, monetary sanctions are not necessary to deter future misconduct, since plaintiff's counsel immediately acknowledged his error and attempted to rectify the situation.

EDITOR'S ANALYSIS: It is possible that the Court treated plaintiff's counsel with lenience in this case, since the action was brought under the Americans with Disabilities Act. As the Court states in its decision, "The Court is aware of the need to avoid 'chilling' Title VII litigation." Generally, Rule 11 sanctions are awarded where the complaint filed asserts patently unmeritorious or frivolous allegations.

[For more information on Rule 11, see Case note Law Outline on Civil Procedure, Chapter 5, Pleading, § VI, Truthfulness in Pleading.]

QUICKNOTES

FRCP 11 - Sets forth the requirement that every pleading or written paper be signed by at least one attorney of record; the representations made by the attorney to the court upon the signing of such document; and the sanctions for violation of the provision.

ADMINISTRATIVE REMEDIES - Relief that is sought before an administrative body as opposed to a court.

NOTES:

BELL v. NOVICK TRANSFER CO.
Automobile passenger (P) v. Trucking company (D)
17 F.R.D. 279 (1955).

NATURE OF CASE: Motion to dismiss for failure to state a claim.

FACT SUMMARY: Bell (P) filed a tort complaint in federal court after removal which stated only that Novick's (D) agent drove a truck which negligently collided with the car in which Bell (P) was riding, causing injury to Bell (P).

CONCISE RULE OF LAW: A complaint which alleges only that a defendant negligently drove a motor vehicle and thereby injured the plaintiff is sufficient under F.R.C.P. 8.

FACTS: After Bell's (P) tort action arising out of an automobile-truck accident was removed to federal court, Bell (P) filed a complaint there, which alleged only that an agent of Novick (D) drove a truck negligently so as to collide with a car in which Bell (P) was riding, causing injury to Bell (P). Novick (D) moved to dismiss the complaint for failure to state a cause of action.

ISSUE: Is a complaint which alleges only that defendant negligently drove a motor vehicle and thereby injured the plaintiff sufficient under F.R.C.P. 8?

HOLDING AND DECISION: (Thomsen, J.) Yes. This tort action was originally filed in Court of Common Pleas of Baltimore City but was removed to federal court. After such a removal, the F.R.C.P. applies rather than the laws of the State of Maryland. Thus, while Maryland law might regard the complaint here as insufficient for failure to state a cause of action, the inquiry here is to be made in light of the F.R.C.P. F.R.C.P. 8 controls the sufficiency of complaints, and requires only "a short and plain statement of the claim showing the pleader is entitled to relief." The complaint in this case contains such a statement and sufficiently states a cause of action under Rule 8. A complaint which alleges only that a defendant negligently drove a motor vehicle and thereby injured the plaintiff is sufficient under F.R.C.P. 8. Motion denied.

EDITOR'S ANALYSIS: A complaint is designed to apprise the defendant of the claim against which he is to defend. The argument against sufficiency in this case is that the defendant is not told what negligent acts he has allegedly committed, giving rise to liability save the general allegation of "negligence." However, the policy of granting everyone access to the courts militates toward permitting generalized allegations and forcing the defendant to move for a more particularized statement under F.R.C.P. 12(e).

[For more information on pleadings, see Case note Law Outline on Civil Procedure, Chapter 5, Pleading, § IV, Special Pleading Requirements.]

QUICKNOTES

FRCP 8 - Sets forth the general rules of pleading a claim for relief.

MOTION TO DISMISS - Motion to terminate a trial based on the adequacy of the pleadings.

REMOVAL - Petition by a defendant to move the case to another court.

NOTES:

TEMPLE v. SYNTHES CORP.

Medical implant user (P) v. Implant manufacturer (D)

498 U.S. 5 (1990).

NATURE OF CASE: Appeal of dismissal with prejudice of action for damages for products liability, medical malpractice, and negligence.

FACT SUMMARY: Temple's (P) federal suit against Synthes (D), the manufacturer of a plate implanted in Temple's (P) back, was dismissed when Temple (P) failed to join the doctor and the hospital responsible for installing the plate.

CONCISE RULE OF LAW: Joint tortfeasors are not necessary parties under Fed. R. Civ. P. 19.

FACTS: A plate and screw device implanted in Temple's (P) back malfunctioned. Temple (P) filed a federal court products liability action against Synthes (D), the manufacturer of the device. Temple (P) also filed a state court medical malpractice and negligence action against the doctor who implanted the device and the hospital where the operation was performed. Synthes (D) filed a motion to dismiss the federal lawsuit under Fed. R. Civ. P. 19 for Temple's (P) failure to join necessary parties. The district court agreed that the doctor and the hospital were necessary parties and gave Temple (P) twenty days to join them. When Temple (P) did not, the court dismissed the suit with prejudice. The court of appeals affirmed, finding that Rule 19 allowed the district court to order joinder in the interest of complete, consistent, and efficient settlement of controversies. It further found that overlapping, separate lawsuits would have prejudiced Synthes (D) because Synthes (D) might claim the device was not defective but that the doctor and the hospital were negligent, and the doctor and the hospital might claim the opposite. Temple (P) appealed, arguing that joint tortfeasors are not necessary parties under Rule 19.

ISSUE: Are joint tortfeasors necessary parties under Fed. R. Civ. P. 19?

HOLDING AND DECISION: [Per curiam.] No. Joint tortfeasors are not necessary parties under Fed. R. Civ. P. 19. It has long been the rule that joint tortfeasors need not be named as defendants in a single lawsuit. Rule 19 does not change that principle. The Advisory Committee Notes to Rule 19(a) state that a tortfeasor with the usual joint and several liability is merely a permissive party. There is a public interest in avoiding multiple lawsuits. However, since the requirements of Rule 19(a) have not been met, the district court had no authority to order dismissal. Reversed and remanded.

EDITOR'S ANALYSIS: The function of compulsory joinder, codified in Fed. R. Civ. P. 19, is to bring all affected parties into the same lawsuit. Joinder is often required where the suit involves jointly-held rights or liabilities, where more than one party claims the same property, or where granting relief necessarily would affect the rights of parties not in the lawsuit. Though there is a strong interest in "complete, consistent, and efficient settlement of controversies," compulsory joinder is limited. There is a strong tradition of allowing the parties themselves to determine who shall be a party, what claims shall be litigated, and what litigation strategies shall be followed.

[For more information on compulsory joinder, see Casenote Law Outline on Civil Procedure, Chapter 6, Joinder of Claims and Parties, § I, Joinder of Claims.]

QUICKNOTES

FRCP 19 - Sets forth the rules governing joinder.

JOINT TORTFEASORS - Two or more parties that either act in concert, or whose individual acts combine to cause a single injury, rendering them jointly and severally liable for damages incurred.

JOINDER - The joining of claims or parties in one lawsuit.

NECESSARY PARTIES - Parties whose joining in a lawsuit is essential to the disposition of the action.

COMPULSORY JOINDER - The joining of parties to a lawsuit that is mandatory if complete relief cannot be afforded to the parties in his absence or his absence will result in injustice.

NOTES:

GOLDINGER v. BORON OIL COMPANY

Employee (P) v. Oil company (D)

60 F.R.D. 562 (W.D.Pa. 1973).

NATURE OF CASE: Motion to compel production of new agreements and reasons for termination of employment contract.

FACT SUMMARY: Goldinger (P) brought this action for wrongful termination of his employment contract with Boron (D) and sought the production of any new agreements with Boron (D) along with the reasons for any changes in those new agreements, and Boron (D) asserted that any changes were made as a result of legal advice and were thus protected by the attorney-client privilege.

CONCISE RULE OF LAW: The reasons for changes in a contract form made as a result of confidential communication between a party and his attorney are protected from discovery by the attorney-client privilege.

FACTS: Goldinger (P) brought an action against Boron (D) for wrongful termination of his employment contract, alleging that Boron (D) forced him to sell gasoline at prices fixed in violation of the antitrust laws of the United States. Goldinger (P) sought production by discovery procedures of any new contracts entered into by Boron (D) with other dealers and the changes contained therein in addition to the reasons for any such changes. Boron (D) challenged the production of any reasons for changes on the ground that the reasons developed as a result of confidential communications with attorneys and thus were protected by the attorney-client privilege.

ISSUE: Are the reasons for changes in a contract form made as a result of confidential communications between a party and his attorney protected from discovery by the attorney client privilege?

HOLDING AND DECISION: (Weber, J.) Yes. Any reasons for changing the contract used by Boron (D) with its dealers would be primarily legal in nature. The advice upon which the reasons were formulated was alleged by Boron (D) to have been obtained from its attorneys during confidential communications. The agreement itself cannot be so protected, however. Even if the privilege once existed as to the agreement, it has been shown to third parties, which has destroyed any possible privilege. Nonetheless, the reasons for changes in a contract form made as a result of confidential communications between a party and his attorney are protected from discovery by the attorney-client privilege. Motion denied.

EDITOR'S ANALYSIS: The F.R.C.P. provides that the laws of privilege of the state in which a district court sits are applicable in federal actions. There is no federal law of privilege in the F.R.E. (Federal Rules of Evidence). The attorney-client privilege is recognized in all United States jurisdictions, however, and this case would be similarly governed by any of them.

[For more information on scope of discovery, see Casenote Law Outline on Civil Procedure, Chapter 7, Discovery, § III, Outline of the Scope of Discovery Under Federal Rules.]

QUICKNOTES

CONFIDENTIAL COMMUNICATIONS - A communication made between specified classes of persons which is privileged.

ATTORNEY-CLIENT PRIVILEGE - A doctrine precluding the admission into evidence of confidential communications between an attorney and his client made in the course of obtaining professional assistance.

NOTES:

HOUCHENS v. AMERICAN HOME ASSURANCE CO.
Decedents' spouse (P) v. Life insurance company (D)
927 F.d. 163 (4th Cir. 1991).

NATURE OF CASE: Appeal of dismissal of action for damages for breach of contract.

FACT SUMMARY: On American's (D) summary judgment motion, the court dismissed Houchens' (P) suit for payment on two accidental death policies because of insufficient evidence that Houchens' (P) husband died accidentally.

CONCISE RULE OF LAW: Under Fed. R. Civ. P. 56, a federal court must enter summary judgment if after complete discovery a party fails to show that the evidence, viewed in the light most favorable to that party, is sufficient to establish the existence of an essential element on which that party has the burden of proof.

FACTS: Houchens' (P) husband disappeared in Thailand in August, 1980, and was not heard from since. Under Virginia law, a person who is missing for seven years is presumed dead. In 1988, Houchens (P) had her husband declared legally dead. Houchens (P) attempted to collect on two life insurance policies issued by American (D), under which the proceeds would only be paid upon proof that the insured's death was accidental. American (D) refused to pay and Houchens (P) sued in federal court for breach of contract. American (D) moved for summary judgment, arguing there was no evidence that the insured had died or that he had died accidentally. The district court granted the motion and dismissed the case, and Houchens (P) appealed.

ISSUE: Under Fed. R. Civ. P. 56, must a federal court enter summary judgment if a party fails to show that the evidence, viewed in the light most favorable to that party, is sufficient to establish the existence of an essential element on which that party has the burden of proof?

HOLDING AND DECISION: (Ervin, C.J.) Yes. Under Fed. R. Civ. P. 56, a federal court must enter summary judgment if a party fails to show that the evidence, viewed in the light most favorable to that party, is sufficient to establish the existence of an essential element on which that party has the burden of proof. Under Rule 56(c), a summary judgment motion must be granted where there is "no genuine issue as to any material fact." Here, Houchens (P) is entitled to the Virginia presumption that her husband is dead. However, for recovery on the policy it still must be shown that her husband's death was accidental. The meager circumstances surrounding his disappearance do not provide sufficient evidence to allow a reasonable jury to conclude that he died accidentally. Under Virginia law, Houchens (D) had the burden of proof as to accident, a necessary element of her case. She had insufficient evidence to meet this burden. Thus, as there was no genuine issue as to a material fact, the summary judgment motion was properly granted. Affirmed.

EDITOR'S ANALYSIS: Houchens (P) cited two cases where the issue was the same and a summary judgment motion by the insurance company defendant was denied. In Valley National Bank of Arizona v. J. C. Penney Ins. Co., Ariz. Ct. App., 129 Ariz. 108, 628 P.d. 991 (1981), the insured disappeared, and his skeletal remains were later found with bullet casings nearby. In Martin v. Insurance Co. of America, 1 Wash. App. 218, 460 P.d. 682 (1969), the insured disappeared in fog and snow on a steep and wooded mountainside after having last been seen without a compass at the 3,000-foot level, asking for directions. In each of these cases, the court found that there was a genuine issue of material fact because there was sufficient evidence, unlike in the Houchens case, for a jury to find that the insured died accidentally.

[For more information on summary judgments, see Case note Law Outline on Civil Procedure, Chapter 8, Pre-Trial Procedure and Dispositions — Alternatives to Trial, Pre-Trial Conferences, Dismissal, Default Judgment, and Summary Judgment, § IV, Summary judgments.]

QUICKNOTES

FRCP 56(c) - Provides that a court arrive at a pre-verdict disposition on the case at bar when one party fails to prove an a\essential element of its case.

BURDEN OF PROOF - The duty of a party to introduce evidence to support a fact that is in dispute in an action.

SUMMARY JUDGMENT - Judgment rendered by a court in response to a motion by one of the parties, claiming that the lack of a question of material fact in respect to an issue warrants disposition of the issue without consideration by the jury.

NOTES:

NORTON v. SNAPPER POWER EQUIPMENT

Gardener (P) v. Lawn mower manufacturer (D)

806 F.d. 1545 (11th Cir. 1987).

NATURE OF CASE: Appeal from judgment notwithstanding the verdict denying damages for personal injuries.

FACT SUMMARY: In Norton's (P) suit for damages against Snapper Power Equipment (D), Snapper (D) moved for and was granted a judgment notwithstanding the verdict, contending that since a reconstruction of Norton's (P) accident with a Snapper (D) riding mower was impossible, the jury could not determine whether a blade-stopping device would have eliminated or lessened Norton's (P) injury.

CONCISE RULE OF LAW: A judgment notwithstanding the verdict should only be granted where the evidence so strongly points in favor of a moving party that reasonable people could not arrive at a contrary verdict.

FACTS: Norton (P), a commercial gardener, was injured while riding a lawn mower manufactured by Snapper Power Equipment (D). Norton (P) sued Snapper (D) for damages based on strict liability. At the close of Norton's (P) case, and against the close of all evidence, Snapper (D) moved for a directed verdict. The court left the strict liability claim for the jury, and the jury returned a verdict for Norton (P), holding Snapper (D) liable for 80% of the injuries. After dismissing the jury, the court indicated that it would enter a judgment notwithstanding the verdict based on Snapper's (D) contention that since a reconstruction of Norton's (P) accident with the mower was impossible, the jury could not determine whether a blade-stopping device would have eliminated or lessened Norton's (P) injury. Norton (P) appealed.

ISSUE: Should a judgment notwithstanding the verdict only be granted where the evidence so strongly points in favor of a moving party that reasonable people could not arrive at a contrary verdict?

HOLDING AND DECISION: (Clark, J.) Yes. A judgment notwithstanding the verdict should only be granted where the evidence so strongly points in favor of a moving party that reasonable people could not arrive at a contrary verdict. The issues here were whether the failure to install "dead man" devices rendered the mower defective, and if the mower was defective, whether the lack of a "dead man" control caused the injury. Snapper (D) claims that there was little or no evidence to support the jury's verdict. The jury is, however, permitted to reconstruct the series of events by drawing an inference upon an inference. The causation evidence here, although circumstantial, was far more impressive than Snapper (D) contends, and Snapper (D) was given every opportunity to point out the weaknesses in Norton's (P) proof, but was unpersuasive to the jury. Reversed and remanded.

EDITOR'S ANALYSIS: Within 10 days of an adverse verdict, the loser may move for a judgment notwithstanding the verdict. This motion asserts that even if all the winner's evidence is true, the loser is entitled to a verdict as a matter of law. A motion for a new trial may be based either on an error of law or an erroneous charge.

[For more information on judgments notwithstanding the evidence, see Case note Law Outline on Civil Procedure, Chapter 9, Trial and Post-Trial Motions, § VI, Post-Verdict Motions.]

QUICKNOTES

JUDGMENT N.O.V. - A judgment entered by the trial judge reversing a jury verdict if the jury's determination has no basis in law or fact.

DIRECTED VERDICT - A verdict ordered by the court in a jury trial.

STRICT LIABILITY - Liability for all injuries proximately caused by a party's conducting of certain inherently dangerous activities without regard to negligence or fault.

NOTES:

RUSH v. CITY OF MAPLE HEIGHTS

Motorcycle passenger (P) v. Municipality (D)

Ohio Ct. App., 167 Ohio St. 221 (1958).

NATURE OF CASE: Action for damages for personal injuries.

FACT SUMMARY: In Rush's (P) action against the City of Maple Heights (D) to recover damages for personal injuries suffered in a motorcycle accident, Rush (P) claimed that she should be permitted to split her cause of action, filing a claim for property damage in one court and a separate action for personal injuries in another court.

CONCISE RULE OF LAW: Where a person suffers both personal injuries and property damage as a result of the same wrongful act, only a single cause for action arises, the different injuries occasioned thereby being separate items of damages from such act.

FACTS: Rush (P) was riding on a motorcycle operated by her husband and was injured when the cycle ran into a hole in the road, throwing her to the ground. Rush (P) brought suit against the City of Maple Heights (D) for damage to the cycle. The lower court found that the City (D) was negligent in not repairing the road and awarded Rush (P) $100. That judgment was affirmed by the court of appeals and the Ohio supreme court. Then, Rush (P) brought the present suit to recover damages for personal injuries suffered in the same accident, contending that she should be permitted to split her cause of action and file separate claims for property damage and personal injuries in separate courts. The trial court held that the issues of negligence and proximate cause had been determined in the prior action against the City (D) and were binding. The jury awarded Rush (P) $12,000 solely on the question of damages, and the court of appeals affirmed this judgment. The City (D) appealed.

ISSUE: Where a person suffers both personal injuries and property damage as a result of the same wrongful act, does only a single cause of action arise, the different injuries occasioned thereby being separate items of damage from such act?

HOLDING AND DECISION: (Herbert, J.) Yes. Where a person suffers both personal injuries and property damage as a result of the same wrongful act, only a single cause of action arises, the different injuries occasioned thereby being separate items of damage from such act. This is the majority rule in this country, and the reasoning behind it is that a single tort can be the basis of but one action. It is not improper to declare in different counts for damages to the person and property when both result from the same tort; it is the better practice to do so where there is any difference in the measure of damages, and all damages must be sued for in one suit. This is necessary to prevent multiplicity of suits, burdensome expense, delay, and vexatious litigation. Here, Rush (P) suffered both personal injuries and property damage as a result of the same wrongful act — nonrepair of the road. The different injuries occasioned by the wrongful act were separate items of damage from such act, but the actions of the City (D) constituted but one tort. A single tort can be the basis of but one suit. Reversed and remanded.

CONCURRENCE: (Stewart, J.) The rule at common law and in a majority of the states of the union is that damages resulting from a single wrongful act, even though they include both property and personal injury damages, are, when suffered by the same person, the subject of only one action against the wrongdoer.

DISSENT: (Zimmerman, J.) Established law should remain undisturbed in order to insure a stability on which the lower courts and the legal profession generally may rely with some degree of confidence.

EDITOR'S ANALYSIS: Former adjudication can be divided into claim preclusion and issue preclusion. Two requirements must be met before the rules of claim preclusion apply: (1) the claim must be the same in the first and second action; and (2) the first decision must be "on the merits." Issue preclusion prevents a litigant from basing a claim, in a second suit, on the same events as those in the first suit if the same issues were determined in the first litigation between the parties.

[For more information on scope of claim or cause of action, see Casenote Law Outline on Civil Procedure, Chapter 12, Preclusion Doctrines — Res Judicata and Collateral Estoppel, § I, Res Judicata Defined.]

QUICKNOTES

CAUSE OF ACTION - A fact or set of facts the occurrence of which entitle a party to seek judicial relief.

RES JUDICATA - The rule of law that a final judgment by a court precludes subsequent litigation between the parties regarding the same cause of action.

COLLATERAL ESTOPPEL - A doctrine whereby issues litigated and determined in a prior proceeding are binding upon all subsequent litigation between the parties regarding that issue.

APEX HOSIERY CO. v. LEADER
Hosiery company (P) v. Appellant (D)
102 F.2d 702 (3d Cir. 1939).

NATURE OF CASE: Appeal from a court order to produce, for inspection, documents for trial in antitrust action.

FACT SUMMARY: Leader (D) appealed from an order of the court for the discovery and production of documents for inspection, copying, and photographing by Apex Hosiery Co. (P) for use at trial.

CONCISE RULE OF LAW: An order of the court made under Federal Rule of Civil Procedure 34 for discovery and production of documents is interlocutory and therefore not appealable.

FACTS: Leader (D), in an action for treble damages under the Sherman Anti-Trust Act note, appealed from an order of the district court made under Fed. R. Civ. P. 34 for the discovery and production by it of documents for inspection, copying, and photographing by Apex Hosiery (D) for use at the trial of the action.

ISSUE: Is an order of the court made under Fed. R. Civ. P. 34 for discovery and production of documents interlocutory and therefore not appealable?

HOLDING AND DECISION: (Per curiam) Yes. An order of the court made under Fed. R. Civ. P. 34 for discovery and production of documents is interlocutory and therefore not appealable. In this case, the disposition made of the motion will necessarily determine the conduct of the trial and may vitally affect the result. In essence, the motion resembles others made before or during a trial to secure or to suppress evidence, such as applications to suppress a deposition, to compel the production of books or documents, or to physically examine a plaintiff. The orders made upon such applications, so far as they affect the rights only of parties to the litigation, are interlocutory. Appeal denied.

EDITOR'S ANALYSIS: The above doctrine is known as the "final judgment" rule. Its application prevents endless litigation of interim rulings that may ultimately be mooted anyway by resolution or settlement of a case. However, some jurisdictions permit appeal of nonfinal rulings at the trial court level, provided they are judged to be sufficiently "significant."

[For more information on appeal, see Casenote Law Outline on Civil Procedure, Chapter 10, § III, The Federal Courts and the Model of Finality.]

QUICKNOTES
FRCP 24 - Governs discovery and the production of documents at trial.

INTERLOCUTORY (ORDER) - An order entered by the court determining an issue that does not resolve the disposition of the case, but is essential to a proper adjudication of the action.

FINAL JUDGMENT - A decision by the court settling a dispute between the parties on its merits and which is appealable to a higher court.

NOTES:

NOTES

CHAPTER 2
PERSONAL JURISDICTION

QUICK REFERENCE RULES OF LAW

1. **The Origins.** Where the object of an action is to determine the personal rights and obligations of the parties, service by publication against a nonresident is ineffective to confer jurisdiction upon the court. (Pennoyer v. Neff)

    [For more information on federal standard for proper notice, see Casenote Law Outline on Civil Procedure, Chapter 2, Controlling the Choice of Forum: Jurisdiction, Process, and Choice of Law, III, Jurisdiction and Valid Judgments.]

2. **Redefining Constitutional Power.** For a state to subject a nonresident defendant to in personam jurisdiction, due process requires that he have certain minimum contacts with it such that the maintenance of the suit does not offend traditional notions of fair play and substantial justice. (International Shoe Co. v. Washington)

    [For more information on minimum contacts analysis, see Casenote Law Outline on Civil Procedure, Chapter 3, Minimum Contacts Analysis, § II, The Birth of Minimum Contracts Doctrine in International Shoe.]

3. **Redefining Constitutional Power.** For there to be "minimal contacts" sufficient to support in personam jurisdiction, it is essential that there be some act by which the defendant purposefully avails himself of the privilege of conducting activities within the forum state, thus invoking the benefits and protections of its laws. (Hanson v. Denckla)

    [For more information on purposeful contacts, see Casenote Law Outline on Civil Procedure, Chapter 3, Minimum Contacts Analysis, § III, Further Development of Minimum Contacts Doctrine. See also, § V, Step-by-Step Guide to Minimum Contacts Analysis.]

4. **Absorbing In Rem Jurisdiction.** Jurisdiction cannot be founded on property within a state unless there are sufficient contacts within the meaning of the test developed in International Shoe. (Shaffer v. Heitner)

    [For more information on in rem jurisdictions; further development, see Casenote Law Outline on Civil Procedure, Chapter 3, Minimum Contacts Analysis, § III, Further Development of Minimum Contracts Doctrine.]

5. **Specific Jurisdiction.** A state court may exercise personal jurisdiction over a nonresident defendant only so long as there exist sufficient "minimum contacts" between him and the forum state such that maintenance of the suit does not offend "traditional notions of fair play and substantial justice." (World-Wide Volkswagen Corp. v. Woodson)

    [For more information on purposefulness of contracts, see Casenote Law Outline on Civil Procedure, Chapter 3, Minimum Contacts Analysis, § III, V.]

6. **Specific Jurisdiction.** Minimum contacts sufficient to sustain jurisdiction are not satisfied simply by the placement of a product into the stream of commerce coupled with an awareness that its product would reach the forum state. (Asahi Metal Industry Co. v. Superior Court)

    [For more information on reasonableness factors, see Casenote Law Outline on Civil Procedure, Chapter 3, Minimum Contacts Analysis, § V, Step-by-Step Guide to Minimum Contacts Analysis.]

7. **Specific Jurisdiction.** Direct and continuous contacts by a franchisee with the franchisor may lead to the franchisee being subject to the jurisdiction of the franchisor's home forum. (Burger King Corp. v. Rudzewicz)

   [For more information on reasonableness factors, see Casenote Law Outline on Civil Procedure, Chapter 3, Minimum Contacts Analysis, § V, Step-by-Step Guide to Minimum Contacts Analysis.]

8. **General Jurisdiction.** General jurisdiction may be found, regardless of the lack of a relationship between a nonresident defendant's contacts with the forum and the cause of action, where the defendant engages in the continuous and systematic pursuit of general business activities in the forum state. (Kenerson v. Lindblade)

   [For more information on personal/general jurisdiction, see Casenote Law Outline on Civil Procedure, Chapter 3, § III, Further Development of Minimum Contacts Doctrine and § IV, Burnham and Transient Jurisdiction.]

9. **General Jurisdiction.** State courts have jurisdiction over nonresidents who are physically present in the state. (Burnham v. Superior Court)

   [For more information on personal jurisdiction, see Casenote Law Outline on Civil Procedure, Chapter 2, § IV, Choice of Law Influences on Choice of Forum.]

10. **Jurisdiction to Determine Jurisdiction.** Under F.R.C.P. 37(b), a court may, as a sanction for failure to comply with a discovery order directed at establishing jurisdictional facts, order that such facts are deemed to be established. (Insurance Corp. of Ireland v. Compagnie des Bauxites de Guinée)

    [For more information on discovery requests, see Casenote Law Outline on Civil Procedure, Chapter 7, Discovery, § VI, Discovery: Abuse and Sanctions: Federal Rules 26(f)-(g) and 37.]

11. **Consent as a Substitute for Power.** Reasonable forum selection clauses contained in passenger tickets are presumptively valid. (Carnival Cruise Lines, Inc. v. Shute)

12. **The Constitutional Requirement of Notice**. In order to satisfy due process challenges, notice must be by means calculated to inform the desired parties, and, where they reside outside of the state and their names and addresses are available, notice by publication is insufficient. (Mullane v. Central Hanover Bank & Trust Co.)

    [For more information on standards for proper notice, see Casenote Law Outline on Civil Procedure, Chapter 2, Controlling the Choice of Forum: Jurisdiction, Process, and Choice of Law, § III, Jurisdiction and Valid Judgment.]

13. **Long-Arm Statutes as a Restraint on Jurisdiction.** A federal court may exercise in personam territorial jurisdiction over a party served outside the federal court's home state only to the extent that such territorial jurisdiction is authorized by the home state's long-arm statute. (Crocker v. Hilton International Barbados, Ltd.)

    [For more information on long-arm statutes, see Casenote Law Outline on Civil Procedure, Chapter 2, § III, Jurisdiction and Valid Judgments.]

14. **Forum Non Conveniens.** A plaintiff may not defeat a motion to dismiss for forum non conveniens merely by showing that the substantive law that would be applied in the alternative forum is less favorable to him than that of the present forum. (Piper Aircraft v. Reyno)

    [For more information on forum non conveniens, see Casenote Law Outline on Civil Procedure, Chapter 2, § V, Other Constraints on Choice of Forum.]

PENNOYER v. NEFF
Purchaser of property (D) v. Real property owner (P)
95 U.S. 714 (1877).

NATURE OF CASE: Action to recover possession of land.

FACT SUMMARY: Neff (P) attacked the validity of a sheriff's sale of his property to satisfy a personal judgment obtained against him where service was by publication.

CONCISE RULE OF LAW: Where the object of an action is to determine the personal rights and obligations of the parties, service by publication against a nonresident is ineffective to confer jurisdiction upon the court.

FACTS: Neff (P) owned real property in Oregon. Mitchell brought suit in Oregon to recover legal fees allegedly owed him by Neff (P). Neff (P), a nonresident, was served by publication and Mitchell obtained a default judgment. The court ordered Neff's (P) land sold at a sheriff's sale to satisfy the judgment. Pennoyer (D) purchased the property. Neff (P) subsequently learned of the sale and brought suit in Oregon to recover possession of the property. Neff (P) alleged that the court ordering the sale had never acquired in personam jurisdiction over him. Therefore, the court could not adjudicate the personal rights between Neff (P) and Mitchell and the default judgment had been improperly entered.

ISSUE: Where an action involves the adjudication of personal rights and obligations of the parties, is service by publication against a nonresident sufficient to confer jurisdiction?

HOLDING AND DECISION: (Field, J.) No. Substituted service of process in actions against nonresidents of a state is effective only in proceedings in rem. Where an action involves the determination of personal rights and obligations of the parties, service by publication is ineffective to confer jurisdiction over the nonresident defendant. No state can exercise direct jurisdiction and authority over persons or property outside of its boundaries. The validity of every judgment depends upon the jurisdiction of the court rendering judgment. Thus, Mitchell could not obtain a personal judgment against Neff (P) without first obtaining in personam jurisdiction. Substituted service by publication is ineffective to confer personal jurisdiction over a nonresident. The sale was therefore void. A different result could have been reached if Mitchell had first obtained in rem jurisdiction by seizing the property at the time suit was commenced.

EDITOR'S ANALYSIS: Although no state can exercise direct jurisdiction and authority over people or property outside the state, the state may exercise jurisdiction over persons and property inside the state in ways that will affect persons and property outside the state. Pennoyer v. Neff established that every state had the power to regulate the way in which property

within the state is acquired, enjoyed, and transferred. But a state cannot bring a person or property outside the stale into its jurisdiction simply by using substituted service.

[For more information on federal standard for proper notice, see Casenote Law Outline on Civil Procedure, Chapter 2, Controlling the Choice of Forum: Jurisdiction, Process, and Choice of Law, III, Jurisdiction and Valid Judgments.]

QUICKNOTES

IN REM JURISDICTION - A court's authority over a thing so that its judgment is binding in respect to the rights and interests of all parties in that thing.

SERVICE OF PROCESS - The communication of reasonable notice of a court proceeding to a defendant in order to provide him with an opportunity to be heard.

IN PERSONAM JURISDICTION - The jurisdiction of a court over a person as opposed to his interest in property.

NOTES:

INTERNATIONAL SHOE CO. v. WASHINGTON
Delaware corporation (D) v. State (P)
326 U.S. 310 (1945).

NATURE OF CASE: Proceedings to recover unemployment contributions.

FACT SUMMARY: A state statute authorized the mailing of notice of assessment of delinquent contributions for unemployment compensation to nonresident employers. International Shoe Co. (D) was a nonresident corporation. Notice of assessment was served on one of its salespersons within the state and was mailed to International's (D) office.

CONCISE RULE OF LAW: For a state to subject a nonresident defendant to in personam jurisdiction, due process requires that he have certain minimum contacts with it such that the maintenance of the suit does not offend traditional notions of fair play and substantial justice.

FACTS: A Washington statute set up a scheme of unemployment compensation which required contributions by employers. The statute authorized the commissioner, Washington (P), to issue an order and notice of assessment of delinquent contributions by mailing the notice to nonresident employers. International (D) was a Delaware corporation having its principal place of business in Missouri. International employed 11 to 13 salespersons under the supervision of managers in Missouri. These salespeople resided in Washington and did most of their work there. They had no authority to enter into contracts or make collections. International (D) did not have any office in Washington and made no contracts there. Notice of assessment was served upon one of International's (D) Washington salespersons and a copy of the notice was sent by registered mail to International's (D) Missouri address.

ISSUE: For a state to subject a nonresident defendant to in personam jurisdiction, does due process require only that he have certain minimum contacts with it, such that the maintenance of the suit does not offend notions of fair play and substantial justice?

HOLDING AND DECISION: (Stone, C.J.) Yes. Historically the jurisdiction of courts to render judgment in personam is grounded on their power over the defendant's person, and his presence within the territorial jurisdiction of a court was necessary to a valid judgment. But now, due process requires only that in order to subject a defendant to a judgment in personam, if he is not present within the territorial jurisdiction, he have certain minimum contacts with the territory such that the maintenance of the suit does not offend traditional notions of fair play and substantial justice. The contacts must be such as to make it reasonable, in the context of our federal system, to require a defendant corporation to defend the suit brought there. An estimate of the inconveniences which would result to the corporation from a trial away from its "home" is relevant. To require a corporation to defend a suit away from home where its contact has been casual or isolated activities has been thought to lay too unreasonable a burden on it. However, even single or occasional acts may, because of their nature, quality and circumstances, be deemed sufficient to render a corporation liable to suit. Hence, the criteria to determine whether jurisdiction is justified is not simply mechanical or quantitative. Satisfaction of due process depends on the quality and nature of the activity in relation to the fair and orderly administration of the laws. In this case International's (D) activities were neither irregular nor casual. Rather, they were systematic and continuous. The obligation sued upon here arose out of these activities. They were sufficient to establish sufficient contacts or ties to make it reasonable to permit Washington (P) to enforce the obligations International (D) incurred there.

DISSENT: (Black, J.) The U.S. Constitution leaves to each state the power to tax and to open the doors of its courts for its citizens to sue corporations who do business in the state. It is a judicial deprivation to condition the exercise of this power on this court's notion of "fair play."

EDITOR'S ANALYSIS: Before this decision three theories had evolved to provide for suits by and against foreign corporations. The first was the consent theory. It rested on the proposition that since a foreign corporation could not carry on its business within a state without the permission of that state, the state could require a corporation to appoint an agent to receive service of process within the state. However, it soon became established law that a foreign corporation could not be prevented by a state from carrying on interstate commerce within its borders. The presence doctrine required that the corporation was "doing business" and "present" in the state. The third theory used either the present or consent doctrine, and it was necessary to determine whether the corporation was doing business within the state either to decide whether its consent could properly be implied or to discover whether the corporation was present.

[For more information on minimum contacts analysis, see Casenote Law Outline on Civil Procedure, Chapter 3, Minimum Contacts Analysis, § II, The Birth of Minimum Contracts Doctrine in International Shoe.]

QUICKNOTES

IN PERSONAM JURISDICTION - The jurisdiction of a court over a person as opposed to his interest in property.

CONSENT JURISDICTION - The forum having jurisdiction over a lawsuit as agreed upon by the parties prior to litigation.

MINIMUM CONTACTS - The minimum degree of contact necessary in order to sustain a cause of action within a particular forum, consistent with the requirements of due process.

HANSON v. DENCKLA
Will legatees (P) v. Trust beneficiaries (D)
357 U.S. 235 (1950).

NATURE OF CASE: Appeal from disposition of property in a trust.

FACT SUMMARY: Legatees under the decedent's will argued that the property in question passed under the will's residuary clause, while beneficiaries under a trust argued that the property passed through the trust.

CONCISE RULE OF LAW: For there to be "minimal contacts" sufficient to support in personam jurisdiction, it is essential that there be some act by which the defendant purposefully avails himself of the privilege of conducting activities within the forum state, thus invoking the benefits and protections of its laws.

FACTS: The decedent established a trust in Delaware. The decedent later became domiciled in Florida, and it was there that her will was admitted to probate. Legatees under the will argued that the money should pass under the residuary clause of the will, while the beneficiaries under the trust argued that the money should be distributed through the Delaware trust. The Florida courts sustained the position of the legatees, but the Delaware courts, on the ground that Florida had failed to acquire in personam jurisdiction over an indispensable party, the Delaware trustee, refused to accord full faith and credit to the Florida decision and found for the beneficiaries.

ISSUE: For there to be "minimal contacts" sufficient to support in personam jurisdiction, is it essential that there be some act by which the defendant purposefully avails himself of the privilege of conducting activities within the forum state?

HOLDING AND DECISION: (Warren, C.J.) Yes. For there to be "minimal contacts" sufficient to support in personam jurisdiction, it is essential that there be some act by which the defendant purposefully avails himself of the privilege of conducting activities with the forum state, thus invoking the benefits and protections of its laws. In this case, no such contacts could be found. The Delaware trustee had no office in Florida and conducted no business there. No trust assets were ever held in Florida or administered there, and there was no solicitation of business in that state either in person or by mail. Consequently, this suit was not one to enforce an obligation that arose from a privilege exercised in Florida. However minimal the burden of defending in a foreign tribunal, a defendant may not be called upon to do so unless he has had the minimum contacts with that state that are a prerequisite to its exercise of power over him. Reversed and remanded.

EDITOR'S ANALYSIS: The case really revolves around the validity of the inter vivos trust. The trust was created in Delaware, and the corpus remains there. The fact that some Florida residents are beneficiaries thereunder, or that they wish to defeat the trust, is not a compelling state interest. It certainly is not a more substantial interest than is Delaware's right to construe the validity of a trust created under its laws and the corpus of which is within its jurisdiction. The fact that the settlor was a Florida resident is immaterial. She was not a resident when the trust was created, nor was she attempting to have the trust set aside.

[For more information on purposeful contacts, see Case note Law Outline on Civil Procedure, Chapter 3, Minimum Contacts Analysis, § III, Further Development of Minimum Contacts Doctrine. See also, § V, Step-by-Step Guide to Minimum Contacts Analysis.]

QUICKNOTES

IN PERSONAM JURISDICTION - The jurisdiction of a court over a person as opposed to his interest in property.

MINIMUM CONTACTS - The minimum degree of contact necessary in order to sustain a cause of action within a particular forum, consistent with the requirements of due process.

RESIDUARY CLAUSE (OF WILL) - A clause contained in a will disposing of the assets remaining following distribution of the estate.

INTER VIVOS TRUST - Property that is held by one person for the benefit of another and which is created by an instrument that takes effect during the life of the grantor.

NOTES:

SHAFFER v. HEITNER
Corporation (D) v. Shareholder (P)
433 U.S. 186 (1977).

NATURE OF CASE: Appeal from a finding of state jurisdiction.

FACT SUMMARY: Heitner (P) brought a derivative suit against Greyhound (D) directors for antitrust losses it had sustained in Oregon. The suit was brought in Delaware, Greyhound's (D) state of incorporation.

CONCISE RULE OF LAW: Jurisdiction cannot be founded on property within a state unless there are sufficient contacts within the meaning of the test developed in International Shoe.

FACTS: Heitner (P) owned one share of Greyhound (D) stock. Greyhound (D) had been subjected to a large antitrust judgment in Oregon. Heitner (P), a nonresident of Delaware, brought a derivative suit in Delaware, the state of Greyhound's (D) incorporation. Jurisdiction was based on sequestration of Greyhound (D) stock which was deemed to be located within the state of incorporation. The Delaware sequestration statute allowed property within the state to be seized ex parte to compel the owner to submit to the in personam jurisdiction of the court. None of the stock was actually in Delaware, but a freeze order was placed on the corporate books. Greyhound (D) made a special appearance to challenge the court's jurisdiction to hear the matter. Greyhound (D) argued that the sequestration statute was unconstitutional under the line of case's beginning with Snidatch. Greyhound (D) also argued that there were insufficient contacts with Delaware to justify an exercise of jurisdiction. The Delaware courts found that the sequestration statute was valid since it was not a per se seizure of the property and was merely invoked to compel out-of-state residents to defend actions within the state. Little or no consideration was given to the "contact" argument based on a finding that the presence of the stock within the state conferred quasi-in-rem jurisdiction.

ISSUE: May a state assume jurisdiction over an issue merely because defendant's property happens to be within the state?

HOLDING AND DECISION: (Marshall, J.) No. Mere presence of property within a state is insufficient to confer jurisdiction on a court absent independent contacts within the meaning of International Shoe, which would make acceptance constitutional. We expressly disapprove that line of cases represented by Harris v. Balk, which permits jurisdiction merely because the property happens to be within the state. If sufficient contacts do not exist to assume jurisdiction absent the presence of property within the state, it cannot be invoked on the basis of property within the court's jurisdiction. We base this decision on the fundamental concepts of justice and fair play required under the due process and equal protection clauses of the Fourteenth Amendment. Here, the stock is not the subject of the controversy. There is no claim to ownership of it or injury caused by it. The defendants do not reside in Delaware or have any contacts there. The injury occurred in Oregon. No activities complained of were done within the forum. Finally, Heitner (P) is not even a Delaware resident. Jurisdiction was improperly granted. Reversed.

CONCURRENCE: (Powell, J.) I would only disagree as to cases involving property permanently within the state, e.g., real property. Such property should confer jurisdiction.

CONCURRENCE: (Stevens, J.) I concur in the result since purchase of stock in the marketplace should not confer in rem jurisdiction in the state of incorporation. I also concur with Mr. Justice Powell's statements.

CONCURRENCE AND DISSENT: (Brennan, J.) A state may exercise jurisdiction over a party only on the basis of the minimum contacts among the parties, the contested transaction and the forum state. In this case, however, the assertion of jurisdiction was based on the presence of property, in the form of capital stock, in Delaware. This is quasi-in-rem jurisdiction and is not based upon minimum contacts. However, even under the minimum contacts analysis that the majority requires today, jurisdiction should not be denied in this case. The state of Delaware has a strong interest in adjudicating claims as to corporations chartered by it. It must provide restitution for its corporations, it has a regulatory interest, and an interest in providing a convenient forum for the entity which is a creature of its law. Thus, jurisdiction should attach.

EDITOR'S ANALYSIS: While the corporation could be sued in its state of incorporation under the dissent's theory, the suit is against the directors and neither the site of the wrong nor the residence of a defendant is in Delaware. The decision will only have a major impact in cases such as herein where the state really has no reason to want to adjudicate the issue. Of course, real property would still be treated as an exception.

[For more information on in rem jurisdictions; further development, see Casenote Law Outline on Civil Procedure, Chapter 3, Minimum Contacts Analysis, § III, Further Development of Minimum Contracts Doctrine.]

QUICKNOTES

IN REM JURISDICTION - A court's authority over a thing so that its judgment is binding in respect to the rights and interests of all parties in that thing.

QUASI-IN REM JURISDICTION - A court's authority over the defendant's property within a specified geographical area.

EX PARTE - A proceeding commenced by one party without providing any opposing parties with notice or which is uncontested by an adverse party.

WORLD-WIDE VOLKSWAGEN CORP. v. WOODSON
Automobile distributor (P) v. Court (D)
444 U.S. 286 (1980).

NATURE OF CASE: Petition for a writ prohibiting the exercise of in personam jurisdiction.

FACT SUMMARY: World-Wide (P) sought a writ of prohibition to keep district court Judge Woodson (D) from exercising in personam jurisdiction over it, alleging it did not have sufficient "contacts" with the forum state of Oklahoma to render it subject to such jurisdiction.

CONCISE RULE OF LAW: A state court may exercise personal jurisdiction over a nonresident defendant only so long as there exist sufficient "minimum contacts" between him and the forum state such that maintenance of the suit does not offend "traditional notions of fair play and substantial justice."

FACTS: World-Wide (P) was the regional distributor of Audi automobile for the tri-state area of New York, New Jersey, and Connecticut. It was the distributor of the particular Audi that the Robinsons purchased from a New York dealer and drove to Oklahoma, where three family members were severely burned when another car struck their Audi in the rear. The Robinsons brought a products liability action in an Oklahoma district court, suing the New York dealership and World-Wide (a New York corporation). Claiming that no evidence showed it had any connection with Oklahoma whatsoever, World-Wide (P) sought a writ of prohibition to keep district court Judge Woodson (D) from exercising in personam jurisdiction. World-Wide (P) argued that a lack of sufficient contacts with the forum state made assertion of such jurisdiction improper under the Due Process Clause. The Supreme Court of Oklahoma denied the writ, noting that World-Wide (P) could foresee that the automobiles it sold would be taken into other states, including Oklahoma. The United States Supreme Court granted certiorari.

ISSUE: Must a defendant have "minimum contacts" with the forum state before it can exercise in personam jurisdiction over him?

HOLDING AND DECISION: (White, J.) Yes. Under the Due Process Clause, the exercise of in personam jurisdiction over a defendant is not constitutional unless he has sufficient "minimum contacts" with the forum state so that maintenance of the suit does not offend "traditional notions of fair play and substantial justice." Here, World-Wide (P) had no "contacts, ties, or relations" with Oklahoma, so personal jurisdiction could not be exercised. As for the notion that it was foreseeable that cars sold in New York would wind up in Oklahoma, the foreseeability that is critical to due process analysis is not the mere likelihood that a product will find its way into the forum state. Rather, it is that the defendant's

conduct and connection with the forum state are such that he should reasonably anticipate being hauled into court there. Such conduct and connection are simply missing in this case. Reversed.

DISSENT: (Brennan, J.) The automobile is designed specifically to facilitate travel from place to place, and the sale of one purposefully injects it into the stream of interstate commerce. Thus, this case is not unlike those where in personam jurisdiction is properly exercised over one who purposefully places his product into the stream of interstate commerce with the expectation it will be purchased by consumers in other states. Furthermore, a large part of the value of automobiles is the extensive, nationwide network of highways. State maintenance of such roads contributes to the value of World-Wide's (P) business. World-Wide (P) also participates in a network of related dealerships with nationwide service facilities. Having such facilities in Oklahoma also adds to the value of World-Wide's (P) business. Thus, it has the required minimum contacts with Oklahoma to render this exercise of personal jurisdiction constitutional.

DISSENT: (Marshall, J.) The majority takes an unnecessarily narrow view of World-Wide's (P) forum-related conduct. Jurisdiction can, in this case, be constitutionally premised on the deliberate and purposeful actions of World-Wide (P) in choosing to become part of a nationwide, indeed a global, network for marketing and servicing automobiles.

DISSENT: (Blackmun, J.) The nature of the automobile is such that it is intended for travel about the country and across state boundary lines. World-Wide (P) is in the business of providing vehicles which spread all over the highways of our several states. In assessing "minimum contacts," foreseeable use in another state seems to me to be little different from foreseeable resale in another state. Yet, the majority would allow jurisdiction in the latter case, but not in the former. At any rate, World-Wide (P) derives substantial benefits from having Oklahoma highways available for its customers in the use of their automobiles, etc.

Continued on next page.

EDITOR'S ANALYSIS: Over the years, modern transportation and communication have made foreign state suits much less of a burden to defendants. This resulted in a relaxing of the due process limits placed on state jurisdiction down to the "minimum contacts" concept. However, even if there were no inconvenience to the defendant, a state could not exercise personal jurisdiction over him if he had no "contacts, ties, or relations." This is true even if that state had a strong interest in applying its law to the controversy, it was the most convenient location for litigation, etc. The reason is that the Due Process Clause serves two distinct functions: the first is as a guarantor against inconvenient litigation but the second is as a guardian of interstate federalism. It is in this second capacity that the Due Process Clause would prevent assumption of jurisdiction in the aforementioned instance by recognizing the "territorial limitations on the power of the respective states."

[For more information on purposefulness of contracts, see Casenote Law Outline on Civil Procedure, Chapter 3, Minimum Contacts Analysis, § III, V.]

QUICKNOTES

IN PERSONAM JURISDICTION - The jurisdiction of a court over a person as opposed to his interest in property.

MINIMUM CONTACTS - The minimum degree of contact necessary in order to sustain a cause of action within a particular forum, consistent with the requirements of due process.

NOTES:

ASAHI METAL INDUSTRY CO., LTD. v. SUPERIOR COURT OF CALIFORNIA, SOLANO COUNTY

Japanese tire corporation (P) v. Court (D)

480 U.S. 102 (1987).

NATURE OF CASE: Appeal from discharge of writ quashing service of summons.

FACT SUMMARY: Asahi (P) appealed from a decision of the California Supreme Court discharging a peremptory writ issued by the appeals court quashing service of summons in Cheng Shin's indemnity action, contending that there did not exist minimum contacts between California and Asahi (P) sufficient to sustain jurisdiction.

CONCISE RULE OF LAW: Minimum contacts sufficient to sustain jurisdiction are not satisfied simply by the placement of a product into the stream of commerce coupled with an awareness that its product would reach the forum state.

FACTS: Asahi (P), a Japanese corporation, manufactured tire valve assemblies in Japan, selling some of them to Cheng Shin, a Taiwanese company who incorporated them into the motorcycles it manufactured. Zurcher was seriously injured in a motorcycle accident, and a companion was killed. He sued Cheng Shin, alleging the motorcycle tire manufactured by Cheng Shin was defective. Cheng Shin sought indemnity from Asahi (P), and the main action settled. Asahi (P) moved to quash service of summons, contending that jurisdiction could not be maintained by California, the state in which Zurcher filed his action, consistent with the Due Process Clause of the Fourteenth Amendment. The evidence indicated that Asahi's (P) sales to Cheng Shin took place in Taiwan, and shipments went from Japan to Taiwan. Cheng Shin purchased valve assemblies from other manufacturers. Sales to Cheng Shin never amounted to more than 1.5% of Asahi's (P) income. Approximately 20% of Cheng Shin's sales in the United States are in California. In declaration, an attorney for Cheng Shin stated he made an informal examination of tires in a bike shop in Solano County, where Zurcher was injured, finding approximately 20% of the tires with Asahi's (P) trademark (25% of the tires manufactured by Cheng Shin). The Superior Court (D) denied the motion to quash, finding it reasonable that Asahi (P) defend its claim of defect in their product. The court of appeals issued a peremptory writ commanding the Superior Court (D) to quash service of summons. The state supreme court reversed and discharged the writ, finding that Asahi's (P) awareness that some of its product would reach California by placing it in the stream of commerce satisfied minimum contacts sufficient to sustain jurisdiction. From this decision, Asahi (P) appealed.

ISSUE: Are minimum contacts sufficient to sustain jurisdiction satisfied by the placement of a product into the stream of commerce, coupled with the awareness that its product would reach the forum state?

HOLDING AND DECISION: (O'Connor, J.) No. Minimum contacts sufficient to sustain jurisdiction are not satisfied by the placement of a product in the stream of commerce, coupled with the awareness that its product would reach the forum state. To satisfy minimum contacts, there must be some act by which the defendant purposefully avails itself of the privilege of conducting activities within the forum state. Although the courts that have squarely addressed this issue have been divided, the better view is that the defendant must do more than place a product in the stream of commerce. The unilateral act of a consumer bringing the product to the forum state is not sufficient. Asahi (P) has not purposefully availed itself of the California market. It does not do business in the state, conduct activities, maintain offices or agents, or advertise. Nor did it have anything to do with Cheng Shin's distribution system, which brought the tire valve assembly to California. Assertion of jurisdiction based on these facts exceeds the limits of due process. [The Court went on to consider the burden of defense on Asahi (P) and the slight interests of the state and Zurcher, finding the assertion of jurisdiction unreasonable and unfair.] Reversed and remanded.

CONCURRENCE: (Brennan, J.) The state supreme court correctly concluded that the stream of commerce theory, without more, has satisfied minimum contacts in most courts which have addressed the issue, and it has been preserved in the decision of this Court.

CONCURRENCE: (Stevens, J.) The minimum contacts analysis is unnecessary; the Court has found by weighing the appropriate factors that jurisdiction under these facts is unreasonable and unfair.

EDITOR'S ANALYSIS: The Brennan concurrence is quite on point in criticizing the plurality for its characterization that this case involves the act of a consumer in bringing the product within the forum state. The argument presented in World-Wide Volkswagen Corp. v. Woodson, 444 U.S. 286 (1980), cited by the plurality, seems more applicable to distributors and retailers than to manufacturers of component parts.

Continued on next page.

——————————————

NOTES:

[For more information on reasonableness factors, see Casenote Law Outline on Civil Procedure, Chapter 3, Minimum Contacts Analysis, § V, Step-by-Step Guide to Minimum Contacts Analysis.]

QUICKNOTES

MINIMUM CONTACTS - The minimum degree of contact necessary in order to sustain a cause of action within a particular forum, consistent with the requirements of due process.

PURPOSEFUL AVAILMENT - An element in determining whether a defendant had the required minimum contacts in a forum necessary in order for a court to exercise jurisdiction over the party, whereby the court determines whether the defendant intentionally conducted activities in the forum and thus knows, or could reasonably expect, that such conduct could give rise to litigation in that forum.

PEREMPTORY WRIT - Writ directing the sheriff to have the defendant appear before the court so long as the plaintiff has provided adequate security in order to prosecute the action.

QUASH - To vacate, annul, void.

BURGER KING CORP v. RUDZEWICZ

Fast food corporation (P) v. Franchisee (D)

471 U.S. 462 (1985).

NATURE OF CASE: Appeal from reversal of award of damages and injunctive relief for breach of contract.

FACT SUMMARY: Burger King Corp. (P) brought an action against Rudzewicz (D), a defaulting franchisee, in Burger King's (P) home forum.

CONCISE RULE OF LAW: Direct and continuous contacts by a franchisee with the franchisor may lead to the franchisee being subject to the jurisdiction of the franchisor's home forum.

FACTS: Rudzewicz (D) contracted for a Burger King franchise in Michigan with Burger King Corp. (P), a Florida corporation. A franchise was granted. The terms of the contract called for substantial supervision of the franchise's operations by Burger King (P), and also for the laws of Florida to apply. Despite the fact that Rudzewicz (D) was a sophisticated businessman, the business failed, and Burger King (P) brought suit for unpaid rent. The Florida district court granted damages and injunctive relief, but the Eleventh Circuit reversed, holding that Rudzewicz (D) was not amenable to Florida jurisdiction. Burger King Corp. (P) appealed.

ISSUE: May direct and continuous contacts by a franchisee with the franchisor lead to the franchisee being subject to the jurisdiction of the franchisor's home forum?

HOLDING AND DECISION: (Brennan, J.) Yes. Direct and continuous contacts by a franchisee with the franchisor may lead to the franchisee being subject to the jurisdiction of the franchisor's home forum. The main test for personal jurisdiction is whether a defendant's actions were such that he should have been put on notice of the possibility of becoming subject to the subject forum's jurisdiction. The yardstick here is the nature of that defendant's contacts with that forum. Here, Rudzewicz (D) contracted with a Florida franchisor and entered into a contract providing for a continuous relationship with that franchisor and constant monitoring by that franchisor. Further, the contract stated that it was to be construed a Florida contract. Considering the nature of Rudzewicz's (D) contacts with Florida, an ample basis for jurisdiction existed. Reversed.

DISSENT: (Stevens, J.) The typical franchise is a large operation connected with the franchisor's home office only in name. Since the business is purely local, only local jurisdiction should apply.

EDITOR'S ANALYSIS: Part of the rationale for the Court's opinion was the clause making the contract a Florida one. Most contracts involving parties in different states have such clauses. Exactly how much weight was given this was not spelled out by the Court, but the opinion did say that such a clause is not determinative.

[For more information on reasonableness factors, see Casenote Law Outline on Civil Procedure, Chapter 3, Minimum Contacts Analysis, § V, Step-by-Step Guide to Minimum Contacts Analysis.]

QUICKNOTES

PERSONAL JURISDICTION - The court's authority over a person or parties to a law suit.

MINIMUM CONTACTS - The minimum degree of contact necessary in order to sustain a cause of action within a particular forum, consistent with the requirements of due process.

INJUNCTIVE RELIEF - A count order issued as a remedy, requiring a person to do, or prohibiting that person from doing, a specific act.

NOTES:

KENERSON v. LINDBLADE

Representative of decedent (P) v. President of hospital (D)

604 F. Supp. 792 (D. Maine 1985).

NATURE OF CASE: Motion to dismiss for lack of personal jurisdiction in malpractice action.

FACT SUMMARY: Kenerson (P) brought a wrongful death action in Maine against Memorial Hospital (D) and its physicians (D), although the medical treatment received by Kenerson's (P) decedent occurred in the State of New Hampshire.

CONCISE RULE OF LAW: General jurisdiction may be found, regardless of the lack of a relationship between a nonresident defendant's contacts with the forum and the cause of action, where the defendant engages in the continuous and systematic pursuit of general business activities in the forum state.

FACTS: Kenerson's (P) decedent, Reginald Kenerson, a Maine resident, fell and was injured in New Hampshire in March 1981. As a result of injuries sustained in the fall, he was taken to Memorial Hospital (D) in North Conway, New Hampshire, of which Lindblade (D) was president and trustee, where he was treated by Dr. Stevenson. Several hours later Mr. Kenerson's condition worsened, and the physician at Memorial Hospital consulted by telephone with a neurosurgeon at the Maine Medical Center in Portland, Maine, and later arranged to have Kenerson transferred to that hospital. He died en route to the Portland hospital. Kenerson (P) brought suit in Maine Superior Court. The action was removed to federal court, and the defendants then brought a motion to dismiss based on lack of personal jurisdiction.

ISSUE: May general jurisdiction be found, in the absence of a relationship between a nonresident defendant's contacts with the forum and the cause of action, where the defendant engages in the continuous and systematic pursuit of general business activities in the forum state?

HOLDING AND DECISION: (Carter) Yes. General jurisdiction may be found, in the absence of a relationship between a nonresident defendant's contacts with the forum and the cause of action, where the defendant engages in the continuous and systematic pursuit of general business activities in the forum state. The most salient and forceful evidence of such contacts in this case is that in the period 1980-1983, the Hospital (D) treated a total of 432 Maine residents as in-patients. This constituted approximately 8.5% of Memorial's in-patient population. The Hospital (D) also treated a total of 7,854 Maine residents as out-patients during the same period of time. In 1981, over 13% of the out-patients were from Maine. Additionally, patients were transferred to other hospitals (D) in Maine by the Hospital (D), which acted more as a regional hospital irrespective of state lines. Motion denied.

EDITOR'S ANALYSIS: General jurisdiction arises where defendants are being sued in what is apparently their base of operations. Base of operations is determined by considering the states of domicile, principal place of business, and incorporation. However, general jurisdiction may extend beyond the base of operations depending on the level of activity engaged in by defendant.

[For more information on personal/general jurisdiction, see Casenote Law Outline on Civil Procedure, Chapter 3, § III, Further Development of Minimum Contacts Doctrine and § IV, Burnham and Transient Jurisdiction.]

QUICKNOTES

FORUM STATE - The state in which a court, or other location in which a legal remedy may be sought, is located.

DOMICILE - A person's permanent home or principal establishment to which he has an intention of returning when he is absent therefrom.

PERSONAL JURISDICTION - The court's authority over a person or parties to a law suit.

GENERAL JURISDICTION - Refers to the authority of a court to hear and determine all cases of a particular type.

NOTES:

BURNHAM v. SUPERIOR COURT
Husband and father (P) v. Court (D)
— U.S.—, 110 S.Ct. 2105 (1990).

NATURE OF CASE: Appeal from denial of motion to quash service of process in dissolution action on the grounds that the court lacked personal jurisdiction.

FACT SUMMARY: Dennis Burnham (P) and his wife were living in New Jersey when they decided to separate. Mrs. Burnham moved with the children to California, filed for divorce in that state and served Mr. Burnham (P) while he was visiting.

CONCISE RULE OF LAW: State courts have jurisdiction over nonresidents who are physically present in the state.

FACTS: Dennis Burnham (P) and his wife were living in New Jersey when they decided to separate. Mrs. Burnham moved with the children to California and filed for divorce in that state. Mr. Burnham (P) visited his children in January of 1988, at which time he was served with a California court summons and a copy of his wife's divorce petition. He made a special appearance in the California Superior Court (D) moving to quash the service of process on the ground that the Court (D) lacked personal jurisdiction over him because his only contacts with California were a few short visits to the state for the purpose of conducting business and visiting his children. The Superior Court (D) denied the motion, and the California Court of Appeal denied mandamus relief. The court held it to be a valid jurisdictional predicate for in personam jurisdiction that Mr. Burnham (P) was present in the forum state and personally served with process. The U.S. Supreme Court granted certiorari.

ISSUE: Do state courts have jurisdiction over nonresidents who are physically present in the state?

HOLDING AND DECISION: (Scalia, J.) Yes. State courts have jurisdiction over nonresidents who are physically present in the state. Jurisdiction based on physical presence alone constitutes due process because it is one of the continuing traditions of our legal system that define the due process standard of traditional notions of fair play and substantial justice. That standard was developed by analogy to physical presence, and it would be perverse to say it could now be turned against that touchstone of jurisdiction. Affirmed.

CONCURRENCE: (Brennan, J.) History is an important factor in establishing whether a jurisdictional rule satisfies due process requirements, but it is not the only factor such that all traditional rules of jurisdiction are, ipso facto, forever constitutional.

CONCURRENCE: (Stevens, J.) It is sufficient to note that the historical evidence and consensus identified by Justice Scalia,

the considerations of fairness identified by Justice Brennan, and the common sense displayed by Justice White, all combine to demonstrate that this is, indeed, a very easy case.

EDITOR'S ANALYSIS: In a footnote to the above case, Justice Scalia explained that in Helicopteros Nacionales de Columbia v. Hall, 466 U.S. at 414 (1984) the U.S. Supreme Court held that due process is not offended by a state's subjecting a corporation to its jurisdiction when there are sufficient contacts between the state and the foreign corporation. However, the only holding supporting that statement involved regular service of summons upon a corporate president while in the forum state acting in that capacity. See Perkins v. Benguet Consolidated Mining Co., 342 U.S. 437 (1952). It may be that whatever special rule exists permitting continuous and systematic contacts to support jurisdiction with respect to matters unrelated to activity in the forum applied only to corporations, which have never fitted comfortably within a jurisdictional regime based primarily upon de facto power over the defendant's person.

[For more information on personal jurisdiction, see Casenote Law Outline on Civil Procedure, Chapter 2, § IV, Choice of Law Influences on Choice of Forum.]

QUICKNOTES

PERSONAL JURISDICTION - The court's authority over a person or parties to a law suit.

SERVICE OF PROCESS - The communication of reasonable notice of a court proceeding to a defendant in order to provide him with an opportunity to be heard.

NOTES:

INSURANCE CORPORATION OF IRELAND v. COMPAGNIE de BAUXITES de GUINEA

Insurance company (D) v. Claimant (P)

456 U.S. 694 (1982).

NATURE OF CASE: Appeal from sanctions for failure to comply with discovery order.

FACT SUMMARY: Insurance Corp. of Ireland (ICI) (D) contended that the district court had no power to order the existence of personal jurisdiction over it as a sanction for its failure to comply with discovery orders.

CONCISE RULE OF LAW: Under F.R.C.P. 37(b), a court may, as a sanction for failure to comply with a discovery order directed at establishing jurisdictional facts, order that such facts are deemed to be established.

FACTS: Compagnie (P) obtained insurance against business interruption from ICI (D), which refused to pay Compagnie's (P) claim. Compagnie (P) sued in federal court in Pennsylvania, and ICI (D) contested the existence of personal jurisdiction. Compagnie (P) made requests for discovery information relevant to the jurisdiction issue, which ICI (D) refused. ICI (D) subsequently failed to comply with an order to disclose the information and the court, under F.R.C.P. 37(b), imposed sanctions which ordered that the facts establishing personal jurisdiction were deemed to exist. ICI (D) appealed, contending the court had no power to order the existence of jurisdiction.

ISSUE: May a court order that facts showing the existence of personal jurisdiction be deemed established as a sanction for the failure to comply with a discovery order under F.R.C.P. 37(b)?

HOLDING AND DECISION: (White, J.) Yes. Under F.R.C.P. 37(b), a court may, as a sanction for the failure to comply with a discovery order, directed at establishing jurisdictional facts, order that such facts be deemed to be established. The requirement of personal jurisdiction is a personal right, it is not a matter of governmental sovereignty, and as such it may be waived. Because it is not an element of sovereignty like subject matter jurisdiction is, personal jurisdiction, as a defense, may be taken from the defendant. The actions of the defendant may amount to legal submission to the jurisdiction of the court whether voluntary or not. Therefore, by failing to comply with discovery orders after being warned of the court's intent to order jurisdiction, ICI (D) submitted to the court's jurisdiction. Affirmed.

CONCURRENCE: (Powell, J.) Although in this case personal jurisdiction existed, the court misapprehended the character of the requirement of personal jurisdiction. It is indeed one of constitutional proportions and no less strong than that of subject matter jurisdiction.

EDITOR'S ANALYSIS: Some commentators argue that this case was not actually decided on the sanctions rationale. Rather, they argue, that the holding is based on prior decisions which articulate the proposition that a presumption of the existence of jurisdictional facts may arise from the defendant's silence.

---

*[For more information on discovery requests, see **Casenote Law Outline on Civil Procedure, Chapter 7, Discovery, § VI, Discovery: Abuse and Sanctions: Federal Rules 26(f)-(g) and 37.**]*

QUICKNOTES

PERSONAL JURISDICTION - The court's authority over a person or parties to a law suit.

DISCOVERY - Pretrial procedure during which one party makes certain information available to the other.

SUBJECT MATTER JURISDICTION - The authority of the court to hear and decide actions involving a particular type of issue or subject.

NOTES:

CARNIVAL CRUISE LINES, INC. v. SHUTE
Cruise company (D) v. Customers (P)
499 U.S. 585 (1991)

NATURE OF CASE: Review of denial of defense motion for summary judgment in personal injury action.

FACT SUMMARY: Shute (P), an injured cruise ship passenger, filed suit in her home state despite a stipulation in her passenger ticket requiring all suits to be filed in Florida.

CONCISE RULE OF LAW: Reasonable forum selection clauses contained in passenger tickets are presumptively valid.

FACTS: The Shutes (P), residents of Washington State, purchased passage for a seven-day cruise on a ship owned by Carnival Cruise Lines (D). The cruise tickets they received contained a forum-selection clause setting the State of Florida as the forum where any disputes arising from the cruise would be litigated. Carnival Cruise (D) had its principal place of business in Florida, and many of its cruises departed from there. During the cruise, Mrs. Shute (P) was injured in a slip-and-fall accident. The Shutes (P) filed a negligence action in Washington. Carnival Cruise (D) moved for summary judgment, contending that the forum clause in the Shutes's (P) ticket required them to bring their suit in a Florida court. The Ninth Circuit denied its motion on the ground that the clause was not a product of negotiation, and the Supreme Court granted certiorari.

ISSUE: Are reasonable forum selection clauses contained in passenger tickets presumptively valid?

HOLDING AND DECISION: (Blackmun, J.) Yes. Reasonable forum selection clauses contained in passenger tickets are presumptively valid. They are permissible because a cruise line has a special interest in limiting the fora in which it potentially could be subject to suit. Such a clause also dispels any confusion about where a suit must be brought, thereby sparing litigants and courts the time and expense of litigating the issue. Finally, the passengers themselves benefit from forum clauses because fares are reduced commensurate with the money saved by the cruise line in limiting the fora where it may be sued. Since in this case there is no bad faith motive apparent in Carnival Cruise's (D) forum provision, and the Shutes (P) have conceded that they had notice of the provision, the Ninth Circuit erred in refusing to enforce the clause. Reversed.

DISSENT: (Stevens, J.) The prevailing rule is that forum selection clauses are not enforceable if they were not freely bargained for, create additional expense for one party, or deny one party a remedy.

EDITOR'S ANALYSIS: Besides forum selection clauses, a contract may contain a choice of law clause, stipulating which jurisdiction's substantive law will govern, or an arbitration clause, requiring parties to use arbitration as their exclusive forum. The most extreme example of a contract provision limiting a defendant's right to appeal or to even raise a defense to an action is the "cognovit." A cognovit note is written authority of a debtor for entry of a judgment against him if the obligation set forth in the note is not paid when due. Such agreements are prohibited in many states.

QUICKNOTES

FORUM SELECTION CLAUSE - Provision contained in a contract setting forth the particular forum in which the parties would resolve a matter if a dispute were to arise.

COGNOVIT NOTE - A note signed by a debtor authorizing an attorney to enter judgment against him if payment is not made thereon.

NOTES:

MULLANE v. CENTRAL HANOVER BANK AND TRUST CO.

Guardian of trust beneficiaries (P) v. Bank (D)

339 U.S. 306 (1950).

NATURE OF CASE: Constitutional challenge of the sufficiency of the notice provision of the New York Banking Law relating to beneficiaries of common trust funds.

FACT SUMMARY: Central Hanover Bank (D) pooled a number of small trust funds, and beneficiaries (some of whom lived out of state) were notified by publication in a local newspaper.

CONCISE RULE OF LAW: In order to satisfy due process challenges, notice must be by means calculated to inform the desired parties, and, where they reside outside of the state and their names and addresses are available, notice by publication is insufficient.

FACTS: A New York statute allowed corporate trustees to pool the assets of numerous small trusts administered by them. This allowed more efficient and economical administration of the funds. Each participating trust shared ratably in the common fund, but the trustees held complete control of all assets. A periodic accounting of profits, losses, and assets were to be submitted to the courts for approval. Beneficiaries were to be notified of the accounting so that they might object to any irregularities in the administration of the common fund. Once approved by the court, their claims would be barred. A guardian would be appointed to protect the interests of principal and income beneficiaries. Central Hanover Bank (D) established a common fund by consolidating the corpus of 113 separate trusts under their control. Notice of the common fund was sent to all interested parties along with the relevant portions of the statute. Notice of accountings were by publication in a local New York newspaper. Mullane (P) was the appointed guardian for all parties known and unknown who had an interest in the trust's income. He objected to the sufficiency of the statutory notice provisions claiming that they violated the Due Process Clause of the Fourteenth Amendment. Notice by publication was not a reasonable method of informing interested parties that their rights were being affected, especially with regard to out-of-state beneficiaries. Mullane's (P) objections were overruled in state courts and the present federal appeal was brought by him.

ISSUE: Is notice by publication sufficient to satisfy due process challenges where the parties to be informed reside out of state and an alternative means, better calculated to give actual notice, is available?

HOLDING AND DECISION: (Jackson, J.) No. The purpose of a notice requirement is to inform parties that their rights are being affected. Therefore, the method chosen should, if at all possible, be reasonably designed to accomplish this end. Notice in a New York legal paper is not reasonably calculated to provide out-of-state residents with the desired information. While the state has a right to discharge trustees of their liabilities through the acceptance of their accounting, it must also provide beneficiaries with adequate notice so that their rights to contest the accounting are not lost. In cases where the identity or whereabouts of beneficiaries or future interest holders is unknown, then publication is the most viable alternate means available for giving notice. Publication is only a supplemental method of giving notice. However, the court will approve its use where alternative methods are not reasonably possible or practical. Where alternative methods, better calculated to give actual notice, are available, publication is an impermissible means of providing notice. Notice to known beneficiaries via publication is inadequate, not because it in fact fails to inform everyone, but, because under the circumstances, it is not readily calculated to reach those who could easily be informed by other means at hand. Since publication to known beneficiaries is ineffective, the statutory requirement violates the Due Process Clause of the Fourteenth Amendment. These parties have, at least potentially, been deprived of property without due process of law. With respect to remote future interest holders and unknown parties, publication is permissible.

EDITOR'S ANALYSIS: Ineffective notice provisions violate procedural due process rights. As in all due process challenges, there must be a legitimate state interest and the means selected must be reasonably adapted to accomplish the state's purpose. While in Mullane the state's ends were permissible, the method of giving notice was unreasonable as it pertained to known parties. As has been previously stated, publication is only a supplementary method for giving notice. It is normally used in conjunction with other means when personal service by hand is unavailable or impractical. Mullane has been applied to condemnation cases where a known owner of property was never personally served. Schroeder v. City of New York, 371 U.S. 208. Factors considered by the Court involve the nature of the action, whether the party's whereabouts or identity are known or unknown, whether he is a resident and whether or not he has attempted to avoid personal service. If an attempt to avoid service is made, then constructive service by publication in conjunction with substitute service by mail is permitted. Finally, foreign corporations are generally required to appoint resident agents authorized to accept service of process.

[For more information on standards for proper notice, see Casenote Law Outline on Civil Procedure, Chapter 2, Controlling the Choice of Forum: Jurisdiction, Process, and Choice of Law, § III, Jurisdiction and Valid Judgment.]

CROCKER v. HILTON INTERNATIONAL-BARBADOS, LTD.
Rape victim (P) v. Hotel (D)
976 F.3d 797 (1st Cir. 1992).

NATURE OF CASE: Appeal from dismissal of negligence action.

FACT SUMMARY: Crocker (P) was raped at the Hilton in Barbados and sought to sue Hilton (D) in Massachusetts.

CONCISE RULE OF LAW: A federal court may exercise in personam territorial jurisdiction over a party served outside the federal court's home state only to the extent that such territorial jurisdiction is authorized by the home state's long-arm statute.

FACTS: The Crockers (P) were guests at Hilton International (D), a hotel in Barbados, when the Crockers (P) alleged that an unknown assailant raped Ms. Crocker (P) at knife-point while at the hotel. The Crockers (P) returned to Massachusetts and commenced action against Hilton International (D), a Barbados corporation, for negligence and loss of consortium. Ms. Crocker (P) alleged she suffered post-traumatic stress syndrome. Hilton International (D) had no telephone number, address, agents, employees, or agent for process in Massachusetts and limited its activities in Massachusetts to soliciting business. The federal district court dismissed the action for lack of jurisdiction. The Crockers (P) appealed.

ISSUE: May a federal court exercise in personam territorial jurisdiction over a party served outside the federal court's home state if such territorial jurisdiction is not authorized by the home state's long-arm statute?

HOLDING AND DECISION: (Torruella, J.) No. A federal court may exercise in personam territorial jurisdiction over a party served outside the federal court's home state only to the extent that such territorial jurisdiction is authorized by the home state's long-arm statute. The Massachusetts long-arm statute does not extend to Hilton International (D) on these facts. Mass. Gen. Laws § 3(a) authorizes jurisdiction when the cause of action arises from the defendant's transacting business in Massachusetts; however, the Crockers's (P) cause of action arises from the rape in Barbados. Similarly, Mass. Gen. Laws § 3(d) authorizes the court to extend jurisdiction when a tortious injury is caused in Massachusetts; but, the Crockers's tortious injury was caused in Barbados. Finally, Mass. Gen. Laws § 38 authorizes service of process for foreign corporations, but it does not extend jurisdiction to cases when the cause of action does not arise in Massachusetts. Affirmed.

EDITOR'S ANALYSIS: The first step in determining whether the court has personal territorial jurisdiction over an out-of-state defendant is to apply the long-arm statute to the facts of the case.

If the long-arm statute does not extend, no due process analysis is needed. However, for exam purposes, it is usually better practice to assume arguendo that the long-arm statute extends to the defendant and then to conduct a federal due process analysis.

[For more information on long-arm statutes, see Casenote Law Outline on Civil Procedure, Chapter 2, § III, Jurisdiction and Valid Judgments.]

QUICKNOTES

IN PERSONAM JURISDICTION - The jurisdiction of a court over a person as opposed to his interest in property.

LONG-ARM STATUTE - A state statute conferring personal jurisdiction to state courts over a defendant not residing in the state, when the cause of action arises as a result of activities conducted within the state or affecting state residents.

NOTES:

PIPER AIRCRAFT COMPANY v. REYNO
Aircraft company (D) v. Crash victims' representative (P)
454 U.S. 235 (1982).

NATURE OF CASE: Appeal from dismissal on the basis of forum non conveniens.

FACT SUMMARY: Reyno (P), the representative of five victims of an air crash, brought suit in California even though the location of the crash and the homes of the victims were in Scotland.

CONCISE RULE OF LAW: A plaintiff may not defeat a motion to dismiss for forum non conveniens merely by showing that the substantive law that would be applied in the alternative forum is less favorable to him than that of the present forum.

FACTS: Reyno (P) was the representative of five air crash victims' estates and brought suit for wrongful death in United States district court in California, even though the accident occurred and all the victims resided in Scotland. Piper (D) moved to dismiss for forum non conveniens, contending that Scotland was the proper forum. Reyno (P) opposed the motion on the basis that the Scottish laws were less advantageous to her than American laws. The district court granted the motion, while the court of appeals reversed. The Supreme Court granted certiorari.

ISSUE: May a plaintiff defeat a motion to dismiss for forum non conveniens merely on the basis that the laws of the alternative forum are less advantageous?

HOLDING AND DECISION: (Marshall, J.) No. A plaintiff may not defeat a motion to dismiss for forum non conveniens merely by showing that the substantive law of the alternative forum is less advantageous than that of the present forum. In this case, all the evidence, witnesses, and interests were in Scotland. Thus, the most convenient forum was there. As a result, the motion was properly granted. Reversed.

EDITOR'S ANALYSIS: The Court in this case specifically noted that under some circumstances, the fact that the chosen state's laws are less attractive to the defendant could be used to defeat a motion to dismiss for forum non conveniens. If the state chosen by the plaintiff has the only adequate remedy for the wrong alleged, then the motion may be denied.

[For more information on forum non conveniens, see Casenote Law Outline on Civil Procedure, Chapter 2, § V, Other Constraints on Choice of Forum.]

QUICKNOTES

FORUM NON CONVENIENS - An equitable doctrine permitting a court to refrain from hearing and determining a case when the matter may be more properly and fairly heard in another forum.

MOTION TO DISMISS - Motion to terminate a trial based on the adequacy of the pleadings.

NOTES:

CHAPTER 3
SUBJECT MATTER JURISDICTION OF THE FEDERAL COURTS

QUICK REFERENCE RULES OF LAW

1. **Federal Question Jurisdiction.** Alleging an anticipated constitutional defense in the complaint does not give a federal court jurisdiction if there is no diversity of citizenship between the litigants. (Louisville & Nashville Railroad v. Mottley)

    [For more information on scope of federal question jurisdiction, see Casenote Law Outline on Civil Procedure, Chapter 4, Federal Subject Matter Jurisdiction and Related Doctrines Affecting the Choice of a Federal Forum, § III, The Federal Question Jurisdiction of the District Courts.]

2. **Diversity Jurisdiction.** A domiciliary of a state remains so for diversity purposes until he formulates an intent to permanently remain in another state. (Mas v. Perry)

    [For more information on definitions of domicile, see Casenote Law Outline on Civil Procedure, Chapter 4, Federal Subject Matter Jurisdiction and Related Doctrines Affecting the Choice of a Federal Forum, § IV, The Diversity Jurisdiction of the District Courts.]

3. **Diversity Jurisdiction.** Diversity jurisdiction does not extend over divorce, alimony, and child custody decrees but does cover tort claims for child abuse. (Ankenbrandt v. Richards)

    [For more information on diversity jurisdiction, see Casenote Law Outline on Civil Procedure, Chapter 4, § IV, The Diversity Jurisdiction of the District Courts.]

4. **Supplemental Jurisdiction.** If a plaintiff's claims based on both federal and state law are such that he would ordinarily be expected to try them all in one proceeding, there is power in the federal courts to hear the whole. (United Mine Workers v. Gibbs)

    [For more information on pendent jurisdiction, see Casenote Law Outline on Civil Procedure, Chapter 6, Joinder of Claims and Parties, § V, Supplemental Jurisdiction in Aid of Liberal Joinder in the Federal Courts.]

5. **Removal.** A federal court may remand a case to a state court upon finding that the claim raises a novel or complex issue of state law, the state law claim substantially predominates, or upon determination that retaining jurisdiction would be inappropriate. (Williams v. Huron Valley School District)

    [For more information on removal, see Casenote Law Outline on Civil Procedure, Chapter 4, § V, Removal Jurisdiction.]

6. **Removal.** A removed case may be remanded to state court at any time it appears that a federal court lacks subject matter jurisdiction. (Powell v. Zoning Board of Appeals of the City of Chicago)

    [For more information on removal, see Casenote Law Outline on Civil Procedure, Chapter 4, § V, Removal Jurisdiction.]

LOUISVILLE & NASHVILLE R.R. v. MOTTLEY

Railroad company (D) v. Injured passengers (P)

211 U.S. 149 (1908).

NATURE OF CASE: Appeal of a decision overruling a demurrer in an action for specific performance of a contract.

FACT SUMMARY: Mottley (P) was injured on a train owned by Louisville & Nashville Railroad (D), which granted Mottley (P) a lifetime free pass which he sought to enforce.

CONCISE RULE OF LAW: Alleging an anticipated constitutional defense in the complaint does not give a federal court jurisdiction if there is no diversity of citizenship between the litigants.

FACTS: In 1871, Mottley (P) and his wife were injured while riding on the Louisville & Nashville R.R. (D). The Mottleys (P) released their claims for damages against the Louisville & Nashville R.R. (D) upon receiving a contract granting free transportation during the remainder of their lives. In 1907, the Louisville & Nashville R.R. (D) refused to renew the Mottleys' (P) passes relying upon an act of Congress which forbade the giving of free passes or free transportation. The Mottleys (P) filed an action in a Circuit Court of the United States for the Western District of Kentucky. The Mottleys (P) and the Louisville & Nashville R.R. (D) were both citizens of Kentucky. Therefore, the Mottleys (P) attempted to establish federal jurisdiction by claiming that the Louisville & Nashville R.R. (D) would raise a constitutional defense in their answer, thus raising a federal question. The Louisville & Nashville R.R. (D) filed a demurrer to the complaint for failing to state a cause of action. The demurrer was denied. On appeal, the Supreme Court did not look at the issue raised by the litigants, but on their own motion raised the issue of whether the federal courts had jurisdiction to hear the case.

ISSUE: Does an allegation in the complaint that a constitutional defense will be raised in the answer raise a federal question which would give a federal court jurisdiction if no diversity of citizenship is alleged?

HOLDING AND DECISION: (Moody, J.) No. The Supreme Court reversed the lower court's ruling and remitted the case to that court with instructions to dismiss the suit for want of jurisdiction. Neither party to the litigation alleged that the federal court had jurisdiction in this case, and neither party challenged the jurisdiction of the federal court to hear the case. Because the jurisdiction of the circuit court is defined and limited by statute, the Supreme Court stated that it is their duty to see that such jurisdiction is not exceeded. Both parties to the litigation were citizens of Kentucky and so there was no diversity of citizenship. The only way that the federal court could have jurisdiction in this case would be if there were a federal question involved. Mottley (P) did allege in his complaint that the Louisville & Nashville R.R.

(D) based their refusal to renew the free pass on a federal statute. Mottley (P) then attempted to allege information that would defeat the defense of the Louisville & Nashville R.R. (D). This is not sufficient. The plaintiff's complaint must be based upon the federal laws of the Constitution to confer jurisdiction on the federal courts. Mottley's (P) cause of action was not based on any federal laws or constitutional privileges; it was based on a contract. Even though it is evident that a federal question will be brought up at the trial, plaintiff's cause of action must be based on a federal statute or the constitution in order to have a federal question which would grant jurisdiction to the federal courts.

EDITOR'S ANALYSIS: If Mottley (P) could have alleged that he was basing his action on a federal right, it would have been enough to have given the federal court jurisdiction. The federal court would have had to exercise jurisdiction at least long enough to determine whether there actually was such a right. If the federal court ultimately concludes that the claimed federal right does not exist, the complaint would be dismissed for failure to state a claim upon which relief can be granted rather than for lack of jurisdiction. The court has the power to determine the issue of subject matter jurisdiction on its own motion as it did in this case. Subject matter jurisdiction can be challenged at any stage of the proceeding.

[For more information on scope of federal question jurisdiction, see Case note Law Outline on Civil Procedure, Chapter 4, Federal Subject Matter Jurisdiction and Related Doctrines Affecting the Choice of a Federal Forum, § III, The Federal Question Jurisdiction of the District Courts.]

QUICKNOTES

FEDERAL QUESTION - The authority of the federal courts to hear and determine in the first instance matters pertaining to the federal Constitution, federal law, or treaties of the United States.

DIVERSITY OF CITIZENSHIP - The authority of a federal court to hear and determine cases involving $10,000 or more and in which the parties are citizens of different states, or in which one party is an alien.

SUBJECT MATTER JURISDICTION - The authority of the court to hear and decide actions involving a particular type of issue or subject.

MAS v. PERRY
Grad assistants (P) v. Apartment owner (D)
489 F.2d 1396 (1974).

NATURE OF CASE: Appeal from award of damages for invasion of privacy.

FACT SUMMARY: Mr. Mas (P), a citizen of France, and Mrs. Mas (P), an American, resided temporarily in Louisiana where Perry (D), their landlord, watched their bedroom and bathroom activities through two-way mirrors, and Perry (D) contested subject matter jurisdiction of the district court on the ground that Mrs. Mas (P) was a Louisiana resident, which would destroy complete diversity among the parties.

CONCISE RULE OF LAW: A domiciliary of a state remains so for diversity purposes until he formulates an intent to permanently remain in another state.

FACTS: Mr. Mas (P) was a citizen of France and Mrs. Mas (P) was an American citizen and they were engaged as graduate assistants at Louisiana State University (LSU). They traveled to Mrs. Mas' (P) home in Mississippi to be married and then returned to LSU. In Baton Rouge they rented an apartment from Perry (D), a Louisiana domiciliary. Mrs. Mas (P) had no intention of returning to Mississippi after the completion of her and her husband's duties at LSU, and they were undecided about their future home. During the period in Louisiana after marriage, Perry (D) observed the Mas' (P) bedroom and bathroom activities through two-way mirrors installed in the rented apartment. Mr. and Mrs. Mas (P) brought this action in federal court alleging diversity of citizenship as a basis for federal jurisdiction. Perry (D) contended that Mrs. Mas' (P) residence in Louisiana constituted a domicile there and that complete diversity did not exist. Perry (D) appealed the district court's denial of his motion to dismiss therefor.

ISSUE: Does a domiciliary of a state remain so for diversity purposes until he formulates an intent to permanently remain in another state?

HOLDING AND DECISION: (Ainsworth, J.) Yes. A person's domicile is his "true, fixed and permanent home and principal establishment and to which he has the intention of returning whenever he is absent therefrom." Two elements are necessary for the changing of domiciles: (1) taking up residence in a different domicile, and (2) having the intention to remain there permanently. While in the past the domicile of a wife is said to be that of her husband, in this case that rule is not applicable because Mr. Mas (P) is a citizen of a foreign nation. Mrs. Mas' (P) domicile therefore is to be determined without reference to that of her husband. Even though she had not the intention to return to her parents' Mississippi home, she had none to remain permanently in Louisiana either. Thus, her moving from her last

domicile, i.e., Mississippi, did not change it, and she was a domiciliary of Mississippi at the time of the action. Complete diversity therefore existed, and the district court had subject matter jurisdiction over the action under 28 U.S.C. § 1332. A domiciliary of a state remains so for diversity purposes until he formulates the intention to remain permanently in another state. Affirmed.

EDITOR'S ANALYSIS: Complete diversity is required between the sides of the litigation in diversity cases. While all parties on one side if the case may be from one state, if any party on the other side is from a state of an opponent, diversity is destroyed. To be "from" a state, one must be a domiciliary of it, which, though not always easily determined, centers around the residence in that state and the intention to permanently remain there at the time of the litigation.

[For more information on definitions of domicile, see Casenote Law Outline on Civil Procedure, Chapter 4, Federal Subject Matter Jurisdiction and Related Doctrines Affecting the Choice of a Federal Forum, § IV, The Diversity Jurisdiction of the District Courts.]

QUICKNOTES

DOMICILE - A person's permanent home or principal establishment to which he has an intention of returning when he is absent therefrom.

DIVERSITY OF CITIZENSHIP - The authority of a federal court to hear and determine cases involving $10,000 or more and in which the parties are citizens of different states, or in which one party is an alien.

NOTES:

ANKENBRANDT v. RICHARDS
Wife (P) v. Husband (D)
112 S. Ct. 2206 (1992).

NATURE OF CASE: Appeal of dismissal of diversity action for damages for child abuse.

FACT SUMMARY: A federal district court dismissed a diversity suit which Ankenbrandt (P) brought against her ex-husband, Richards (D), for abusing their children because the case was within the domestic relations exception to jurisdiction.

CONCISE RULE OF LAW: Diversity jurisdiction does not extend over divorce, alimony, and child custody decrees but does cover tort claims for child abuse.

FACTS: Ankenbrandt (P) filed a diversity suit for damages against her ex-husband, Richards (D), for sexually and physically abusing their two daughters. The district court dismissed the action because it decided that the case fell within the "domestic relations" exception to diversity jurisdiction. According to the district court, this exception bars jurisdiction over the "whole subject of the domestic relations of husband and wife, parent and child." The court of appeals affirmed this ruling. Ankenbrandt (P) appealed.

ISSUE: Does diversity except tort claims for child abuse from the domestic relations exception to federal court jurisdiction?

HOLDING AND DECISION: (White, J.) Yes. Although diversity jurisdiction does not extend over divorce, alimony, and child custody decrees, it does cover tort claims for child abuse. The Court has recognized a domestic relations exception to diversity jurisdiction since Barber v. Barber in 1859. In that case, the Court held that the Judiciary Act of 1789 establishing diversity jurisdiction did not intend to provide federal courts with jurisdiction over divorce and alimony actions. When Congress amended the diversity statute in 1948, it did not intend to alter this "domestic relations" exception. Therefore, diversity jurisdiction does not extend to divorce, alimony, and child custody decrees. Ankenbrandt's (P) allegation, however, that Richards (D) committed torts against the children does not come within the domestic relations exception. Reversed.

CONCURRENCE: (Blackmun, J.) The federal courts' refusal to hear divorce, alimony, and custody cases should be a matter of discretionary abstention rather than a jurisdictional concern.

EDITOR'S ANALYSIS: Divorce was a rare occurrence at the time of the Judiciary Act of 1789, and some commentators believe that Congress' intentions regarding the matter are too difficult to ascertain. Other commentators have suggested that the federal judiciary's hesitation to hear these cases is a type of sex discrimination against women. See Resnik, "Naturally" Without Gender: Women, Jurisdiction, and the Federal Courts, 66 N.Y.U. L. Rev. 1682 (1991).

[For more information on diversity jurisdiction, see Casenote Law Outline on Civil Procedure, Chapter 4, § IV, The Diversity Jurisdiction of the District Courts.]

QUICKNOTES

DIVERSITY OF CITIZENSHIP - The authority of a federal court to hear and determine cases involving $10,000 or more and in which the parties are citizens of different states, or in which one party is an alien.

FEDERAL JURISDICTION - The authority of federal courts to hear and determine cases of a particular nature derived from the United States Constitution and rules promulgated by Congress pursuant thereto.

NOTES:

UNITED MINE WORKERS v. GIBBS
Mine workers union (D) v. Affiliate of mine company (P)
383 U.S. 715 (1966).

NATURE OF CASE: Appeal from award of damages for conspiracy.

FACT SUMMARY: Gibbs (P) alleged a conspiracy under state and federal law on the part of UMW (D) in preventing him from executing contracts for coal haulage and supervision of workers when UMW's (D) members forcibly prevented the opening of a mine operated by a subsidiary of a former employer of UMW's (D) miners. The district court dismissed the federal claim but sustained a damage award based on the state law claim.

CONCISE RULE OF LAW: If a plaintiff's claims based on both federal and state law are such that he would ordinarily be expected to try them all in one proceeding, there is power in the federal courts to hear the whole.

FACTS: Gibbs (P) brought this action alleging a conspiracy on the part of UMW (D) based on the laws of Tennessee and federal law. UMW's (D) members, without the sanction, knowledge or approval of UMW (D), prevented the opening of a mine by force which included beatings. Gibbs (P) was party to a contract with the company which operated the mines. The company was a subsidiary of a company which had recently fired 100 UMW (D) miners, and the members involved in the violence regarded the opening of the new mine as a violation of their contract with the parent company. After the incident, Gibbs (P) filed this action against UMW (D) because of the interference with his contracts for coal haulage and for worker supervision with the subsidiary. The complaint alleged conspiracy on UMW's (D) part and was based on the laws of Tennessee and federal law. The district court dismissed the federal claim, but sustained the damage award based on state law. UMW (D) appealed.

ISSUE: If a plaintiff's claims based on both federal and state law are such that he would ordinarily be expected to try them all in one proceeding, is there power in the federal courts to hear the whole?

HOLDING AND DECISION: (Brennan, J.) Yes. Pendent jurisdiction exists whenever there is a claim "arising under the Constitution or laws of the United States or the Treaties made, or which shall be made, under their authority" and the relationship between that claim and the state claim comprises one "case." It is not required that a district judge exercise that power, but it is within his discretion. In this case, the district judge did not abuse that discretion in hearing both Gibbs' (P) state and federal claims. The fact that the claims under federal law failed did not preclude the award of damages based upon the state claim, even though the proceeding took place in federal court. If a plaintiff's claims

based on both state and federal law are such that he would ordinarily be expected to try them all in one judicial proceeding, there is power in federal courts to hear the whole. Thus, there was no error in hearing both claims and awarding damages based on the state claim.

EDITOR'S ANALYSIS: The Court in this case went on to hold that Gibbs (P) could not recover under Tennessee law for conspiracy here. The main thrust of the case, however, is on the matter of pendent jurisdiction in federal court. Pendent jurisdiction permits the addition of state claims to federal claims in order to further the interests of judicial economy, as opposed to ancillary jurisdiction, which relates to the addition of a new party involved in the same transaction or occurrence giving rise to the action.

[For more information on pendent jurisdiction, see Casenote Law Outline on Civil Procedure, Chapter 6, Joinder of Claims and Parties, § V, Supplemental Jurisdiction in Aid of Liberal Joinder in the Federal Courts.]

QUICKNOTES

PENDENT JURISDICTION - A doctrine granting authority to a federal court to hear a claim that does not invoke diversity jurisdiction if it arises from the same transaction or occurrence as the primary action.

CONSPIRACY - Concerted action by two or more persons to accomplish some unlawful purpose.

CLAIM - The demand for a right to payment or equitable relief; the fact or facts giving rise to such demand.

NOTES:

WILLIAMS v. HURON VALLEY SCHOOL DISTRICT
Religious claimant (P) v. School district (D)
858 F. Supp. 97 (E.D. Mich. 1994).

NATURE OF CASE: Motion to remand religious discrimination claim to state court.

FACT SUMMARY: Williams (P) sued in state court for religious discrimination, the case was removed to federal court, and Williams (P) moved to remand to state court.

CONCISE RULE OF LAW: A federal court may remand a case to a state court upon finding that the claim raises a novel or complex issue of state law, the state law claim substantially predominates, or upon determination that retaining jurisdiction would be inappropriate.

FACTS: Williams (P) sued Huron Valley School District (D) and other school officials (D), alleging a claim for religious discrimination based upon their refusal to grant her time off to observe Jewish "Holy Days." Within two days, Williams (P) amended her complaint to state three state claims and two federal claims involving Title VII which were all related to the original claim. The School District (D) sought and was granted removal to federal court based upon the federal questions raised by the Title VII claims. Williams (P) moved to remand the case to state court, alleging that the state claims predominated.

ISSUE: May a federal court remand a case to a state court when the claim raises a novel or complex issue of state law, the state law claims substantially predominate, or upon finding jurisdiction is inappropriate?

HOLDING AND DECISION: (Cook, J.) Yes. A federal court may remand a case to a state court upon finding that the claim raises a novel or complex issue of state law, the state law claim substantially predominates, or upon determination that retaining jurisdiction would be inappropriate. Because the complaint in this case does not appear to raise novel issues of state law, three state claims versus two federal claims do not meet the requisite "substantially dominates" test, and it is no more economical or convenient for the federal court to render a decision than the state court, it is not inappropriate to retain jurisdiction. Motion to remand denied.

EDITOR'S ANALYSIS: The general rule is that removal is proper in any civil action within the original jurisdiction of the federal district court that was filed instead in a state court. Defendants may not remove a case to federal court by pleading federal issues in the answer.

[For more information on removal, see Casenote Law Outline on Civil Procedure, Chapter 4, § V, Removal Jurisdiction.]

QUICKNOTES

REMOVAL - Petition by a defendant to move the case to another court.

NOTES:

POWELL v. ZONING BOARD OF APPEALS OF THE CITY OF CHICAGO

Building owner (P) v. Zoning board (D)

1994 U.S. Dist. LEXIS 4772 (N.D. IL. 1994).

NATURE OF CASE: Motion to dismiss and motion to remand in action alleging wrongful denial of a zoning permit.

FACT SUMMARY: Powell (P) sued in state court, the case was removed to federal court, and Powell (P) moved to remand to state court.

CONCISE RULE OF LAW: A removed case may be remanded to state court at any time it appears that a federal court lacks subject matter jurisdiction.

FACTS: Powell (P) sued the Zoning Board of Appeals of the City of Chicago (D) to compel judicial review of the denial of a zoning certification for her building. A section of Powell's (P) complaint stated, "said decision denies Plaintiff due process of law, equal protection of law and deprives Plaintiff the full use and enjoyment of her property." The Zoning Board (D) asserted that this language raised a federal question and removed the case to federal court. Once in federal court, the Zoning Board (D) sought dismissal pursuant to Fed. R. Civ. P. 12(b)(6) for failure to state a federal cause of action. Powell (P) defended that the complaint was a garden-variety zoning petition, the complaint was intended to assert only a state claim, and the case had been improperly removed. Powell (P) moved to remand, and the Zoning Board (D) moved to dismiss.

ISSUE: If it later appears that a federal court lacks subject matter jurisdiction, may the case be remanded to state court?

HOLDING AND DECISION: (Kocoras, J.) Yes. A removed case may be remanded to state court at any time it appears that a federal court lacks subject matter jurisdiction. The language in Powell's (P) complaint is found in both the state and federal constitution. Because Powell (P) makes no federal claim, no federal question exists. Motion to remand to state court is granted.

EDITOR'S ANALYSIS: Plaintiff attorneys often prefer state court over federal court because procedural rules are more relaxed. To avoid federal question jurisdiction, attorneys cite only to state statutes in the complaint. To avoid diversity jurisdiction, attorneys name a non-diverse defendant. Of course, ethical rules must be considered.

[For more information on removal, see Casenote Law Outline on Civil Procedure, Chapter 4, § V, Removal Jurisdiction.]

QUICKNOTES

REMOVAL - Petition by a defendant to move the case to another court.

SUBJECT MATTER JURISDICTION - The authority of the court to hear and decide actions involving a particular type of issue or subject.

PROP 12(b)(6) - Motion to dismiss for failure to state a claim.

NOTES:

CHAPTER 4
THE ERIE PROBLEM

QUICK REFERENCE RULES OF LAW

1. **Constitutionalizing the Issue.** Although the 1789 Rules of Decision Act left federal courts unfettered to apply their own rules of procedure in common law actions brought in federal court, state law governs substantive issues. State law includes not only statutory law, but case law as well. (Erie Railroad v. Tompkins)

    [For more information on substantive law and procedure, see Casenote Law Outline on Civil Procedure, Chapter 4, Federal Subject Matter Jurisdiction and Related Doctrines Affecting the Choice of a Federal Forum, § VIII, The Erie Doctrine.]

2. **Interpreting the Constitutional Command of *Erie*.** Where a state statute that would completely bar recovery in state court has significant effect on the outcome-determination of the action, even though the suit be brought in equity, the federal court is bound by the state law. (Guaranty Trust Co. v. York)

    [For more information on balancing state and federal interests, see Casenote Law Outline on Civil Procedure, Chapter 4, Federal Subject Matter Jurisdiction and Related Doctrines Affecting the Choice of a Federal Forum, § VIII, The Erie Doctrine.]

3. **Interpreting the Constitutional Command of *Erie*.** The *Erie* doctrine requires that federal courts in diversity cases must respect the definitions of rights and obligations created by state courts, but state laws cannot alter the essential characteristics and functions of the federal courts, and the jury function is such an essential function (provided for in the Seventh Amendment). (Byrd v. Blue Ridge Rural Electric Cooperative)

    [For more information on balancing state and federal interests, see Casenote Law Outline on Civil Procedure, Chapter 4, Federal Subject Matter Jurisdiction and Related Doctrines Affecting the Choice of a Federal Forum, § VIII, The Erie Doctrine.]

4. **De-Constitutionalizing *Erie*.** The *Erie* doctrine mandates that federal courts are to apply state substantive law and federal procedural law, but, where matters fall roughly between the two and are rationally capable of classification as either, the Constitution grants the federal court system the power to regulate their practice and pleading (procedure). (Hanna v. Plumer)

    [For more information on the outcome-determinative conflict, see Casenote Law Outline on Civil Procedure, Chapter 4, Federal Subject Matter Jurisdiction and Related Doctrines Affecting the Choice of a Federal Forum, § VIII, The Erie Doctrine.]

ERIE RAILROAD CO. v. TOMPKINS
Train company (D) v. Pedestrian (P)
304 U.S. 64 (1938).

NATURE OF CASE: Action to recover damages for personal injury allegedly caused by negligent conduct.

FACT SUMMARY: In a personal injury suit, a federal district court trial judge refused to apply applicable state law because such law was "general" (judge-made) and not embodied in any statute.

CONCISE RULE OF LAW: Although the 1789 Rules of Decision Act left federal courts unfettered to apply their own rules of procedure in common law actions brought in federal court, state law governs substantive issues. State law includes not only statutory law, but case law as well.

FACTS: Tompkins (P) was walking in a right of way parallel to some railroad tracks when an Erie Railroad (D) train came by. Tompkins (P) was struck and injured by what he would, at trial, claim to be an open door extending from one of the rail cars. Under Pennsylvania case law (the applicable law since the accident occurred there), state courts would have treated Tompkins (P) as a trespasser in denying him recovery for other than wanton or willful misconduct on Erie's (D) part. Under "general" law, recognized in federal courts, Tompkins (P) would have been regarded as a licensee and would only have been obligated to show ordinary negligence. Because Erie (D) was a New York corporation, Tompkins (P) brought suit in a federal district court in New York, where he won a judgment for $30,000. Upon appeal to a federal circuit court, the decision was affirmed.

ISSUE: Was the trial court in error in refusing to recognize state case law as the proper rule of decision in deciding the substantive issue of liability?

HOLDING AND DECISION: (Brandeis, J.) Yes. The Court's opinion is in four parts: (1) Swift v. Tyson, 41 U.S. (16 Pet.) 1 (1842), which held that federal courts exercising jurisdiction on the ground of diversity of citizenship need not, in matters of general jurisprudence, apply the unwritten law of the state as declared by its highest court, is overruled. Section 34 of the Federal Judiciary Act of 1789, c. 20, 28 U.S. § 725 requires that federal courts in all matters except those where some federal law is controlling, apply as their rules of decision the law of the state, unwritten as well as written. Up to this time, federal courts had assumed the power to make "general law" decisions even though Congress was powerless to enact "general law" statutes. (2) Swift had numerous political and social defects. The hoped-for uniformity among state courts had not occurred; there was no satisfactory way to distinguish between local and general law. On the other hand, Swift introduced grave discrimination by noncitizens against citizens. The privilege of selecting the court for resolving disputes rested with the noncitizen who could pick the more favorable forum. The resulting far-reaching discrimination was due to the broad province accorded "general law" in which many matters of seemingly local concern were included. Furthermore, local citizens could move out of the state and bring suit in a federal court if they were disposed to do so; corporations, similarly, could simply reincorporate in another state. More than statutory relief is involved here; the unconstitutionality of Swift is clear. (3) Except in matters governed by the Federal Constitution or by acts of Congress, the law to be applied in any case is the law of the state. There is no federal common law. The federal courts have no power derived from the Constitution or by Congress to declare substantive rules of common law applicable in a state whether they be "local" or "general" in nature. (4) The federal district court was bound to follow the Pennsylvania case law which would have denied recovery to Tompkins (P).

CONCURRENCE IN PART: (Reed, J.) It is unnecessary to go beyond interpreting the meaning of "laws" in the Rules of Decision Act. Article III, and the Necessary and Proper Clause of Article I of the Constitution, might provide Congress with the power to declare rules of substantive law for federal courts to follow.

EDITOR'S ANALYSIS: Erie can fairly be characterized as the most significant and sweeping decision on civil procedure ever handed down by the U.S. Supreme Court. As interpreted in subsequent decisions, Erie held that while federal courts may apply their own rules of procedure, issues of substantive law must be decided in accord with the applicable state law — usually the state in which the federal court sits. Note, however, how later Supreme Court decisions have made inroads into the broad doctrine enunciated here.

[For more information on substantive law and procedure, see Casenote Law Outline on Civil Procedure, Chapter 4, Federal Subject Matter Jurisdiction and Related Doctrines Affecting the Choice of a Federal Forum, § VIII, The Erie Doctrine.]

QUICKNOTES

DIVERSITY OF CITIZENSHIP - The authority of a federal court to hear and determine cases involving $10,000 or more and in which the parties are citizens of different states, or in which one party is an alien.

FEDERAL JURISDICTION - The authority of federal courts to hear and determine cases of a particular nature derived from the United States Constitution and rules promulgated by Congress pursuant thereto.

SUBJECT MATTER JURISDICTION - The authority of the court to hear and decide actions involving a particular type of issue or subject.

GUARANTY TRUST CO. OF NEW YORK v. YORK

Trustee (D) v. Note holder (P)

326 U.S. 99 (1945).

NATURE OF CASE: Class action alleging fraud and misrepresentation.

FACT SUMMARY: York (P), barred from filing suit in state court because of the state statute of limitations, brought an equity action in federal court based upon diversity of citizenship jurisdiction.

CONCISE RULE OF LAW: Where a state statute that would completely bar recovery in state court has significant effect on the outcome-determination of the action, even though the suit be brought in equity, the federal court is bound by the state law.

FACTS: Van Swerigen Corporation, in 1930, issued notes and named Guaranty Trust Co. (D) as trustee with power and obligations to enforce the rights of the note holders in the assets of the corporation and the Van Swerigens. In 1931, when it was apparent that the corporation could not meet its obligations, Guaranty (D) cooperated in a plan for the purchase of the outstanding notes for 50% of the notes' face value and an exchange of 20 shares of the corporation's stock for each $1,000 note. In 1934, York (P) received some cash, her donor not having accepted the rate of exchange. In 1940, three accepting note holders sued Guaranty (D), charging fraud and misrepresentation, in state court. York (P) was not allowed to intervene. Summary judgment in favor of Guaranty (D) was affirmed. In 1942, York (P) brought a class action suit in federal court based on diversity of citizenship and charged Guaranty (D) with breach of trust. Guaranty (D) moved for and was granted summary judgment on the basis of the earlier state decision. The court of appeals reversed on the basis that the earlier state decision did not foreclose this federal court action, and held that even though the state statute of limitations had run, the fact that the action was brought in equity releases the federal court from following the state rule.

ISSUE: Does a state statute of limitations, which would bar a suit in state court, also act as a bar to the same action if the suit is brought in equity in federal court and jurisdiction being based on diversity of citizenship?

HOLDING AND DECISION: (Frankfurter, J.) Yes. Erie Railroad Co. v. Tompkins overruled a particular way of looking at law after its inadequacies had been laid bare. Federal courts have traditionally given state-created rights in equity greater respect than rights in law since the former are more frequently defined by legislative enactment. Even though federal equity may be thought of as a separate legal system, the substantive right is created by the state, and federal courts must respect state law which governs that right. While state law cannot define the remedies which a federal court must give simply because a federal court in diversity jurisdiction is available as an alternative, a federal court may afford an equitable remedy for a substantive right recognized by a state even though state court cannot give it. Federal courts enforce state-created substantive rights if the mode of proceeding and remedy were consonant with the traditional body of equitable remedies, practice, and procedure. Matters of "substance" and of "procedure" turn on different considerations. Here, since the federal court is adjudicating a state-created right solely because diversity of citizenship of the parties is, in effect, only another court of the state, it cannot afford recovery if the right to recovery is made unavailable by the state. The question is not whether a statute of limitation is "procedural," but whether the statute so affects the result of litigation as to be controlling in state law. It is, therefore, immaterial to make a "substantive-procedure" dichotomy — Erie Railroad Co. v. Tompkins was not an endeavor to formulate scientific legal terminology, but rather an expression of a policy that touches the distribution of judicial power between state and federal courts. Erie insures that insofar as legal rules determine the outcome of litigation, the result should not be any different in a federal court extending jurisdiction solely on the basis of diversity of citizenship. Through diversity jurisdiction, Congress meant to afford out-of-state litigants another tribunal, and not another body of law.

EDITOR'S ANALYSIS: While clarifying Erie, the legal foundation supporting Guaranty Trust may be undergoing a process of slow erosion by contemporary courts. Hanna v. Plumer held that where state law conflicts with the Federal Rules of Civil Procedure, the latter prevails regardless of the effect on outcome of the litigation. And in Byrd v. Blue Ridge Elec. Cooperative, the Court suggested that some constitutional doctrines (there, the right to a jury trial in federal court) are so important as to be controlling over state law, regardless of whether application of such constitutional doctrines would result in an outcome different than that which would result under the law of the state in which the federal court sits.

[For more information on balancing state and federal interests, see Casenote Law Outline on Civil Procedure, Chapter 4, Federal Subject Matter Jurisdiction and Related Doctrines Affecting the Choice of a Federal Forum, § VIII, The Erie Doctrine.]

QUICKNOTES

DIVERSITY OF CITIZENSHIP - The authority of a federal court to hear and determine cases involving $10,000 or more and in which the parties are citizens of different states, or in which one party is an alien.

COMITY - A rule pursuant to which courts in one state give deference to the statutes and judicial decisions of another.

BYRD v. BLUE RIDGE ELECTRIC COOPERATIVE, INC.
Injured employee (P) v. Electric utility (D)
356 U.S. 525 (1958).

NATURE OF CASE: Negligence action for damages.

FACT SUMMARY: Byrd (P) was injured while connecting power lines for a subcontractor of Blue Ridge Electric Cooperative, Inc. (D).

CONCISE RULE OF LAW: The Erie doctrine requires that federal courts in diversity cases must respect the definitions of rights and obligations created by state courts, but state laws cannot alter the essential characteristics and functions of the federal courts, and the jury function is such an essential function (provided for in the Seventh Amendment).

FACTS: Byrd (P) was injured while connecting power lines as an employee of a subcontractor of Blue Ridge Electric Cooperative, Inc. (D). He sued Blue Ridge (D) in federal court on a negligence theory. Because he is a citizen of North Carolina and Blue Ridge (D) is a South Carolina corporation, jurisdiction is grounded in diversity of citizenship. At trial, Blue Ridge (D) offered an affirmative defense based on a South Carolina law which would limit Byrd (P) to worker's compensation benefits by defining him as a statutory employee of Blue Ridge (D) as well as the subcontractor (thereby precluding any collateral negligence action). The trial court refused to allow the defense to be offered, but the U.S. Supreme Court reversed and remanded the case to the trial court for a new trial allowing the defense. Under South Carolina law, however, this issue of immunity from negligence is to be tried by a judge. Blue Ridge (D), however, claims that despite the Erie doctrine, South Carolina law cannot be allowed to preclude his right to a jury.

ISSUE: Do Erie doctrine considerations require that all state determinations of rights be upheld regardless of their intrusions into federal determinations?

HOLDING AND DECISION: (Brennan, J.) No. The Erie doctrine requires that federal courts in diversity cases must respect the definitions of rights and obligations created by state courts, but state laws cannot alter the essential characteristics and functions of the federal courts, and the jury function is such an essential function (provided for in the Seventh Amendment). The South Carolina determination here that immunity is a question of law to be tried by a judge is merely a determination of the form and mode of enforcing immunity. It does not involve any essential relationship or determination of right created by the state. Of course, the Erie doctrine will reach even such form and mode determinations where no affirmative countervailing considerations can be found. Here, however, the Seventh Amendment makes the jury function an essential factor in the federal process protected by the Constitution. On remand, the court must permit a jury trial.

EDITOR'S ANALYSIS: This case points up a major retreat by the Court in its interpretation of the Erie doctrine. The Guaranty Trust case had stated that the Erie doctrine required that federal courts not tamper with state remedies for violations of state-created rights. In Byrd, the Court retreats, stating that questions of mere "form and mode" of remedy (i.e., trial by jury or judge) is not necessarily the province of the states where essential federal rights (i.e., Seventh Amendment) are involved. Note that the Court does not abandon the Guaranty Trust rationale, however (that the outcome of a case should not be affected by the choice of court in which it is filed). The Court expresses doubt that the permitting of trial by jury here will make any difference in the final determination of the case. Note the inconsistency of argument here since the Court first states that trial by jury is an essential right, then states that it is really insignificant after all.

[For more information on balancing state and federal interests, see Casenote Law Outline on Civil Procedure, Chapter 4, Federal Subject Matter Jurisdiction and Related Doctrines Affecting the Choice of a Federal Forum, § VIII, The Erie Doctrine.]

NOTES:

HANNA v. PLUMER
Injured claimant (P) v. Executor of defendant (D)
280 U.S. 460 (1965).

NATURE OF CASE: Appeal of summary judgment In federal diversity tort action.

FACT SUMMARY: Plumer (D) filed tort action in federal court in Massachusetts, where Hanna (P) resided, for an auto accident that occurred in South Carolina.

CONCISE RULE OF LAW: The Erie doctrine mandates that federal courts are to apply state substantive law and federal procedural law, but, where matters fall roughly between the two and are rationally capable of classification as either, the Constitution grants the federal court system the power to regulate their practice and pleading (procedure).

FACTS: Hanna (P), a citizen of Ohio, filed a tort action in federal court in Massachusetts against Plumer (D), the executor of the estate of Louise Plumer Osgood, a Massachusetts citizen. It was alleged that Mrs. Osgood caused injuries to Hanna (P) in an auto accident in South Carolina. Service on Plumer (D) was accomplished pursuant to F.R.C.P. 4(d)(1) by leaving copies of the summons with Plumer's (D) wife. At trial, motion for summary judgment by Plumer (D) was granted on the grounds that service should have been accomplished pursuant to Massachusetts law (by the Erie doctrine) which required service by hand to the party personally. On appeal, Hanna (P) contended that Erie should not affect the application of the Federal Rules of Civil Procedure to this case. Plumer (D), however, contended that (1) a substantive law question under Erie is any question in which permitting application of federal law would alter the outcome of the case (the so-called "outcome determination" test), (2) the application of federal law here (i.e., 4[d][1]) will necessarily affect the outcome of the case (from a necessary dismissal to litigation); and, so, therefore (3) Erie requires that the state substantive law requirement of service by hand be upheld along with the trial court's summary judgment.

ISSUE: Does the Erie doctrine classification of "substantive law questions" extend to embrace questions involving both substantive and procedural considerations merely because such a question might have an effect on the determination of the substantive outcome of the case?

HOLDING AND DECISION: (Warren, C.J.) No. The Erie doctrine mandates that federal courts are to apply state substantive law and federal procedural law, and, where matters fall roughly between the two and are rationally capable of classification as either, the Constitution grants the federal court system the power to regulate their practice and pleading (procedure). It is well settled that the Enabling Act for the Federal Rules of Civil Procedure requires that a procedural effect of any

rule on the outcome of a case be shown to actually "abridge, enlarge, or modify" the substantive law in a case for the Erie doctrine to come into play. Where, as here, the question only goes to procedural requirements (i.e., service of summons, a dismissal for improper service here would not alter the substantive right of Hanna [P] to serve Plumer [D] personally and refile or effect the substantive law of negligence in the case), Article III and the Necessary and Proper Clause provide that the Congress has a right to provide rules for the federal court system such as F.R.C.P. 4(d)(1). "Outcome determination analysis was never intended to serve as a talisman" for the Erie doctrine. The judgment of the trial court must be reversed.

CONCURRENCE: (Harlan, J.) Justice Harlan agrees with the result of the Court and its rejection of the outcome determination test. He argues, however, that the Court was wrong in stating that anything arguably procedural is constitutionally placed within the province of the federal government to regulate. His test for "substantive" would be whether "the choice of rule would substantially affect those primary decisions respecting human conduct which our constitutional system leaves to state regulation."

EDITOR'S ANALYSIS: This case points up a return to the basic rationales of Erie R. Co. v. Tompkins. First, the Court asserts that one important consideration in determining how a particular question should be classified (substantive or procedural) is the avoidance of "forum shopping" (the practice of choosing one forum such as federal, to file in, in order to gain the advantages of one), which permits jurisdictions to infringe on the substantive law-defining powers of each other. Second, the Court seeks to avoid inequitable administration of the laws which would result from allowing jurisdictional considerations to determine substantive rights. Justice Warren here, in rejecting the "outcome determination" test, asserts that any rule must be measured ultimately against the Federal Rules Enabling Act and the Constitution.

[For more information on the outcome-determinative conflict, see Casenote Law Outline on Civil Procedure, Chapter 4, Federal Subject Matter Jurisdiction and Related Doctrines Affecting the Choice of a Federal Forum, § VIII, The Erie Doctrine.]

QUICKNOTES
SUBSTANTIVE LAW - Law that pertains to the rights and interests of the parties and upon which a cause of action may be based.

PROCEDURAL LAW - Law relating to the process of carrying out a lawsuit and not to the substantive rights asserted by the parties.

NOTES

CHAPTER 5
INCENTIVES TO LITIGATE

QUICK REFERENCE RULES OF LAW

1. **Compensatory Damages.** The fundamental principle of damages is to restore the injured party, as nearly as possible, to the position he would have been in had it not been for the wrong of the other party. (United States v. Hatahley)

2. **Liquidated, Statutory, and Punitive Damages.** To be constitutional, state law permitting punitive damage awards must make the awards subject to judicial review. (Honda Motor Co. v. Oberg)

3. **Remedial Hierarchy.** The main prerequisite to obtaining injunctive relief is a finding that plaintiff is being threatened by some injury for which he has no adequate legal remedy. (Sigma Chemical Co. v. Harris)

4. **Separating Lawyer and Client.** A court may in its discretion accept a settlement that denies statutorily authorized fees. (Evans v. Jeff D.)

5. **Restraining Orders.** A preliminary injunction should be granted if the moving party demonstrates either a combination of probable success and the possibility of irreparable harm, or that serious questions are raised and the balance of hardship tips sharply in his favor. (William Inglis & Sons Baking Co. v. ITT Continental Baking Co.)

6. **Provisional Remedies and Due Process.** Procedural due process requires that parties whose rights are to be affected are entitled to be heard at a meaningful time; and in order that they may enjoy that right they must be notified. (Fuentes v. Shevin)

[For more information on prejudgment attachment, see Casenote Law Outline on Civil Procedure, Chapter 11, Enforcement of Judgments, § III, Enforcement of Coercive Judgments.]

UNITED STATES v. HATAHLEY
Federal government (D) v. Cattle owner (P)
257 F.2d 920 (10th Cir. 1958).

NATURE OF CASE: Action to recover the value of livestock sold to a glue factory.

FACT SUMMARY: In Hatahley's (P) action against the Government (D) to recover damages for livestock owned by the Navajo tribe which the Government (D) and white ranchers rounded up and sold to a glue factory, Hatahley (P) contended that such roundups violated federal law, which requires notice before a roundup takes place.

CONCISE RULE OF LAW: The fundamental principle of damages is to restore the injured party, as nearly as possible, to the position he would have been in had it not been for the wrong of the other party.

FACTS: Hatahley (P) was a member of the Navajo tribe. He and other tribe members grazed their cattle on federal range lands. The Government (D) and white ranchers alleged that the Navajo cattle were not entitled to graze on federal lands and filed a lawsuit to stop the practice. Before the suit was decided, federal agents and the ranchers rounded up and sold the livestock to a glue factory. The Navajos, including Hatahley (P), then filed suit against the Government (D), contending that the roundup violated federal law, which required notice before such an action took place. The United States Supreme Court held that the Navajos had stated a claim and sent the case back to the district court for a determination of damages.

ISSUE: Is the fundamental principle of damages to restore the injured party, as nearly as possible, to the position he would have been in had it not been for the wrong of the other party?

HOLDING AND DECISION: (Pickett, J.) Yes. The fundamental principle of damages is to restore the injured party, as nearly as possible, to the position he would have been in had it not been for the wrong of the other party. Applying this rule, Hatahley (P) was entitled to the market value, or replacement cost, of their livestock as of the time of taking, and the time they, acting prudently, could have replaced the animals. However, the right to such damages does not extend forever, and it is limited to the time in which a prudent person would replace the destroyed livestock. The district court here awarded Hatahley (P) not only the value of each animal, but a sum for mental pain and suffering and damages for one-half the value of the diminution of the individual herds between the date the livestock was taken and the last date of the hearing. This was error. It is true that animals of a particular strain and trained for a special purpose are different from other animals, but that does not mean they cannot be replaced by animals similarly developed. The law requires only that the Government (D) make full reparation for the pecuniary loss which their agents inflicted. Reversed and remanded.

EDITOR'S ANALYSIS: When litigants go to court, the relief most often sought is money damages. Damages are the form of relief preferred by the court as well. Equitable relief is traditionally unavailable unless money damages would be inadequate.

QUICKNOTES
MONEY DAMAGES - Monetary compensation sought by, or awarded to, a party who incurred loss as a result of a breach of contract or tortious conduct on behalf of another party.

EQUITABLE RELIEF - A remedy that is based upon principles of fairness as opposed to rules of law.

PECUNIARY LOSS - Monetary loss or the loss of something of monetary value.

NOTES:

HONDA MOTOR CO. v. OBERG
Vehicle manufacturer (D) v. Injured ATV driver (P)
___U.S.___, 114 S. Ct. 2331 (1994).

NATURE OF CASE: Review of judgment awarding punitive damages in product liability action.

FACT SUMMARY: After a jury awarded Oberg (P) punitive damages in the amount of $5 million dollars against Honda Motor Co. (D), Honda (D) argued that the award violated the Due Process Clause because Oregon courts were not permitted to correct excessive verdicts.

CONCISE RULE OF LAW: To be constitutional, state law permitting punitive damage awards must make the awards subject to judicial review.

FACTS: Oberg (P), injured in an accident while driving a three-wheel all-terrain vehicle, sued Honda Motor Co. (D), the manufacturer of his ATV. A jury awarded Oberg (P) $735,512.31 compensatory damages and $5 million punitive damages. Per the Oregon constitution, the punitive damage award was not subject to judicial review. Honda (D) appealed anyway, claiming that this unreviewability violated due process. The Oregon Court of Appeals and Oregon Supreme Court affirmed, and the U.S. Supreme Court granted review.

ISSUE: To be constitutional, must state law permitting punitive damage awards make the awards subject to judicial review?

HOLDING AND DECISION: (Stevens, J.) Yes. To be constitutional, state law permitting punitive damage awards must make the awards subject to judicial review. Since common law, punitive damages have always been subject to both trial court and appellate review. This appears to result from a recognition that punitive damages present a great danger of arbitrariness. The Fourteenth Amendment guarantees citizens protection of life and property against arbitrary deprivation. The only way that this guarantee can be enforced is to ensure judicial review of such awards or at least some substitute form of protection against arbitrariness. Here, Oregon law prohibited judicial review and afforded no comparable protection. Consequently, the system of punitive damage awards is unconstitutional. Reversed.

CONCURRENCE: (Scalia, J.) The deprivation of property without observing an important traditional procedure for enforcing limits upon such deprivation violates due process.

DISSENT: (Ginsburg, J.) Oregon has substituted, for traditional appellate review, procedural obstacles to the awarding of punitive damages, such as precise instructions to guide the jury and a clear and convincing evidentiary standard. This satisfies due process.

EDITOR'S ANALYSIS: The issue of punitive damage awards is one that the Court has visited several times in recent years. In cases such as Pacific Mutual v. Haslip, 499 U.S. 1 (1991) and T.X.O. Production Corp. v. Alliance, 509 U.S.___, 113 S. Ct. 2711 (1993), the Court held that a punitive damage award may be so excessive as to violate due process. However, the Court has never specified where the line is to be drawn.

QUICKNOTES

PUNITIVE DAMAGES - Damages exceeding the actual injury suffered for the purposes of punishment, deterrence and comfort to plaintiff.

NOTES:

SIGMA CHEMICAL COMPANY v. HARRIS

Chemical company employer (P) v. Purchasing agent (D)

605 F. Supp. 1253 (E.D. Mo. 1985).

NATURE OF CASE: Action for permanent injunction and determination of the validity of a restrictive covenant.

FACT SUMMARY: In Sigma Chemical's (P) action against Harris (D) for breach of a restrictive covenant, Sigma (P) contended that a permanent injunction should be entered against Harris (D) for violating the terms of the employment contract because he was aware of the restrictions imposed upon him by the contract, and that he took a voluntary risk by deciding to violate the contract.

CONCISE RULE OF LAW: The main prerequisite to obtaining injunctive relief is a finding that plaintiff is being threatened by some injury for which he has no adequate legal remedy.

FACTS: Sigma Chemical (P) employed Harris (D) as a purchasing agent whose job consisted of matching the right chemical supplier with a chemical product sold by Sigma (P). Harris (D) signed an agreement, when he went to work for Sigma (P), that he would not work for a competitor for two years after leaving Sigma (P), and even after that period would not disclose any confidential information acquired from Sigma (P). Harris (D) became dissatisfied with Sigma (P), began looking for another job and, after finding one with a competitor of Sigma's (P), quit his Sigma (P) job. At the new job, Harris (D) used information acquired during his employment at Sigma (P) which helped his new employer find new sources of various chemicals. Sigma (P) then sued Harris(D) for breach of his employment contract, contending that a permanent injunction should be entered against Harris (D) for violating the terms of the contract because Harris (D) was aware of the restrictions imposed upon him by that contract, and that he took a voluntary risk by deciding to violate the contract.

ISSUE: Is the main prerequisite to obtaining injunctive relief a finding that plaintiff is being threatened by some injury for which he has no adequate legal remedy?

HOLDING AND DECISION: (Nangle, C.J.) Yes. The main prerequisite to obtaining injunctive relief is a finding that plaintiff is being threatened by some injury for which he has no adequate legal remedy. Also, a determination whether to issue an injunction involves a balancing of the interests of the parties who might be affected by the court's decision — the hardship on plaintiff if relief is denied as opposed to the hardship to defendant if it is granted. Here, it is clear that Harris (D) is violating the restrictive covenant by working for Sigma's (P) competitor. Under these circumstances, there is a strong threat of irreparable injury to Sigma (P). The harm that would occur to Harris (D) if the injunction should be granted is not insubstantial, but the threat of

harm to Sigma (P) greatly outweighs the threat of harm to Harris (D).

EDITOR'S ANALYSIS: Courts consider two factors in discussing the propriety of issuing an injunction. These are: the inadequacy of legal remedy and the balance of hardships to the two parties. Injunctions are by far the most prevalent form of equitable relief and with an injunction, courts will order parties to do things or to refrain from doing them.

QUICKNOTES

INJUNCTION - A remedy imposed by the court ordering a party to cease the conduct of a specific activity.

EQUITABLE RELIEF - A remedy that is based upon principles of fairness as opposed to rules of law.

RESTRICTIVE COVENANT - A promise contained in a deed to limit the uses to which the property will be made.

NOTES:

EVANS v. JEFF D.
Mentally disabled children (P) v. State (D)
475 U.S. 717 (1986).

NATURE OF CASE: Review of settlement approved by court in class action for injunctive relief.

FACT SUMMARY: The legal aid attorney representing a class of handicapped children (P) accepted settlement offer that denied attorney fees.

CONCISE RULE OF LAW: A court may in its discretion accept a settlement that denies statutorily authorized fees.

FACTS: Johnson, an Idaho Legal Aid Society attorney, represented a class of emotionally and mentally disturbed children (P) seeking injunctive relief from the State of Idaho (D) to improve their treatment. Johnson accepted a settlement offer which granted the plaintiff class generous injunctive relief, but denied Johnson his statutorily authorized fees. Legal Aid contended that the court abused its discretion in accepting a settlement conditioned on the denial of attorney fees and sought appellate review. Legal Aid argued that Johnson was forced to accept the settlement to obtain the most favorable relief for his clients because of his ethical obligation to his clients, and, therefore, the court had a duty to reject the settlement. The appellate court found an abuse of discretion. The State (D) appealed.

ISSUE: May a court in its discretion accept a settlement that denies statutorily authorized fees?

HOLDING AND DECISION: (Stevens, J.) Yes. A court may in its discretion accept a settlement which denies statutorily authorized fees. The Fees Act and its legislative history do not indicate that Congress intended to ban fee waivers conditioned on favorable settlement terms. Courts may appraise the reasonableness of settlement offers that deny fees on a case-by-case basis until Congress commands that fees be paid. Reversed.

EDITOR'S ANALYSIS: Ethical issues abound in the area of attorney fees. It is good practice to discuss the issue of fees with clients early on in representation. Many states have statutes that require the attorney fee agreement to be in writing if the fees are likely to exceed a set amount. If Johnson had a written fee agreement with his clients, this might have provided him with some leverage. If Johnson had disclosed the fact that he had a written fee agreement and the State (D) had continued to push for a settlement without fees, this might be construed as tortious interference with contract.

QUICKNOTES

INJUNCTIVE RELIEF - A count order issued as a remedy, requiring a person to do, or prohibiting that person from doing, a specific act.

SETTLEMENT OFFER - An offer made by one party to a lawsuit to the other agreeing upon the determination of rights and issues between them, thus disposing of the need for judicial determination.

NOTES:

WILLIAM INGLIS & SONS BAKING CO. v. ITT CONTINENTAL BAKING CO.

Baker (P) v. Baking company (D)

526 F.d. 86 (1976).

NATURE OF CASE: Appeal from denial of preliminary injunction.

FACT SUMMARY: Inglis (P) brought this suit for a preliminary injunction against ITT (D) for violations of antitrust provisions, and the district court denied the injunction on the ground of the lack of probability that Inglis (P) would succeed on the merits.

CONCISE RULE OF LAW: A preliminary injunction should be granted if the moving party demonstrates either a combination of probable success and the possibility of irreparable harm, or that serious questions are raised and the balance of hardship tips sharply in his favor.

FACTS: Inglis (P) brought suit for a preliminary injunction against ITT (D) and other bakers for alleged violations of the Sherman Act, the Robinson-Patman Act, and applicable California laws. The district court applied only the probable success-irreparable injury test and denied the injunction on the ground that the court was not convinced of the probability that Inglis (P) would succeed on the merits. Inglis (P) appealed.

ISSUE: Should a preliminary injunction be granted if the moving party demonstrates either a combination of probable success and the possibility of irreparable harm, or that serious questions are raised and the balance of hardship tips sharply in his favor?

HOLDING AND DECISION: (Skopil, J.) Yes. A grant or denial of a preliminary injunction is subject to reversal only if the lower court based its decision upon an erroneous legal premise or abused its discretion. The district court in this case did not abuse its discretion. However, it did fail to apply an alternative test as to whether a moving party is entitled to a preliminary injunction. A preliminary injunction should be granted if the moving party demonstrates either a combination of probable success and the possibility of irreparable harm, or that serious questions are raised and the balance of hardship tips sharply in his favor. The district court applied only the first part of the test. Reversed and remanded.

EDITOR'S ANALYSIS: This decision does not ensure Inglis (P) that it will obtain the preliminary injunction sought. It means only that the district court upon remand must consider whether there has been a raising of a serious question and a sharp tip of the balance of hardship. A court has wide latitude in this sort of equitable decision.

CHAPTER 6
PLEADING

QUICK REFERENCE RULES OF LAW

1. **Stating a Claim.** Ultimate facts which support each element of a claim must be pleaded to state a cause of action. (People ex rel. Department of Transportation v. Superior Court)

    [For more information on pleading, see Casenote Law Outline on Civil Procedure, Chapter 5, § II, Code-Pleading Requirements—The Complaint.]

2. **Stating a Claim**. Although only a short and plain statement is necessary, a claim which is illegibly stated or asserts a bald conclusion fails to state a federal claim. (Duncan v. AT&T Communications, Inc.)

    [For more information on pleading, see Casenote Law Outline on Civil Procedure, Chapter 5, § III, Notice Pleading Requirements—The Complaint.]

3. **The Question of "Detail."** A short statement in a complaint, giving the defendant fair notice of what the claim is, is sufficient under F.R.C.P. 8. (Rannels v. S.E. Nichols, Inc.)

    [For more information on pleading requirements, see Casenote Law Outline on Civil Procedure, Chapter 5, Pleading, § III, Notice Pleading Requirements—The Complaint.]

4. **Ethical Principles as a Limitation.** It is a violation of Fed. R. Civ. P. 11 to file or to cause the filing of a suit without a reasonable belief in its validity or without making a reasonable inquiry into the facts of the case. (Business Guides v. Chromatic Communications Enterprises)

5. **Ethical Principles as a Limitation.** Concise rule of law not stated. (Gerbode v. Religious Technology Center)

    [For more information on attorney fees and Rule 11, see Casenote Law Outline on Civil Procedure, Chapter 5, § VI, Truthfulness in Pleading.]

6. **Disfavored Claims.** A plaintiff must plead the circumstances constituting fraud with specificity. (DiLeo v. Ernst & Young)

7. **Civil Rights.** A pleading need not fully anticipate the official immunity defense, but, once the defense is raised, a detailed reply may be required. (Schultea v. Wood)

    [For more information on pleading, see Casenote Law Outline on Civil Procedure, Chapter 5, § IV, Special Pleading Requirements.]

8. **Allocating the Elements.** In an action to redress the deprivation of rights secured by the U.S. Constitution and laws under 42 U.S.C. § 1983, the complaint need not allege the defendant's bad faith in order to state a claim for relief. (Gomez v. Toledo)

    [For more information on pleading requirements, see Casenote Law Outline on Civil Procedure, Chapter 5, Pleading, § III, Notice Pleading Requirements—The Complaint.]

9. **Denials.** In the federal courts, a defendant who knowingly makes inaccurate statements may be estopped from denying those inaccurate statements at the trial. (Zielinksi v. Philadelphia Piers, Inc.)

   [For more information on pleading requirements, see Casenote Law Outline on Civil Procedure, Chapter 5, Pleading, § V, Answers. See also § VI, Truthfulness in Pleading.]

10. **Affirmative Defenses.** It is the obligation of a defendant in an action for trespass to affirmatively plead and prove matters in justification. (Layman v. Southwestern Bell Telephone Co.)

    [For more information on pleading requirements, see Casenote Law Outline on Civil Procedure, Chapter 5, Pleading, § V, Answers.]

11. **Prejudice.** The opponent of a motion for leave to amend must show he will be prejudiced by the grant of leave under F.R.C.P. 15(a). (Beeck v. Aquaslide 'N Dive Corp.)

    [For more information on Rule 15, see Casenote Law Outline on Civil Procedure, Chapter 5, Pleading, § VII, Amendments to Pleadings.]

12. **Statutes of Limitations and Relation Back.** A claim that does not arise out of the same conduct, transaction, or occurrence as the original claim does not relate back to the original pleading. (Moore v. Baker)

    [For more information on the statute of limitations and relation back, see Casenote Law Outline on Civil Procedure, Chapter 5, § VII, Amendments to Pleadings.]

13. **Statutes of Limitations and Relation Back.** When allegations in an amended complaint and the original complaint derive from the same nucleus of operative facts, the amended complaint relates back to the date of the original complaint. (Bonerb v. Richard J. Caron Foundation)

    [For more information on statute of limitations and Relation Back, see Casenote Law Outline on Civil Procedure, Chapter 5, § VII, Amendments to Pleadings.]

PEOPLE ex. rel. DEPARTMENT of TRANSPORTATION v. SUPERIOR COURT

Department of transportation (D) v. Court (P)

Cal. Ct. App., 5 Cal. App. 4th 1480 (1992).

NATURE OF CASE: Writ of mandamus to review ruling on motion in personal injury action.

FACT SUMMARY: A form complaint omitted essential elements of a claim.

CONCISE RULE OF LAW: Ultimate facts which support each element of a claim must be pleaded to state a cause of action.

FACTS: An attorney used a form complaint approved by the Judicial Council and asserted a cause of action for premises liability without alleging sufficient facts to support each element of the claim. The Department of Transportation (D) sought a demurrer in the trial court, stating that the complaint failed to plead sufficient facts to support a cause of action. The trial judge denied the motion, stating that Judicial Council form complaints cannot be demurred. The Department (D) requested a writ of mandamus to review the trial judge's decision.

ISSUE: Must ultimate facts which support each element of a claim be pleaded to state a cause of action in all complaints?

HOLDING AND DECISION: (Gilbert, J.) Yes. Ultimate facts which support each element of a claim must be pleaded in all complaints, even form complaints approved by the Judicial Council. Inadequate pleading prevented The Department (D) from determining the theory upon which the plaintiff was seeking relief and prevented the Department (D) from asserting all possible defenses. Writ of mandate issued to set aside the superior court's overruling of the demurrer and to order a new order sustaining the demurrer with leave to amend.

EDITOR'S ANALYSIS: Code pleading states like California require that the complaint state ultimate facts which support a cause of action. As in the present case, litigation often results when the plaintiff fails to allege enough essential facts to assert a claim. On the other hand, if the complaint includes too many factual allegations, the plaintiff may be limited in asserting all possible theories upon which the defendant caused injury. Thus, drafting complaints is more of an art than a science.

[For more information on pleading, see Casenote Law Outline on Civil Procedure, Chapter 5, § II, Code-Pleading Requirements — The Complaint.]

QUICKNOTES

ULTIMATE FACT - A fact upon which a judicial determination is made and which is inferred from the evidence presented at trial.

COMPLAINT - The initial pleading commencing litigation which sets forth a claim for relief.

WRIT OF MANDAMUS - A court order issued commanding a public or private entity, or an official thereof, to perform a duty required by law.

DEMURRER - The assertion that the opposing party's pleadings are insufficient and that the demurring party should not be made to answer.

NOTES:

DUNCAN v. AT&T COMMUNICATIONS, INC.
Claimant (P) v. Utility company (D)
668 F. Supp. 232 (S.D.N.Y. 1987).

NATURE OF CASE: Motion to dismiss complaint alleging discrimination, breach of duty of fair representation, and infliction of emotional distress.

FACT SUMMARY: Duncan's (P) complaint omitted essential elements to state a federal claim.

CONCISE RULE OF LAW: Although only a short and plain statement is necessary, a claim which is illegibly stated or asserts a bald conclusion fails to state a federal claim.

FACTS: In her suit against AT&T (D), Duncan (P) made claims for race- and disability-based discrimination, breach of the duty of fair representation, and intentional infliction of emotional distress. However, Duncan's (P) complaint omitted to assert Duncan's (P) membership in a protected minority group, or that Duncan (P) was qualified for a position for which AT&T (D) was seeking applicants. It also failed to assert that despite Duncan's (P) qualifications, Duncan (P) was not offered the position, or that AT&T (D) kept the position open and continued to see applicants with Duncan's (P) qualifications. AT&T (D) sought dismissal on a Fed. R. Civ. P. 12(b)(6) motion..

ISSUE: Does a statement of a claim which is illegible and asserts a bald conclusion state a federal claim?

HOLDING AND DECISION: (Carter, J.) No. Although only a short and plain statement of the claim is necessary, a claim which is illegibly stated or baldly conclusory fails. AT&T (D) is entitled to notice of the federal claim and the grounds upon which it rests. Motion to dismiss is granted.

EDITOR'S ANALYSIS: Under the federal rules, the complaint must give the defendant notice of some set of circumstances under which the pleader is entitled to relief, unlike code pleading states which require the pleader to state ultimate facts upon which the pleader is entitled to relief. Thus, federal pleading standards are more liberal than code pleading standards.

[For more information on pleading, see Casenote Law Outline on Civil Procedure, Chapter 5, § III, Notice Pleading Requirements — The Complaint.]

QUICKNOTES
FRCP 12(b)(6) - Motion to dismiss for failure to state a claim.

NOTES:

DILEO v. ERNST & YOUNG

Shareholder (P) v. Corporate accountant (D)

901 F.2d 624 (7th Cir.), cert. denied, -- U.S. --, 111 S.Ct 347 (1990).

NATURE OF CASE: Appeal from dismissal of action for damages for fraud.

FACT SUMMARY: DiLeo (P) brought a class action suit against Ernst (D) for securities fraud under Rule 10b-5, but failed to include any specific circumstances which constituted fraud in his pleadings.

CONCISE RULE OF LAW: A plaintiff must plead the circumstances constituting fraud with specificity.

FACTS: DiLeo (P) owned stock in Continental Illinois Bank. For some time during the 1980s, Continental made increasingly risky loans. Continental identified some nonperforming loans and established reserves to cover anticipated losses. During this period, Ernst (D), the corporate accountant for Continental, certified the financial statements, including the accounts receivable. When large numbers of the bad loans became uncollectible, DiLeo's (P) Continental stock became nearly worthless because the bank did not increase its reserves fast enough to prevent failure. DiLeo (P) filed a class action suit under SEC Rule 10b-5, alleging securities fraud. The pleadings contained only general information gleaned from the various annual reports certified by Ernst (D). DiLeo (P) did not identify any specific problem loans or how Ernst (D) could have recognized that Continental's reserves were inadequate. The district court declined to certify the class because the action duplicated a suit which was already settled. The court then dismissed the suit because DiLeo (P) failed to give any examples in his pleadings of how he was defrauded by Ernst (D) or how Ernst (D) aided and abetted Continental in violating securities laws. DiLeo (P) appealed.

ISSUE: Must a plaintiff plead, with specificity, the circumstances constituting fraud?

HOLDING AND DECISION: (Easterbrook, J.) Yes. The plaintiff must plead, with specificity, the circumstances constituting fraud. Those investors who seek relief under SEC Rule 10b-5 must plead how they are damaged differently from anyone else who was injured. Fed. R. Civ. P. 9(b) requires that the plaintiff state "with particularity" the "circumstances constituting fraud." This means that the plaintiff must bring forward facts which are attributable to fraud. Without these facts, the pleadings are deficient and the action must be dismissed. Here, DiLeo (P) primarily alleged that Ernst (D) should have realized that large amounts of Continental's accounts receivable were uncollectible. The pleadings failed, however, to identify what specific loans were problem loans or how Ernst (D) could or should have recognized that the reserves established by Continental were inadequate. DiLeo (P) presented only information contained within various financial statements and alleged that the differences between them were due to fraud. Securities laws do not guarantee good business practices nor do they protect investors from financial reverses. While states of mind may be pled in generalities, circumstances must be pled with specificity, including the who, what, where, and when of the allegations. Because DiLeo's (P) pleadings lacked any specifics as to what fraudulent acts were committed by Ernst (D), his claim was properly dismissed. Affirmed.

EDITOR'S ANALYSIS: Fraud is a basis to excuse a party of the contractual obligation to perform. Historically, at common law, the courts were reluctant to put aside contractual duties to perform. Because of the reluctance of the common law courts, actions alleging fraud had a higher pleading threshold than other actions, and American courts continued to follow this view. This higher pleading threshold has been codified in Fed. R. Civ. P. 9.

QUICKNOTES

FRCP 9(b) - Sets forth the requirements for pleading fraud or mistake and requires the circumstances constituting fraud or mistake to be plead with particularity; malice, intent, knowledge and other conditions of the mind of a person may be plead generally.

FRAUD - A false representation of facts with the intent that another will rely on the misrepresentation to his detriment.

SEC RULE 106-5 - Provides penalties against anyone who uses misrepresentation or fraud in conjunction with the sale of securities.

NOTES:

SCHULTEA v. WOOD
Chief of police (P) v. City council member (D)
47 F. 3d 1427 (5th Cir. 1995) (en banc).

NATURE OF CASE: Motion to dismiss and motion to amend due process complaint.

FACT SUMMARY: Schultea (P), a chief of police, investigated allegations that a city council member (D) was involved in criminal activity, and, after the council demoted him, he sued.

CONCISE RULE OF LAW: A pleading need not fully anticipate the official immunity defense, but, once the defense is raised, a detailed reply may be required.

FACTS: Council members demoted Schultea (P), the chief of police, after Schultea (P) investigated allegations of criminal wrongdoing by a council member (D). Schultea (P) sued several council members (D), alleging violations of due process and infringements of his First Amendment rights. The council members (D) alleged that the pleading failed to fully anticipate the official immunity defense and moved to dismiss. Schultea (P) moved to amend.

ISSUE: Must a pleading fully anticipate the official immunity defense?

HOLDING AND DECISION: (Hugginbotham, J.) No. A pleading need not fully anticipate the official immunity defense, but, once the defense is raised, a detailed reply may be required. The qualified immunity doctrine creates a new role for the Rule 7(a) reply. The district court has narrow discretion not to require a reply when greater detail might assist the court in determining the adequacy of the claim. Remanded to district court with motion to amend granted.

CONCURRENCE: (Jones, J.) The official immunity defense cannot be abrogated by the Federal Rules of Civil Procedure. Absent a demand for pleadings with particularity, government officials will sacrifice some of their right to immunity. Utilizing Rule 7 is the next best approach available.

EDITOR'S ANALYSIS: As the present case indicates, government officials enjoy qualified immunity if they reasonably believe their actions were constitutional. Thus, the issue of state of mind is relevant in substantive law. Fed. R. Civ. P. 9(b) requires pleadings to be stated with particularity when fraud or mistake are alleged; however, malice, intent, knowledge, and other conditions of mind may be averred generally. The present case indicates a judicial preference that a reply be stated with particularity when the answer raises the doctrine of qualified immunity in order to balance the conflict of substantive law with procedural law.

[For more information on pleading, see Casenote Law Outline on Civil Procedure, Chapter 5, § IV, Special Pleading Requirements.]

QUICKNOTES

PLEADING - A statement setting forth the plaintiff's cause of action or the defendant's defenses to the plaintiff's claims.

QUALIFIED IMMUNITY - An affirmative defense relieving officials from civil liability for the performance of activities within their discretion so long as such conduct is not in violation of an individual's rights pursuant to law as determined by a reasonable person standard.

FRCP 9(b) - Sets forth the requirements for pleading fraud or mistake and requires the circumstances constituting fraud or mistake to be plead with particularity; malice, intent, knowledge and other conditions of the mind of a person may be plead generally.

FRCP 7 - Provides that a party need not respond to any new claims or issues returned in a responsive pleading, to prevent any undue admission that may arise as the result of addressing the new assertions.

NOTES:

LAYMAN v. SOUTHWESTERN BELL TELEPHONE COMPANY

Real estate owner (P) v. Telephone company (D)

Mo. Ct. App., 554 S.W.2d 477 (1977).

NATURE OF CASE: Appeal from denial of damages for trespass.

FACT SUMMARY: In Layman's (P) suit against Southwestern Bell (D) for trespass, Layman (P) contended that Bell (D) had entered her land and had installed underground telephone wires and cables without her consent and, in doing so, had depreciated the value of her land.

CONCISE RULE OF LAW: It is the obligation of a defendant in an action for trespass to affirmatively plead and prove matters in justification.

FACTS: Layman (P) owned real estate in Jefferson County, Missouri. Layman (P) brought suit for trespass against Southwestern Bell (D), contending that Bell (D) had entered her land and had installed underground telephone wires and cables without her consent and, in doing so, had depreciated the value of her land. After hearing the evidence, the court rendered judgment in Bell's (D) favor, stating that there was "insufficient evidence to establish the trespass pleaded and sought to be proved." Layman (P) appealed.

ISSUE: Is it the obligation of a defendant in an action for trespass to affirmatively plead and prove matters in justification?

HOLDING AND DECISION: (Weier, J.) Yes. It is the obligation of a defendant in an action for trespass to affirmatively plead and prove matters in justification. Here, Layman (P) contends that the trial court erred when it permitted Bell (D) to introduce evidence that it had received an assignment of an easement originally executed by owners of the land previous to Layman (P). Layman (P) argued that Bell (D) had pleaded only as general denial and not an affirmative defense of easement to Layman's (P) claim of trespass. Layman (P) further argued that affirmative defenses, such as easement in a trespass case, must be affirmatively pleaded as a condition to the admissibility of such evidence at the trial, and that because Bell (D) did not do so, such evidence should not be admissible. It seems clear that the right of Bell (D) to enter upon Layman's (P) land would have to be proven by some competent evidence which would give that right to Bell (D). If Bell (D) avers that Layman's (P) theory of liability does not apply because of additional facts which placed Bell (D) in a position to avoid any legal responsibility for its action, that defense, rather than a general denial, must be set forth in its answer. Bell (D) did not do this, and, thus, Layman's (P) objection to introduction of the easement evidence when it was not pleaded in justification of the trespass should have been sustained. Reversed.

EDITOR'S ANALYSIS: In some situations, a plaintiff must allege a certain matter and a defendant must allege the opposite in the form of an affirmative defense, rather than just denying plaintiff's allegations. For example, the plaintiff in a defamation suit must allege the falsity of the statement, but the truth of the statement is an affirmative defense that must be pleaded. The rationale for this rule seems to be that the facts in question are such an integral part of the claim that plaintiff must make the initial allegation, but that the responsibility for pleading and proving such matters will be placed on the defendant.

[For more information on pleading requirements, see Casenote Law Outline on Civil Procedure, Chapter 5, Pleading, § V, Answers.]

QUICKNOTES

AFFIRMATIVE DEFENSE - A manner of defending oneself against a claim not by denying the truth of the charge but by the introduction of some evidence challenging the plaintiff's right to bring the claim.

GENERAL DENIAL - Type of pleading contradicting all the assertions of a former pleading.

NOTES:

BEECK v. AQUASLIDE 'N DIVE CORP.
Injured slide user (P) v. Slide manufacturer (D)
562 F.2d 537 (1977).

NATURE OF CASE: Appeal from grant of leave to amend.

FACT SUMMARY: Beeck (P) was injured on a pool slide alleged to have been manufactured by Aquaslide (D), and after Aquaslide (D) admitted manufacture in its answer, the district court granted it leave to amend to deny manufacture over Beeck's (P) objection.

CONCISE RULE OF LAW: The opponent of a motion for leave to amend must show he will be prejudiced by the grant of leave under F.R.C.P. 15(a).

FACTS: Beeck (P) was injured while using the slide at a social gathering at Kimberly Village, Davenport, Iowa. Beeck (P) then brought this action in district court under diversity jurisdiction alleging that Aquaslide (D) was liable under theories of negligence, strict liability, and breach of implied warranty. Aquaslide (D) answered the complaint, admitting that it manufactured the slide in question in reliance upon the opinions of insurance investigators. The district court then granted Aquaslide (D) leave to amend the answer to deny this fact and permitted a separate trial on the question of manufacture over the objection of Beeck (P). The jury found for Aquaslide (D) and the court entered summary judgment against Beeck (P). By the time of the amendment, the statute of limitations for Beeck's (P) cause of action had run, and Beeck (P) appealed.

ISSUE: Must an opponent of a motion for leave to amend show he will be prejudiced by the grant of leave under F.R.C.P. 15(a)?

HOLDING AND DECISION: (Benson, J.) Yes. F.R.C.P. 15(a) provides that "leave shall be freely given when justice so requires." The grant or denial of such leave to amend is within the sound discretion of the trial judge. The party opposing the motion for leave must show he will be prejudiced by the grant of leave under F.R.C.P. 15(a). In this case, Aquaslide (D) relied upon the conclusions of three separate insurance companies and their investigators and were thus not negligent in determining the facts in question, and it was not an abuse of discretion to give Aquaslide (D) a chance to correct a fact disputed. Beeck (P) alleged that he was prejudiced because his action was foreclosed by the running of the statute of limitations. This argument required the trial judge to assume that Aquaslide (D) would prevail on the manufacturing issue, and the judge properly refused to so presume. Neither was the grant of separate trials improper. A substantial issue of material fact was raised which would exonerate Aquaslide (D) if resolved in its favor. There was thus no abuse of discretion. Affirmed.

EDITOR'S ANALYSIS: Because of the running of the statute of limitations, it would be unlikely, if not impossible, that Beeck (P) would be able to move against any other party. The court had to counterbalance this injustice against that of precluding Aquaslide (D) from proving that it did not manufacture the slide which caused the injury. Since the amendment and the separate trial gave Beeck (P) a chance to disprove Aquaslide's (D) argument, and since the F.R.C.P. technically permitted the amendment and severance, the balance was struck in Aquaslide's (D) favor.

[For more information on Rule 15, see Casenote Law Outline on Civil Procedure, Chapter 5, Pleading, § VII, Amendments to Pleadings.]

QUICKNOTES

FRCP 15(a) - Sets forth the rule that a party may amend its pleading once as a matter of course at any time before a responsive pleading is served, or within 20 days if no responsive pleading is permitted and the action has not been placed on the trial calendar; otherwise a party may amend its pleading only by leave of court or written consent of the opposing party; a party is required to plead in response to an amended pleading within the time remaining for response to the original pleading or within ten days of service of the amended pleading, whichever is longer, unless otherwise stated by court order.

AMENDMENT TO PLEADING - The modification of a pleading either as a matter of course upon motion to the court or by consent of both parties; a party is entitled to change its pleading once as a matter of course before a responsive pleading has been served.

ISSUE OF MATERIAL FACT - A fact that is disputed between two or more parties to litigation that is essential to proving an element of the cause of action or a defense asserted or would otherwise affect the outcome of the proceeding.

NOTES:

MOORE v. BAKER

Patient (P) v. Physician (D)

989 F. 2d 1129 (11th Cir. 1993).

NATURE OF CASE: Appeal of denial of motion to amend pleading in non-consent action.

FACT SUMMARY: Moore (P) initially alleged that Dr. Baker (D) violated the informed consent law, but then sought to include a claim for medical malpractice.

CONCISE RULE OF LAW: A claim that does not arise out of the same conduct, transaction, or occurrence as the original claim does not relate back to the original pleading.

FACTS: Moore (P) consulted Dr. Baker (D) to correct a blockage of her carotid artery. Baker (D) recommended surgery and warned Moore (P) of the risks. The operation left Moore (P) permanently disabled. Moore's (P) initial complaint alleged only a violation of Georgia's informed consent law. The trial court granted Baker's (D) motion for summary judgment. The statute of limitations ran the day after Moore (P) filed the original complaint. Moore (P) then sought to amend the complaint to include a claim for negligence, asserting that the new claim should relate back to the date of the original complaint. The trial court denied Moore's (P) motion, and Moore (P) appealed.

ISSUE: May a claim that does not arise out of the same conduct, transaction, or occurrence as the original claim relate back to the original pleading?

HOLDING AND DECISION: (Morgan, J.) No. A claim that does not arise out of the same conduct, transaction, or occurrence as the original claim may not relate back to the original pleading. In this case, the new claim arises out of alleged actions which are distinct in time and involve separate and distinct conduct. The failure-to-warn claim focused on actions prior to surgery, while the negligence claim focuses on actions during and post-surgery. Motion to amend denied.

EDITOR'S ANALYSIS: Whether the conduct, transaction, or occurrence in the amended complaint relates back to the original complaint to avoid the bar of a statute of limitations is a subjective test open to argument and interpretation. The role of the appellate court is to decide whether the trial court abused its discretion in applying this test to the facts of the case.

[For more information on the statute of limitations and relation back, see Casenote Law Outline on Civil Procedure, Chapter 5, § VII, Amendments to Pleadings.]

QUICKNOTES

RELATION BACK DOCTRINE - Doctrine which holds that a party may not amend its pleading to set forth a new or different claim or defense unless it involves the subject matter of the original pleading; under FRCP 15, if a party amends its pleading as a matter of course before a responsive pleading is served, such amendment is said to relate back to the original pleading if it involves the subject matter of the original pleading.

AMENDMENT TO PLEADING - The modification of a pleading either as a matter of course upon motion to the court or by consent of both parties; a party is entitled to change its pleading once as a matter of course before a responsive pleading has been served.

NOTES:

BONERB v. RICHARD J. CARON FOUNDATION

Injured basketball player (P) v. Foundation (D)

159 F.R.D. 16 (W.D.N.Y. 1994).

NATURE OF CASE: Motion to amend complaint in personal injury action.

FACT SUMMARY: After Bonerb (P) filed suit for injuries received on a basketball court while he was being treated at the Richard J. Caron Foundation (D), he sought to amend his complaint to add a cause of action for "counseling malpractice."

CONCISE RULE OF LAW: When allegations in an amended complaint and the original complaint derive from the same nucleus of operative facts, the amended complaint relates back to the date of the original complaint.

FACTS: Bonerb (P) slipped and fell while playing basketball at the Richard J. Caron Foundation (D) while participating in the Foundation's (D) mandatory exercise program. Bonerb's (P) original complaint alleged the Foundation's (D) basketball court was negligently maintained. Bonerb (P) sought to amend the complaint to include a new claim for counseling malpractice. Bonerb (P) sought to relate back the malpractice claim to the date of the original complaint since the statute of limitations had expired for asserting a malpractice claim.

ISSUE: May allegations in an amended complaint relate back to the date of the original complaint when the new claim derives from the same nucleus of operative facts as the original complaint?

HOLDING AND DECISION: (Heckman, J.) Yes. Allegations in an amended complaint may relate back to the date of the original complaint when the new claim derives from the same nucleus of operative facts as the original complaint. The determining factor is whether the facts stated in the original complaint put the defendant on notice of the claim which plaintiff later seeks to add. Here, Bonerb (P) is using the same factual allegations in the amended complaint as in the original complaint. Bonerb (P) has merely changed the legal theory upon which the claim is based. Motion to amend is granted.

EDITOR'S ANALYSIS: Amendment to a pleading may occur in an answer as well as a complaint. Fed. R. Civ. P. 15© allows relation back for claims and defenses asserted in the original pleading or attempted to be set forth in the original pleading which arose from the conduct, transaction, or occurrence of the original pleading.

[For more information on statute of limitations and Relation Back, see Casenote Law Outline on Civil Procedure, Chapter 5, § VII, Amendments to Pleadings.]

QUICKNOTES

RELATION BACK DOCTRINE - Doctrine which holds that a party may not amend its pleading to set forth a new or different claim or defense unless it involves the subject matter of the original pleading; under FRCP 15, if a party amends its pleading as a matter of course before a responsive pleading is served, such amendment is said to relate back to the original pleading if it involves the subject matter of the original pleading.

NUCLEUS OF OPERATIVE FACTS - An underlying fact situation common to those pleadings asserting it.

FRCP 15(a) - Sets forth the rule that a party may amend its pleading once as a matter of course at any time before a responsive pleading is served, or within 20 days if no responsive pleading is permitted and the action has not been placed on the trial calendar; otherwise a party may amend its pleading only by leave of court or written consent of the opposing party; a party is required to plead in response to an amended pleading within the time remaining for response to the original pleading or within ten days of service of the amended pleading, whichever is longer, unless otherwise stated by court order.

NOTES:

CHAPTER 7
DISCOVERY

QUICK REFERENCE RULES OF LAW

1. **Relevance.** In an action alleging sex discrimination in hiring practices, information as to advancement policies within the defendant's organization is sufficiently "relevant" for purposes of discovery under F.R.C.P. 26. (Blank v. Sullivan & Cromwell)

   [For more information on scope of discovery, see Casenote Law Outline on Criminal Procedure, Chapter 7, Discovery, § III, Outline of the Scope of Discovery Under the Federal Rules.]

2. **Relevance**. Only evidence which is relevant to the issue being litigated may be discovered. (Steffan v. Cheney)

3. **The General Problem of Privacy.** A protective order entered upon a showing of good cause which does not restrict the dissemination of information if gained from other sources does not violate the First Amendment. (Seattle Times Co. v. Rhinehart)

   [For more information on the general problem of Privacy, see Casenote Law Outline on Civil Procedure, Chapter 7, § IV, Specific Discovery Devices.]

4. **Physical and Mental Examinations.** Under Federal Rule of Civil Procedure 35: (1) the rule which provides for physical and mental examinations of parties is applicable to defendants as well as plaintiffs; (2) though the person to be examined under the rule must be a party to the action, he need not be an opposing party vis-a-vis the movant; and (3) a person who moves for a mental or physical examination of a party who has not asserted her mental or physical condition either in support of or in defense of a claim must affirmatively show that the condition sought to be examined is really in controversy and that good cause exists for the particular examination requested. (Schlagenhauf v. Holder)

   [For more information on physical and mental examinations, see Casenote Law Outline on Civil Procedure, Chapter 7, Discovery, § IV, Specific Discovery Devices.]

5. **Privilege and Trial Preparation Material.** Material obtained by counsel in preparation for litigation is the work product of the lawyer, and while such material is not protected by the attorney-client privilege, it is not discoverable on mere demand without a showing of necessity or justification. (Hickman v. Taylor)

   [For more information on attorney work product privilege, see Casenote Law Outline on Criminal Procedure, Chapter 7, Discovery, § III, Outline of the Scope of Discovery Under the Federal Rules.]

6. **Expert Information.** Under exceptional circumstances, if it is impractical for the party seeking discovery to obtain facts or opinions on the same subject by other means, a party may, by interrogatories or by deposition, discover information by an expert who has been retained or specially employed by another party in anticipation of litigation and who is not to be called as a witness. (Thompson v. The Haskell Co.)

   [For more information on discovery in the adversary system, see Casenote Law Outline on Civil Procedure, Chapter 7, § III, Outline of the Scope of Discovery under the Federal Rules.]

7. **Expert Information.** A nontestifying expert is immune from discovery unless exceptional circumstances apply. (Chiquita International Ltd. v. M/V Bolero Reefer)

   [For more information on discovery in the adversary system, see Casenote Law Outline on Civil Procedure, Chapter 7, § III, Outline of the Scope of Discovery Under the Federal Rules.]

8. **Sanctions as a Remedy.** An attorney who impedes, delays, or frustrates a deposition may be subject to sanctions. (Phillips v. Manufacturers Hanover Trust Co.)

    [For more information on Controlling Abuse of Discovery, see Casenote Law Outline on Civil Procedure, Chapter 7, §VI, Discovery.]

9. **Sanctions as a Remedy.** The exclusion of critical evidence is an extreme sanction that is not normally imposed absent a showing of willful deception or flagrant disregard of a court order by the proponent of the evidence. (Kotes v. Super Fresh Food Markets, Inc.)

    [For more information on discovery, see Casenote Law Outline on Civil Procedure, Chapter 7, § III, Outline of the Scope of Discovery Under the Federal Rules.]

BLANK v. SULLIVAN & CROMWELL

Sex discrimination claimant (P) v. Law firm (D)

16 F.E.P. Cases (BNA) 87 (S.D.N.Y. 1976).

NATURE OF CASE: Motion for rehearing of order denying discovery.

FACT SUMMARY: In a sex discrimination action, Blank (P) sought to determine from Sullivan & Cromwell (D), a law firm, the identities of all female associates offered or refused partnership with the firm and the identities of male associates offered partnership and their lengths of employment, times of offer, and areas of specialization.

CONCISE RULE OF LAW: In an action alleging sex discrimination in hiring practices, information as to advancement policies within the defendant's organization is sufficiently "relevant" for purposes of discovery under F.R.C.P. 26.

FACTS: Blank (P) brought this action for sex discrimination against Sullivan & Cromwell (D), a law firm which did not hire her. She sought to discover under F.R.C.P. 26 the identities of female associates of the firm and whether each was offered a partnership in the firm and whether any became a partner. Blank (P) also sought the identities of male associates and the lengths of their employment, the dates they were offered partnership if they were, and the areas of specialization. The court denied a motion to compel answers to the interrogatories requesting this information, and Blank (P) moved for rehearing and modification of the order of denial.

ISSUE: In an action alleging sex discrimination in hiring practices, is information as to the advancement policies within the defendant's organization sufficiently "relevant" for purposes of discovery under F.R.C.P. 26?

HOLDING AND DECISION: (Motley, J.) Yes. Material sought on discovery need not be "relevant" in the sense that it is admissible evidence at trial. However, such material cannot be so unrelated as not to be calculated to lead to the discovery of admissible evidence. Here, the advancement policies of a firm may be related to their hiring practices with respect to women. In an action alleging sex discrimination in hiring practices, information as to the advancement policies within the defendant's organization is sufficiently "relevant" for purposes of discovery under F.R.C.P. 26. Even though numerous factors play a part in the decision to hire or to advance an applicant in a law firm, sex discrimination on one level may be probative of the same on another. Defendant is directed to answer the interrogatories.

EDITOR'S ANALYSIS: F.R.C.P. 26(b)(1) permits the discovery of any material "reasonably calculated to lead to the discovery of admissible evidence." This is a broad rule and is normally construed with an eye toward revelation of all "good cause shown" to protect a party against "annoyance, embarrassment, oppression or undue burden or expense."

[For more information on scope of discovery, see Case note Law Outline on Criminal Procedure, Chapter 7, Discovery, § III, Outline of the Scope of Discovery Under the Federal Rules.]

QUICKNOTES

FRCP 26 - Protects work product revealing an attorney's mental processes absent a strong showing of necessity and unavailability.

DISCOVERY - Pretrial procedure during which one party makes certain information available to the other.

INTERROGATORY - A method of pretrial discovery in which written questions are provided by one party to another who must respond in writing under oath.

NOTES:

STEFFAN v. CHENEY

Homosexual naval candidate (P) v. Secretary of Defense (D)

920 F.2d 74 (D.C. Cir. 1990).

NATURE OF CASE: Appeal from dismissal of action for wrongful discharge from U.S. Naval Academy.

FACT SUMMARY: Steffan (P), who was discharged from the U.S. Naval Academy after he truthfully responded in the affirmative to a superior's inquiry as to whether he was homosexual, argued that his wrongful discharge action should not have been dismissed because the district court erroneously allowed irrelevant questions as to whether he had engaged in homosexual activities during or after his tenure as a midshipman.

CONCISE RULE OF LAW: Only evidence which is relevant to the issue being litigated may be discovered.

FACTS: Steffan (P), while he was a midshipman at the U.S. Naval Academy, responded truthfully to a superior who ask him if he was a homosexual. Steffan (P) resigned from the Academy after an administrative board, shortly before he was to graduate at the head of his class, recommended that Steffan (P) be discharged, based solely on his statement. Steffan (P) brought suit against Secretary of Defense Cheney (D), alleging that he was constructively discharged from the service and challenging the constitutionality of the regulation that provided for discharge of homosexuals. During discovery, Steffan (P), invoking his Fifth Amendment privilege against self-incrimination, refused to answer questions as to whether he had ever engaged in homosexual activities during the time he was a midshipman or after his discharge. Additionally, he objected that the questions were not relevant to the legality of his separation. After giving a warning, the district court dismissed Steffan's (P) action for failure to comply with discovery orders, but the court acknowledged that Steffan (P) was discharged for his statement, not for acts. The court held, however, that the questions were relevant because the Navy could "refuse reinstatement on the grounds an individual has engaged in homosexual acts." Steffan (P) appealed.

ISSUE: May evidence which is irrelevant to the issue being litigated be discovered?

HOLDING AND DECISION: [Per curiam.] No. Only evidence which is relevant to the issue being litigated may be discovered. The law is quite clear on this issue. Further, judicial review must be confined to the grounds upon which the action was based. Here, the action was brought for invalid separation from the Naval Academy. If the basis for separation from the Academy was homosexual conduct, then the questions may have been relevant and the information discoverable. However, in the instant case, the basis for separation was a statement made by Steffan (P) in response to an inquiry by Academy supervisors. This does not

put into question whether he engaged in the potentially disqualifying activity. Therefore, this area was not discoverable, unless the court could find another ground to assert relevance. Reversed and remanded.

EDITOR'S ANALYSIS: Discovery is allowed on issues which are admissible or will lead to admissible evidence. However, discovery may be denied even when the issue is relevant if it invades the right of privacy of the individual. In these instances, the court must weigh the judicial concept of fair play requiring disclosure of evidence relevant to a claim against the constitutional rights of the individual. Clearly, if the right being invaded is a fundamental right, then discovery will be denied, unless the government can demonstrate a compelling need.

QUICKNOTES

DISCOVERY - Pretrial procedure during which one party makes certain information available to the other.

FUNDAMENTAL RIGHT - A liberty that is either expressly or impliedly provided for in the United States Constitution, the deprivation or burdening of which is subject to a heightened standard of review.

RELEVANT EVIDENCE - Evidence having any tendency to prove or disprove a disputed fact.

NOTES:

SEATTLE TIMES CO. v. RHINEHART
Publishing company (D) v. Spiritual leader (P)
467 U.S. 20 (1984).

NATURE OF CASE: Review of protective order in defamation suit.

FACT SUMMARY: Seattle Times Co. (D) sought to publish information obtained through the discovery process about Rhinehart (P), an alleged spiritual cult leader, and his cult members.

CONCISE RULE OF LAW: A protective order entered upon a showing of good cause which does not restrict the dissemination of information if gained from other sources does not violate the First Amendment.

FACTS: Seattle Times Co. (D) published derogatory stories about Rhinehart (P), a spiritual leader of the Aquarian Foundation. Rhinehart (P) responded with claims for defamation and invasion of privacy against the Times (D) and others. The Times (D) answered the complaint and immediately instituted extensive discovery regarding the membership and financial affairs of Rhinehart's (P) Aquarian Foundation. Rhinehart (P) refused to release all the information that the Times (D) requested, asserting that members had been threatened and that release of the information would subject members to additional attacks. The Times (D) sought an order to compel discovery, and Rhinehart (P) sought a protective order that information obtained could not be published. Both orders were granted. Both the Times (D) and Rhinehart (P) appealed. The Washington Supreme Court affirmed both orders. The Times (D) appealed the protective order asserting a First Amendment violation.

ISSUE: Does a protective order entered upon a showing of good cause which does not restrict the dissemination of information if gained from other sources violate the First Amendment?

HOLDING AND DECISION: (Powell, J.) No. A protective order entered upon a showing of good cause which does not restrict the dissemination of information if gained from other sources does not violate the First Amendment. Discovery is only for the purpose of preparing for trial and is not subject to the First Amendment.

EDITOR'S ANALYSIS: Fed. R. Civ. Proc. 26 (c) allows the federal court to grant an order which justice requires to protect a party or person from annoyance, embarrassment, oppression, or undue burden or expense. The party seeking the protective order has the burden of proving the need for the order. Without protective orders, litigants might drop their claims to avoid embarrassment or oppression.

[For more information on the general problem of Privacy, see Casenote Law Outline on Civil Procedure, Chapter 7, § IV, Specific Discovery Devices.]

QUICKNOTES

PROTECTIVE ORDER - Court order protecting a party against potential abusive treatment through use of the legal process.

DISCOVERY - Pretrial procedure during which one party makes certain information available to the other.

FRCP 26 - Protects work product revealing an attorney's mental processes absent a strong showing of necessity and unavailability.

NOTES:

HICKMAN v. TAYLOR

Surviving crew member (P) v. Tug owner (D)

392 U.S. 495 (1947).

NATURE OF CASE: Action for damages for wrongful death.

FACT SUMMARY: Five crew members drowned when a tug sank. In anticipation of litigation, the attorney for Taylor (D), the tug owner, interviewed the survivors. Hickman (P), as representative of one of the deceased, brought this action and tried by means of discovery to obtain copies of the statements Taylor's (D) attorney obtained from the survivors.

CONCISE RULE OF LAW: Material obtained by counsel in preparation for litigation is the work product of the lawyer, and while such material is not protected by the attorney-client privilege, it is not discoverable on mere demand without a showing of necessity or justification.

FACTS: Five of nine crew members drowned when a tug sank. A public hearing was held at which the four survivors were examined. Their testimony was recorded and was made available to all interested parties. A short time later, the attorney for Taylor (D), the tug owner, interviewed the survivors, in preparation for possible litigation. He also interviewed other persons believed to have information on the accident. Ultimately, claims were brought by representatives of all five of the deceased. Four were settled. Hickman (P), the fifth claimant, brought this action. He filed interrogatories asking for any statements taken from crew members as well as any oral or written statements, records, reports, or other memoranda made concerning any matter relative to the towing operation, the tug's sinking, the salvaging and repair of the tug, and the death of the deceased. Taylor (D) refused to summarize or set forth the material on the ground that it was protected by the attorney-client privilege.

ISSUE: Does a party seeking to discover material obtained by an adverse party's counsel in preparation for possible litigation have a burden to show a justification for such production?

HOLDING AND DECISION: (Murphy, J.) Yes. The deposition-discovery rules are to be accorded a broad and liberal treatment, since mutual knowledge of all the relevant facts gathered by both parties is essential to proper litigation. But discovery does have ultimate and necessary boundaries. Limitations arise upon a showing of bad faith or harassment or when the inquiry seeks material which is irrelevant or privileged. In this case, the material sought by Hickman (P) is not protected by the attorney-client privilege. However, such material as that sought here does constitute the work product of the lawyer. The general policy against invading the privacy of an attorney in performing his various duties is so well recognized and so essential to the orderly working of our legal system that the party seeking work product material has a burden to show reasons to justify such production. Interviews, statements, memoranda, correspondence, briefs, mental impressions, etc., obtained in the course of preparation for possible or anticipated litigation fall within the work product. Such material is not free from discovery in all cases. [1]Where relevant and nonprivileged facts remain hidden in an attorney's file and where production of those facts is essential to the preparation of one's case, discovery may be had. But there must be a showing of necessity and justification. In this case, Hickman (P) seeks discovery of oral and written statements of witnesses whose identity is well known and whose availability to Hickman (P) appears unimpaired. Here no attempt was made to show why it was necessary that Taylor's (D) attorney produce the material. No reasons were given to justify this invasion of the attorney's privacy. Hickman's (P) counsel admitted that he wanted the statements only to help him prepare for trial. That is insufficient to warrant an exception to the policy of protecting the privacy of an attorney's professional activities.

EDITOR'S ANALYSIS: The Hickman decision left open a number of questions as to the scope of the work product doctrine and the showing needed to discover work product material. In 1970, Federal Rule 26(b)(3) was added to deal with the discovery of work product. It provides that documents and tangible things which were prepared in anticipation of litigation or for trial are discoverable only upon a showing that the party seeking such materials has substantial need of them and that he is unable without undue hardship to obtain the substantial equivalent of the materials by other means. The rule states that mental impressions, conclusions, opinions, or legal theories of an attorney or other representative of a party are to be protected against disclosure.

[For more information on attorney work product privilege, see Casenote Law Outline on Criminal Procedure, Chapter 7, Discovery, § III, Outline of the Scope of Discovery Under the Federal Rules.]

QUICKNOTES

DEPOSITION - A pretrial discovery procedure whereby oral or written questions are asked by one party of a witness of the opposing party under oath in preparation for litigation.

DISCOVERY - Pretrial procedure during which one party makes certain information available to the other.

ATTORNEY-CLIENT PRIVILEGE - A doctrine precluding the admission into evidence of confidential communications between an attorney and his client made in the course of obtaining professional assistance.

FED. R. CIV. P. 26 (b) (3) - Codifies the work product doctrine.

SCHLAGENHAUF v. HOLDER
Bus driver/bus company (D) v. Injured passengers (P)
379 U.S. 104 (1964).

NATURE OF CASE: Action to recover damages for negligence.

FACT SUMMARY: Passengers injured in a bus collision sued Greyhound, Schlagenhauf (D), the bus driver, and the owners of the trailer with which the bus collided. The trailer owners claimed the accident was due to Schlagenhauf's (D) negligence and moved for a physical and mental examination of him.

CONCISE RULE OF LAW: Under Federal Rule of Civil Procedure 35: (1) the rule which provides for physical and mental examinations of parties is applicable to defendants as well as plaintiffs; (2) though the person to be examined under the rule must be a party to the action, he need not be an opposing party vis-a-vis the movant; and (3) a person who moves for a mental or physical examination of a party who has not asserted her mental or physical condition either in support of or in defense of a claim must affirmatively show that the condition sought to be examined is really in controversy and that good cause exists for the particular examination requested.

FACTS: A bus collided with a tractor-trailer. The injured passengers brought a negligence action against Greyhound, owner of the bus (D), Schlagenhauf (D), the bus driver, Contract Carriers (D), owner of the tractor, and against the tractor driver and the trailer owner. Greyhound (D) cross-claimed against Contract (D) and the trailer owner. Contract (D) filed an answer to this cross-claim, stating that the collision was caused by Schlagenhauf's (D) negligence. Contract (D) petitioned for a mental and physical examination of Schlagenhauf (D) under Federal Rule of Civil Procedure 35. The district court judge, Holder, granted the petition. Schlagenhauf (D) applied for a writ of mandamus to have Holder's order requiring his (D) mental and physical examinations set aside.

ISSUES: (1) Would the application of the rule providing for physical and mental examinations of parties to defendants (F.R.C.P. 35) be an unconstitutional invasion of their privacy? (2) Must the party to be examined under the rule (F.R.C.P. 35) be an opposing party vis-a-vis the movant? (3) Must a person who moves for a mental or physical examination of a party (under F.R.C.P. 35) who has not asserted his mental or physical condition either in support of or in defense of a claim affirmatively show that the condition sought to be examined is really in controversy and that good cause exists for the particular examination requested?

HOLDING AND DECISION: (Goldberg, J.) (1) No. The rule which provides for physical and mental examinations of parties is Federal Rule of Civil Procedure 35. On its face, it applies to all parties to an action, and there is no basis for holding it applicable to plaintiffs and inapplicable to defendants. Issues cannot be resolved by a doctrine of favoring one class of litigants over another. In this case, the fact that Schlagenhauf (D) is a defendant does not make the rule inapplicable to him. (2) No. Rule 35 only requires that the person to be examined is a party to the action. It does not require that he be an opposing party, vis-a-vis the movant. Insistence that the movant have filed a pleading against the person to be examined would have the undesirable effect of an unnecessary proliferation of cross-claims and counterclaims and would not be in keeping with the aims of a federal discovery policy. Here, Schlagenhauf (D) was a party to this action by virtue of the original complaint. (3) Yes. Rule 35 expressly requires that the condition sought to be examined must be in controversy, and there must be good cause for the examination. These requirements are not mere formalities and are not met by mere conclusory allegations of the pleadings nor by mere relevance to the case. They require an affirmative showing by the movant that each condition sought to be examined is really and genuinely in controversy and that good cause exists for each examination. Here, Schlagenhauf (D) did not assert his mental or physical condition in support of or in defense of a claim. Hence, Contract (D), as movant, must make an affirmative showing that Schlagenhauf's (D) mental or physical condition was in controversy and that there was good cause for the examinations requested. Contract (D) requested examinations by an internist, an ophthalmologist, a neurologist, and a psychiatrist. Yet, the only allegations it made in respect to Schlagenhauf's (D) physical or mental condition were conclusory statements that he was not mentally or physically capable of driving a bus. The attorney's affidavit does have some additional statements about his vision and what an eye witness saw. There is nothing in the pleadings to support the examinations by the neurologist, internist, or psychiatrist. There was a specific allegation that Schlagenhauf's (D) vision was impaired. Were this the only exam requested, it would not be set aside. However, as the case must be remanded to the district court because of the other guidelines ordered, it would be appropriate for the district judge to reconsider this also in light of the guidelines set forth herein.

Continued on next page.

DISSENT: (Douglas, J.) Neither the Court nor Congress up to today has determined that any person whose physical or mental condition is brought into question during some lawsuit must surrender his right to keep his person inviolate.

EDITOR'S ANALYSIS: Rule 35 provides that when the physical or mental condition of a party is at issue, the court, upon motion and for good cause, may order the party to submit to an examination by a physician. The party examined is, upon request, entitled to receive a copy of the written report of the examining physician. The rule provides that, by requesting and receiving a copy of the report, the party examined must, upon request, furnish copies of written reports made by his physicians.

[For more information on physical and mental examinations, see Case note Law Outline on Civil Procedure, Chapter 7, Discovery, § IV, Specific Discovery Devices.]

QUICKNOTES

FRCP 35 - Provides that physical and mental examinations of all parties litigating the action are constitutional.

DISCOVERY - Pretrial procedure during which one party makes certain information available to the other.

WRIT OF MANDAMUS - A court order issued commanding a public or private entity, or an official thereof, to perform a duty required by law.

NOTES:

THOMPSON v. THE HASKELL CO.

Sexually-harassed employee (P) v. Employer (D)

65 F. Empl. Prac. Cas. (BNA) 1088 (M.D. Fl. 1994).

NATURE OF CASE: Motion for protective order in sexual harassment suit.

FACT SUMMARY: Thompson (P) sought to protect her psychologist's report from discovery.

CONCISE RULE OF LAW: Under exceptional circumstances, if it is impractical for the party seeking discovery to obtain facts or opinions on the same subject by other means, a party may, by interrogatories or by deposition, discover information by an expert who has been retained or specially employed by another party in anticipation of litigation and who is not to be called as a witness.

FACTS: Thompson (P) sued The Haskell Co. (D) and Zona (D), a supervisor of the Haskell Co. (D), alleging sexual harassment and that her employment with The Haskell Co. (D) was terminated when she refused to acquiesce to Zona's (D) advances. Thompson's (P) former counsel employed Dr. Lucas, a psychologist, to perform a diagnostic review and personality profile ten days after Thompson (P) was terminated. Thompson (P) sought an order to protect the psychological records possessed by Dr. Lucas.

ISSUE: May a party, under exceptional circumstances, obtain discovery of information by an opposing party's expert who has been retained or employed by a party in anticipation of litigation and who is not to be called as a witness?

HOLDING AND DECISION: (Syder, J.) Yes. Under exceptional circumstances, a party may obtain discovery of information by an opposing party's expert who has been retained or employed by a party in anticipation of litigation and who is not to be called as a witness. Here, Dr. Lucas's report was made ten days after Thompson (P) was terminated and is the only evidence available which is probative of Thompson's (P) emotional state at that time. Motion denied.

EDITOR'S ANALYSIS: Thompson (P) did not file her complaint until several months after she was terminated. Thus, opposing counsel had no opportunity to obtain psychological information from Thompson (P) shortly after her termination which would be probative of her emotional state during that time. This factor provided the exceptional circumstance in the present case.

[For more information on discovery in the adversary system, see Casenote Law Outline on Civil Procedure, Chapter 7, § III, Outline of the Scope of Discovery under the Federal Rules.]

QUICKNOTES

DISCOVERY - Pretrial procedure during which one party makes certain information available to the other.

EXPERT WITNESS - A witness providing testimony at trial who is specially qualified regarding the particular subject matter involved.

INTERROGATORY - A method of pretrial discovery in which written questions are provided by one party to another who must respond in writing under oath.

DEPOSITION - A pretrial discovery procedure whereby oral or written questions are asked by one party of a witness of the opposing party under oath in preparation for litigation.

NOTES:

CHIQUITA INTERNATIONAL LTD. v. M/V BOLERO REEFER

Shipper (P) v. Cargo carrier (D)

1994 U.S. Dist. LEXIS 5820 (S.D.N.Y. 1994).

NATURE OF CASE: Motion to compel discovery.

FACT SUMMARY: International Reefer (D), a carrier, sought to compel discovery of a marine surveyor who had evaluated its loading cranes and side ports.

CONCISE RULE OF LAW: A nontestifying expert is immune from discovery unless exceptional circumstances apply.

FACTS: Shipper Chiquita International Ltd. (P) sued International Reefer Services, S.A. (D), a cargo carrier, for cargo loss and damage. Chiquita (P) alleged that loading cranes and side ports on International Reefer's (D) carrier failed to function properly, which prevented the carrier from shipping the full load of Chiquita (P) bananas to Germany and unloading them before spoilage in accord with their contract. International Reefer (D) requested an order compelling discovery from Winer, a marine surveyor Chiquita (P) had employed to inspect the carrier upon arrival in Germany. International Reefer (D) asserted that Winer was a fact witness rather than an expert and that even if Winer were a nontestifying expert exceptional circumstances existed to compel discovery. Chiquita (P) objected.

ISSUE: May a non-testifying expert be subject to discovery?

HOLDING AND DECISION: (Francis, J.) No. A nontestifying expert may not be subject to discovery unless exceptional circumstances apply. A fact witness is a witness whose information was obtained in the normal course of business; however, a nontestifying expert is a person hired to make an evaluation in connection with expected litigation. Winer was hired by Chiquita (P) to make an observation in anticipation of litigation; thus, he is a nontestifying expert. Because International Reefer (D) could have employed its own expert to examine its carrier, and Chicquita (P) did not prevent another expert from being retained, no exceptional circumstances apply here. Application for Winer's deposition is denied.

EDITOR'S ANALYSIS: It is often not clear whether a person is a fact witness or nontestifying expert; thus, this is a favorite topic for law school examinations. Another favorite topic is determining if exceptional circumstances apply which would warrant compelling discovery from a nontestifying expert.

[For more information on discovery in the adversary system, see Casenote Law Outline on Civil Procedure, Chapter 7, § III, Outline of the Scope of Discovery Under the Federal Rules.]

QUICKNOTES

EXPERT WITNESS - A witness providing testimony at trial who is specially qualified regarding the particular subject matter involved.

DEPOSITION - A pretrial discovery procedure whereby oral or written questions are asked by one party of a witness of the opposing party under oath in preparation for litigation.

DISCOVERY - Pretrial procedure during which one party makes certain information available to the other.

NOTES:

PHILLIPS v. MANUFACTURERS HANOVER TRUST CO.
Employee (P) v. Employer trust company (D)

1994 U.S. Dist. LEXIS 3748 (S.D.N.Y. 1994).

NATURE OF CASE: Motion for sanctions in employment discrimination action.

FACT SUMMARY: Opposing counsel objected at least forty-nine times in an hour-and-a-half-deposition by Phillips's (P) attorney.

CONCISE RULE OF LAW: An attorney who impedes, delays, or frustrates a deposition may be subject to sanctions.

FACTS: During the deposition of Mr. Sztejnberg, a Manufacturers Hanover Trust Co. (D) witness for an employment discrimination case, defense counsel objected at least forty-nine times within an hour and a half. Many objections were related to the form of the question; however, many objections had no discernable basis. Sixty percent of the pages of the deposition transcript contained interruptions by Manufacturers's (D) defense counsel. Phillips (P) sought sanctions, costs, and attorney fees against Manufacturers Hanover (D) and its attorney for the allegedly abusive, unreasonable, and dilatory behavior of the attorney during Sztejnberg's deposition.

ISSUE: May an attorney who impedes, delays, or frustrates a deposition be subject to sanctions?

HOLDING AND DECISION: (Francis, J.) Yes. An attorney who impedes, delays, or frustrates a deposition may be subject to sanctions. Under Fed. R. Civ. P. 30(d)(1), sanctions may be awarded for conduct which the court finds has frustrated the fair examination of the deponent. Although this is a close case, since Rule 30 is new and Phillips's (P) counsel was not prevented from completing the deposition, the court chooses not to exercise its discretion. Motion denied.

EDITOR'S ANALYSIS: During oral depositions, attorneys may state objections in precise and nonargumentative terms which are related to question form or are for the purpose of preserving a privilege. They may not object merely because they perceive a question as unclear. Objections not made at the time of deposition are waived.

[For more information on Controlling Abuse of Discovery, see Casenote Law Outline on Civil Procedure, Chapter 7, §VI, Discovery.]

QUICKNOTES

DEPOSITION - A pretrial discovery procedure whereby oral or written questions are asked by one party of a witness of the opposing party under oath in preparation for litigation.

FRCP 30 - Sets forth the general provisions regarding the taking of oral depositions.

SANCTION - A penalty imposed in order to ensure compliance with a statute or regulation.

NOTES:

KOTES v. SUPER FRESH FOOD MARKETS, INC.

Injured customer (P) v. Supermarket (D)

157 F.R.D. 18 (E.D. Pa. 1994).

NATURE OF CASE: Cross-motions to exclude witnesses in federal personal injury action for lost wages and medical expenses.

FACT SUMMARY: Kotes (P) and Super Fresh Foods (D) sought to preclude the testimony of certain witnesses who had not been disclosed in a timely fashion as required by a scheduling order and by Rule 26 duties of disclosure.

CONCISE RULE OF LAW: The exclusion of critical evidence is an extreme sanction that is not normally imposed absent a showing of willful deception or flagrant disregard of a court order by the proponent of the evidence.

FACTS: Kotes (P) brought a personal injury action against Super Fresh Food Markets, Inc. (D) after she suffered a slip and a fall. The action was brought in U.S. District Court based on diversity jurisdiction. The court issued a pretrial discovery order, mandating that witness lists be exchanged by a certain date in anticipation of a calendered trial date. Both Kotes (P) and Super Fresh (D) failed to exchange witness lists in a timely fashion. Each filed a motion to exclude the other's witnesses from testifying. In the meantime, the trial date was postponed on the court's own motion.

ISSUE: Is the exclusion of critical evidence an extreme sanction that is not normally imposed absent a showing of willful deception or flagrant disregard of a court order?

HOLDING AND DECISION: (Joyner, J.) Yes. The exclusion of critical evidence is an extreme sanction that is not normally imposed absent a showing of willful deception or flagrant disregard of a court order. A witness not disclosed in a timely fashion per court order may nonetheless testify. Fed. R. Civ. P. 26 requires that a party disclose its witnesses and grants broad powers to district courts to adopt local rules governing such disclosure, as this court has done. A failure to disclose may result in witness disqualification. However, witness disqualification is a drastic sanction that should not be lightly imposed. Factors to be considered include willfulness of the violation, prejudice, and extent to which calling the undisclosed witness would disrupt the trial. Here, neither party's conduct, albeit questionable, clearly evidences bad faith. Furthermore, trial has been postponed, so each side may conduct discovery upon the other side's witness. As this ameliorates any prejudice that might otherwise occur, witness disqualification is an inappropriate sanction. Motions denied.

EDITOR'S ANALYSIS: Fed. R. Civ. P. 26 was initially an introductory rule, merely setting the stage for subsequent rules relating to specific types of discovery. This was changed in 1993. That year, amendments were adopted to make discovery obligations self-executing. The disclosure obligations discussed in the present case are an example of this.

[For more information on discovery, see Casenote Law Outline on Civil Procedure, Chapter 7, § III, Outline of the Scope of Discovery Under the Federal Rules.]

QUICKNOTES

FRCP 26 - Sets forth the general provisions regarding discovery including the required disclosures, the permissible scope of discovery and the limitations thereon.

SANCTIONS - A penalty imposed in order to ensure compliance with a statute or regulation.

DISCOVERY - Pretrial procedure during which one party makes certain information available to the other.

NOTES:

CHAPTER 8
RESOLUTION WITHOUT TRIAL

QUICK REFERENCE RULES OF LAW

1. **Default Judgments.** A meritorious defense is not required to set aside a default entered after improper service. (Peralta v. Heights Medical Center)

   [For more information on the effects of improper service, see Casenote Law Outline on Civil Procedure, Chapter 2, Controlling the Choice of Forum: Jurisdiction, Process, and Choice of Law, § III, Jurisdiction and Valid Judgments.]

2. **Contracting for Confidentiality.** Where a protective order or confidentiality agreement can be modified to place private litigants in a position they would otherwise reach only after repetition of another's discovery, modification can be denied only if it would tangibly prejudice substantial rights of the party opposing modification. (Kalinauskas v. Wong)

3. **Contracting for a Judgment.** Litigants should be entitled to a stipulated reversal to effectuate settlement absent a showing of extraordinary circumstances. (Neary v. University of California)

4. **Contracting for a Judgment.** Federal appellate courts should not vacate civil judgments of lower courts in cases that are settled after an appeal is filed. (U.S. Bancorp Mortgage Co. v. Bonner Mall)

5. **The Possibilities of Arbitration.** Judicial review of arbitration proceedings is limited to whether the parties agreed to arbitration, whether the arbitration procedures provide a fair opportunity to be heard, and whether the arbitrators exceeded their powers. (Ferguson v. Writers Guild of America, West)

   [For more information on arbitration, see Casenote Law Outline on Civil Procedure, Chapter 8, Pre-Trial Procedures and Dispositions—Alternatives to Trial, Pre-Trial Conferences, Dismissal, Default Judgment, and Summary Judgment, § I, Alternatives to Trial.]

6. **Curtailed Adjudication.** The plain language of Federal Rule of Civil Procedure 56(c) mandates the entry of summary judgment, after adequate time for discovery, against a party who fails to make a showing sufficient to establish the existence of an element essential to that party's case. (Celotex Corp. v. Catrett)

   [For more information on evidence to establish essential elements, see Casenote Law Outline on Civil Procedure, Chapter 8, Pre-Trial Procedure and Disposition, § IV, Summary Judgments.]

7. **Curtailed Adjudication.** Under Fed. R. Civ. P. 56, a district court will enter summary judgment if, on the evidence presented during the summary judgment proceeding, no rational jury could find for the party opposing summary judgment. (Visser v. Packer Engineering Associates)

   [For more information on summary judgments, see Casenote Law Outline on Civil Procedure, Chapter 8, Pre-Trial Procedures and Dispositions—Alternatives to Trial, Pre-Trial Conferences, Dismissal, Default Judgment, and Summary Judgment, § IV, Summary Judgments.]

8. **Managing a Settlement.** The authority of a federal court to order the attendance of attorneys, parties, and insurers at settlement conferences and to impose sanctions for disregard of the court's orders is so well established as to be beyond doubt. (Lockhart v. Patel)

   [For more information on pre-trial management, see Casenote Law Outline on Civil Procedure, Chapter 8, Pre-Trial Procedure and Disposition, § II, Pre-Trial Conferences and Pre-Trial Orders.]

9. **Managing Litigation Bound for Trial.** A trial judge has broad discretion to exclude evidence supporting a theory of recovery not raised in the complaint. (McKey v. Fairbairn)

[For more information on amendments to pleadings, see Casenote Law Outline on Civil Procedure, Chapter 5, Pleading, § VII, Amendments to Pleadings.]

PERALTA v. HEIGHTS MEDICAL CENTER, INC.

Employer/guarantor (P) v. Hospital (D)

U.S. Sup. Ct., 108 S. Ct. 896 (1988).

NATURE OF CASE: Review of summary judgment dismissing bill of review.

FACT SUMMARY: A trial court refused to set aside a default entered after improper service when Peralta (P) could not show a meritorious defense to the action.

CONCISE RULE OF LAW: A meritorious defense is not required to set aside a default entered after improper service.

FACTS: Heights Medical Center, Inc. (D) sued Peralta (P) on a guarantee to pay medical expenses on an employee of Peralta (P). Peralta (P) was improperly served. Heights Medical (D) nonetheless entered a default on Peralta's (P) failure to respond and a judgment lien was placed on certain real estate belonging to Peralta (P). The property was sold at a marshal's sale at a large discount. Peralta (P), upon discovering the sale, filed an action to void the sale and have the default set aside, as the service was invalid. The trial court granted summary judgment, dismissing the action, holding that Peralta (P) had to show meritorious defense to the underlying action, which he could not do. The Texas court of appeals affirmed. The Supreme Court accepted review.

ISSUE: Is a meritorious defense required to set aside a default entered after improper service?

HOLDING AND DECISION: (White, J.) No. A meritorious defense is not required to set aside a default entered after improper service. It is basic to due process that before a judgment can be entered against a person, he must be given legally sufficient notice of the action and be given an opportunity to defend. It is no defense to a due process claim that the defendant would have lost on the merits. There are avenues that can be employed by a litigant in a losing posture, such as settling or impleading other parties. For the defendant to do this, he must have notice of the suit. Here, Peralta (P) was not given such notice, and due process therefore demands that the default be set aside. Reversed.

EDITOR'S ANALYSIS: Various avenues exist to challenge a default. The most direct manner is to move for relief in the same action in which the default is entered. However, most states place time limitations on this, as did Texas in this instance. This forced Peralta (P) to file a bill of review, a collateral proceeding.

[For more information on the effects of improper service, see Casenote Law Outline on Civil Procedure, Chapter 2, Controlling the Choice of Forum: Jurisdiction, Process, and Choice of Law, § III, Jurisdiction and Valid Judgments.]

QUICKNOTES

SHERIFF'S SALE - A sale of property by a sheriff pursuant to a judgment.

SERVICE OF PROCESS - The communication of reasonable notice of a court proceeding to a defendant in order to provide him with an opportunity to be heard.

DEFAULT JUDGMENT - A judgment entered against a defendant due to his failure to appear in a court or defend himself against the allegations of the opposing party.

NOTES:

KALINAUSKAS v. WONG

Former employee (P) v. Employer (D)

151 F.R.D. 363 (D. Nev. 1993).

NATURE OF CASE: Motion for protective order.

FACT SUMMARY: Caesars Palace Hotel & Casino (D) sought to enforce a confidential settlement agreement with a former employee.

CONCISE RULE OF LAW: Where a protective order or confidentiality agreement can be modified to place private litigants in a position they would otherwise reach only after repetition of another's discovery, modification can be denied only if it would tangibly prejudice substantial rights of the party opposing modification.

FACTS: Kalinauskas (P) sued Desert Palace, Inc. (D), doing business as Caesars (D), for sexual discrimination. She sought to depose Thomas, a former Caesars (D) employee, who had sued Caesars (D) for sexual harassment the previous year. Thomas had settled her claim with Caesars (D) and agreed to a confidential settlement agreement which stated in part that Thomas "shall not discuss any aspect of plaintiff's employment at Caesars other than to state the dates of her employment and her job title." Caesars (D) sought a protective order to enforce the confidential settlement agreement and to bar Thomas's deposition. Kalinauskas (P) opposed the order.

ISSUE: May a protective order or confidentiality agreement be modified to place private litigants in a position they would otherwise reach only after repetition of another's discovery if modification would not tangibly prejudice substantial rights of the party opposing modification?

HOLDING AND DECISION: (Johnston, J.) Yes. A protective order or confidentiality agreement can be modified to place private litigants in a position they would otherwise reach only after repetition of another's discovery if modification would not tangibly prejudice substantial rights of the party opposing modification. Here, Kalinauskas's (P) claim duplicates Thomas's claim both factually and legally. Thus, to force Kalinauskas (P) to duplicate all of Thomas's work would be wasteful. The protective order is granted to the extent that during the deposition of Thomas no information regarding the settlement itself may be disclosed and is denied as to all other aspects. Protective order granted in part and denied in part.

EDITOR'S ANALYSIS: The party seeking to enforce a protective order against a party seeking discovery information has the burden of showing that allowing modification of the order would substantially prejudice that party's rights. As the case above indicates, this burden could be met by showing that an applicable privilege applies to the information sought to be disclosed or that the party would suffer potential injury or prejudice if the information were to be disclosed.

QUICKNOTES

DISCOVERY - Pretrial procedure during which one party makes certain information available to the other.

PROTECTIVE ORDER - Court order protecting a party against potential abusive treatment through use of the legal process.

NOTES:

NEARY v. UNIVERSITY OF CALIFORNIA
Libel claimant (P) v. University (D)
Cal. Sup. Ct., 3 Cal. 4th 273, 834 P.2d 119 (1992).

NATURE OF CASE: Appeal of denial of a stipulated reversal of award of damages for libel.

FACT SUMMARY: Neary (P) was awarded libel damages by a jury against the University of California (D), which agreed to settle with Neary (P) in return for a stipulation to a reversal of the verdict.

CONCISE RULE OF LAW: Stipulated reversals of trial judgments to effectuate settlement should be granted unless extraordinary circumstances warrant an exception to the general rule.

FACTS: Neary (P) obtained a jury verdict of $7 million against the University of California (D) for libel. The judgment was appealed, and while the appeal was pending, the parties agreed to settle. Under the agreement, Neary (P) would receive $3 million and would join the University (D) in a stipulation to vacate the judgment and dismiss the appeals. The parties filed a joint application in the court of appeals, which was denied. Both parties joined in appealing the ruling to the California Supreme Court. Amicus briefs in opposition, asserting that stipulated reversals following trial discourage pretrial settlements, were also filed.

ISSUE: Should stipulated reversals of trial judgments be granted to effectuate posttrial settlements?

HOLDING AND DECISION: (Baxter, J.) Yes. Stipulated reversals should be granted unless extraordinary circumstances warrant an exception to this general rule. The practical benefits of settlement are significant even after trial. Courts would expend substantial resources in deciding appeals, the parties would incur substantial costs in litigating appeals, and nonmonetary costs such as bad publicity would be suffered without settlement. The primary purpose of the judiciary is to provide a forum for the settlement of disputes, and the presumption in favor of granting stipulated reversals advances that policy. Therefore, Neary (P) and the University's (D) application to vacate the judgment should have been granted. Reversed.

DISSENT: (Kennard, J.) Granting stipulated reversals erodes public confidence in the judiciary, discourages pretrial settlements, and fails to take into account the public value of a judgment.

EDITOR'S ANALYSIS: The court did not explain what type of extraordinary circumstances would warrant an exception to the presumption in favor of granting stipulated reversals. The court did note that the potential collateral estoppel effects of a judgment could be one of the factors, but since this was not an issue in Neary, it failed to decide the issue.

QUICKNOTES

SETTLEMENT - An agreement entered into by the parties to a civil lawsuit agreeing upon the determination of rights and issues between them, thus disposing of the need for judicial determination.

REVERSAL - The annulment of a trial court decision by a reviewing court.

STIPULATION - An agreement by the parties regarding an issue before the court not in dispute so as to avoid unnecessary expense and delay.

TRIAL ON THE MERITS - A judicial determination of the facts or issues brought before it pursuant to its jurisdictional authority.

NOTES:

U.S. BANCORP MORTGAGE CO. v. BONNER MALL
Mortgage company (P) v. Property owner (D)
__U.S.__, 115 S. Ct. 386 (1994).

NATURE OF CASE: Motion to vacate judgment in bankruptcy proceeding.

FACT SUMMARY: U.S. Bancorp Mortgage Co. (P) sought to vacate an adverse judgment pending an appeal after the parties settled.

CONCISE RULE OF LAW: Federal appellate courts should not vacate civil judgments of lower courts in cases that are settled after an appeal is filed.

FACTS: U.S. Bancorp Mortgage Co. (P) held a mortgage on property owned by Bonner Mall (D). The day before Bancorp (D) was scheduled to foreclose, Bonner (D) filed under Chapter 11. Bonner (D) subsequently filed a reorganization plan, which Bancorp (D) opposed. The bankruptcy court rejected the plan, but the district court reversed. Bancorp (P) appealed. The Ninth Circuit affirmed, but the U.S. Supreme Court granted review. Pending review, the parties settled. Bancorp (P) moved for an order vacating the judgment. Bonner (D) opposed the motion.

ISSUE: Should federal appellate courts vacate civil judgments of lower courts in cases that are settled after appeal is filed?

HOLDING AND DECISION: (Scalia, J.) No. Federal appellate courts should not vacate civil judgments of lower courts in cases that are settled after appeal is filed. Under 28 U.S.C. § 2106, federal appellate courts are authorized to vacate lower court judgments prior to review. The fact that they are authorized, however, does not necessarily mean they should do so. Judicial proceedings are presumptively correct. They should not be vacated lightly. A party who is unhappy with a judgment has his appellate remedies. Should he decide to settle, he has voluntarily waived his appellate rights. Judicial proceedings belong not only to litigants, but to the community as a whole, and one who voluntarily relinquishes his appellate rights does not necessarily have an interest in a litigation paramount to society as a whole. Finally, to allow vacatur as a matter of right might discourage early settlement, as a party might not be as afraid of the possibility of adverse collateral estoppel if he knows a judgment on appeal will be vacated if he settles. Therefore, this court holds that vacatur will be granted only on a showing of extraordinary circumstances, something not shown here. Motion denied.

EDITOR'S ANALYSIS: Compare this case to Neary v. University of California, 834 P.d. 119 (1992), in which the California Supreme Court decided a similar issue in an opposite manner. The facts of Neary, however, were somewhat different. In Neary, unlike here, vacatur of the judgment was stipulated. Also, federal courts have mootness concerns that state courts do not face due to Article III's live controversy requirement.

QUICKNOTES

28 U.S.C. § 2106 - Provides that a federal appellate court be permitted, but not required, to vacate the lower courts judgment before initiating its own review.

COLLATERAL ESTOPPEL - A doctrine whereby issues litigated and determined in a prior proceeding are binding upon all subsequent litigation between the parties regarding that issue.

NOTES:

FERGUSON v. WRITERS GUILD OF AMERICA, WEST
Screenwriter (P) v. Professional organization (D)
226 Cal.App.3d 1382, 277 Cal. Rptr. 450 (1991).

NATURE OF CASE: Appeal of dismissal of action to set aside arbitration decision.

FACT SUMMARY: After a Writers Guild (D) arbitration proceeding supported a Guild (D) determination that Ferguson (P) should get only a partial writing credit on a film, Ferguson (P) sued to set aside the arbitration proceeding.

CONCISE RULE OF LAW: Judicial review of arbitration proceedings is limited to whether the parties agreed to arbitration, whether the arbitration procedures provide a fair opportunity to be heard, and whether the arbitrators exceeded their powers.

FACTS: A collective bargaining agreement gave the Writers Guild (D) the power to make determinations on writing credits for films. The agreement also provided that disputes could not be taken to court. Instead, any dispute had to be submitted to arbitration by the Guild (D). Anonymous arbitrators were chosen through a specified procedure. Their decision could be appealed to the Guild's (D) policy review board only for deviation from Guild (D) policy or procedure, not for matters of substance. Board approval of a determination was final. The Guild (D) gave Ferguson (P) partial credit on a film. Ferguson (P) initiated arbitration proceedings to have himself declared the sole writer. Ferguson (P) lost his arbitration and appealed to the review board on the substance of the dispute. After the review board declared the determination of partial credit final, Ferguson (P) sued in state court, urging the court to make its own determination and award him sole writing credit. In the alternative, Ferguson (P) asked the court to vacate the arbitration decision based on certain procedural defects and to require the Guild (D) to make a new determination of the writing credits. The Guild (D) argued that the collective bargaining agreement made disputes over writing credits nonjusticiable. The trial court dismissed Ferguson's (P) case, and he appealed.

ISSUE: Is judicial review of arbitration proceedings limited to whether the parties agreed to arbitration, whether the arbitration procedures provide a fair opportunity to be heard, and whether the arbitrators exceeded their powers?

HOLDING AND DECISION: (Klein, J.) Yes. Judicial review of arbitration proceedings is limited to whether the parties agreed to arbitration, whether the arbitration procedures provide a fair opportunity to be heard, and whether the arbitrators exceeded their powers. Courts accord considerable deference to the determination of arbitration review boards because of their expertise, which courts lack, in their specialized field. The Guild's (D) review board is such a body. Additionally, the principle of exhaustion of administrative remedies prevented Ferguson (P) from pursuing a judicial remedy for any alleged procedural defects in the Guild's (D) conduct of the arbitration and review, since he failed to raise them before the policy review board. Even if he had preserved the procedural defects issue, Ferguson's (P) claims were without merit. There was no material and prejudicial departure from the Guild's (D) procedures. Affirmed.

EDITOR'S ANALYSIS: The use of arbitration in place of judicial resolution has increased significantly in recent years. Parties often prefer arbitration because they can control the substantive and procedural rules which apply to their dispute, they can ensure having a fact finder with expertise in the area of the dispute, and they can save time and money as arbitration is often faster and cheaper. Moreover, while courts traditionally looked with disfavor on arbitration agreements, modern courts usually uphold arbitration agreements because they are a mechanism for reducing the increasingly heavy caseloads of civil courts.

[For more information on arbitration, see Casenote Law Outline on Civil Procedure, Chapter 8, Pre-Trial Procedures and Dispositions — Alternatives to Trial, Pre-Trial Conferences, Dismissal, Default Judgment, and Summary Judgment, § I, Alternatives to Trial.]

QUICKNOTES

ARBITRATION - An agreement to have a dispute heard and decided by a neutral third party, rather than through legal proceedings.

ADMINISTRATIVE REMEDIES - Relief that is sought before an administrative body as opposed to a court.

NOTES:

CELOTEX CORP. v. CATRETT

Asbestos product manufacturer (D) v. Wife of decedent (D)

477 U.S. 317 (1986).

NATURE OF CASE: Appeal from reversal of summary judgment denying damages for asbestos exposure.

FACT SUMMARY: In Catrett's (P) action against Celotex Corp. (D) for the death of her husband as a result of his exposure to asbestos manufactured by Celotex (D), Celotex (D) moved for summary judgment, contending that Catrett (P) had failed to identify, in answering interrogatories specifically requesting such information, any witnesses who could testify about the decedent's exposure to Celotex's (D) asbestos.

CONCISE RULE OF LAW: The plain language of Federal Rule of Civil Procedure 56© mandates the entry of summary judgment, after adequate time for discovery, against a party who fails to make a showing sufficient to establish the existence of an element essential to that party's case.

FACTS: Catrett (P) sued Celotex Corp. (D), alleging that the death of her husband resulted from his exposure to products containing asbestos manufactured by Celotex (D). At trial, Celotex (D) moved for summary judgment, contending that Catrett (P) had failed to identify, in answering interrogatories specifically requesting such information, any witnesses who could testify about the decedent's exposure to Celotex's (D) asbestos products. The district court granted Celotex's (D) motion because there was no showing that the decedent was exposed to Celotex's (D) product within the statutory period. Catrett (P) appealed.

ISSUE: Does the plain language of Federal Rule of Civil Procedure 56© mandate the entry of summary judgment, after adequate time for discovery, against a party who fails to make a showing sufficient to establish the existence of an element essential to that party's case?

HOLDING AND DECISION: (Rehnquist, J.) Yes. The plain language of Federal Rule of Civil Procedure 56© mandates the entry of summary judgment, after adequate time for discovery, against a party who fails to make a showing sufficient to establish the existence of an element essential to that party's case. In such a situation, there can be "no genuine issue as to any material fact," since a complete failure of proof concerning an essential element of the nonmoving party's case necessarily renders all other facts immaterial. Here, Catrett (P) failed to identify any witnesses who could testify about her husband's exposure to Celotex's (D) asbestos products. There was also no showing that the decedent was exposed to Celotex's (D) product within the statutory period. Catrett's (P) failure to show sufficient evidence to establish essential elements of her case makes summary judgment proper. Affirmed.

CONCURRENCE: (White, J.) If respondent Catrett (P) had named a witness to support her claim, summary judgment could not have been granted without Celotex (D) somehow showing that the named witness' testimony raised no genuine issue of material fact.

DISSENT: (Brennan, J.) The nonmoving party may defeat a motion for summary judgment that asserts that the nonmoving party has no evidence by calling the court's attention to the supporting evidence in the record that was overlooked by the moving party.

EDITOR'S ANALYSIS: Celotex is an important case in two ways. First, it integrates the burden of proof borne by the parties at trial with the corresponding burdens on a summary judgment motion. Second, it hints at a larger, more significant role for summary judgment in deciding cases.

[For more information on evidence to establish essential elements, see Case note Law Outline on Civil Procedure, Chapter 8, Pre-Trial Procedure and Disposition, § IV, Summary Judgments.]

QUICKNOTES

FRCP 56 - Provides that summary judgment be entered for a party who fails to make a showing sufficient to support a material element of its case.

SUMMARY JUDGMENT - Judgment rendered by a court in response to a motion by one of the parties, claiming that the lack of a question of material fact in respect to an issue warrants disposition of the issue without consideration by the jury.

MATERIAL FACT - A fact without the existence of which a contract would not have been entered.

NOTES:

LOCKHART v. PATEL

Patient (P) v. Physician (P)

115 F.R.D. 44 (E.D. Ky. 1987).

NATURE OF CASE: Contempt proceedings stemming from medical malpractice action.

FACT SUMMARY: In Lockhard's (P) action against Patel (D) for medical malpractice, Patel's (D) insurer, St. Paul Fire and Marine Insurance Company, was directed by the court to attend a settlement conference, and when St. Paul did not send a representative to the conference who had authority to settle the case, the court ordered a hearing to show cause why St. Paul should not be punished for criminal contempt.

CONCISE RULE OF LAW: The authority of a federal court to order the attendance of attorneys, parties, and insurers at settlement conferences and to impose sanctions for disregard of the court's orders is so well established as to be beyond doubt.

FACTS: Lockhart (P), a teenager, filed a medical malpractice action against Patel (D), a physician, alleging that Lockhart (P) lost the sight in one eye due to Patel's (D) negligence. In a summary jury trial, an advisory jury offered Lockhart (P) $200,000. Following the trial, the court held several formal settlement conferences, and at one of these conferences, Patel's (D) insurer, St. Paul Fire and Marine Insurance Company, advised the court that he had been authorized to offer Lockhart (P) $125,000 and no more. At this time, Lockhart's (P) demand was $175,000. The court then directed the parties to appear at another conference and told St. Paul to send a representative to the conference who had authority to negotiate and settle the case. St. Paul instead sent an adjuster to the conference who told the court that she was to reiterate the offer previously made and not to call St. Paul back if it were not accepted. The court then struck Patel's (D) pleadings, declared him in default, and ordered a hearing to show cause why St. Paul should not be punished for criminal contempt. St. Paul then settled with Lockhart (P) for $175,000 and appealed the court's order.

ISSUE: Is the authority of a federal court to order the attendance of attorneys, parties, and insurers at settlement conferences and to impose sanction for disregard of the court's orders so well established as to be beyond doubt?

HOLDING AND DECISION: (Bertelsman, J.) Yes. The authority of a federal court to order the attendance of attorneys, parties, and insurers at settlement conferences and to impose sanctions for disregard of the court's orders is so well established as to be beyond doubt. The clear intention of the recent amendments to Federal Rule of Civil Procedure 16 was to provide courts with the tools that are required to manage their caseloads effectively and efficiently. A settlement conference without all the necessary parties present is not productive. Neither is a conference of persons who have no authority to settle. Here, the court has been provided with a letter of apology from the Chief Executive Officer of St. Paul. St. Paul has also settled the case, and, therefore, it will be permitted to purge itself of contempt. It is clear that the court cannot require any party to settle a case, but it can require that party to make reasonable efforts, as the court did here.

EDITOR'S ANALYSIS: Lockhart v. Patel shows a pretrial conference focused on settlement. Another different function served by such a conference is to ready the parties for trial by encouraging a precise identification of questions and legal theories which are to be contested at trial. Pretrial conference practices vary among judges, with some courts requiring parties to submit elaborate pretrial statements and others allowing a number of conferences during the progress of the case.

[For more information on pre-trial management, see Casenote Law Outline on Civil Procedure, Chapter 8, Pre-Trial Procedure and Disposition, § II, Pre-Trial Conferences and Pre-Trial Orders.]

QUICKNOTES

SETTLEMENT - An agreement entered into by the parties to a civil lawsuit agreeing upon the determination of rights and issues between them, thus disposing of the need for judicial determination.

FED. R. CIV. P. 16 - Addresses the use of pretrial conferences to formulate and narrow issues for trial and discuss means for dispersing with the need for litigation.

NECESSARY PARTIES - Parties whose joining in a lawsuit is essential to the disposition of the action.

PRETRIAL CONFERENCE - A pretrial procedure in order to determine the issues to be resolved at trial and to otherwise facilitate the resolution of the suit.

NOTES:

McKEY v. FAIRBAIRN

Lessee of premises (P) v. Agent of lessor (D)

345 F.2d 739 (1965).

NATURE OF CASE: Appeal from directed verdict and denial of motion to amend.

FACT SUMMARY: McKey's (P) decedent slipped on water which had leaked through the roof of a house rented from Fairbairn (D) as agent, and the trial court denied McKey's (P) motion to amend her complaint to include certain housing regulations after her counsel had orally agreed with the judge that negligence was their theory of recovery.

CONCISE RULE OF LAW: A trial judge has broad discretion to exclude evidence supporting a theory of recovery not raised in the complaint.

FACTS: Fairbairn (D) was acting as the agent of Haynes in renting a dwelling house to McKey (P). McKey's (P) decedent was occupying a room of the house where some wetness was discovered by Fairbairn's (D) inspectors, and before Fairbairn (D) eliminated the wetness as agreed, an all-night rain caused more leaking in the room. McKey's (P) decedent mopped up some of the wetness, but on returning to the room to get a coat, she slipped and fell, sustaining injuries (which were unrelated to her later death). McKey (P) brought this action for damages, and at trial her counsel agreed with the trial judge's assessment of the case as one in negligence. Thereafter, McKey (P) moved to amend her complaint to include citations to certain allegedly relevant housing regulations, but the judge denied the motion and directed a verdict or Fairbairn (D). McKey (P) appealed.

ISSUE: Has a trial judge broad discretion to exclude evidence supporting a theory of recovery not raised in the complaint?

HOLDING AND DECISION: (Miller, J.) Yes. The questions on appeal are whether a directed verdict was error where evidence of a lease and a promise to repair it was offered and whether denial of the motion to amend to include housing regulations was error. The landlord did not have a duty to make the repairs alleged, so that a directed verdict on the issue of negligence liability was proper. Similarly, it was not error to refuse to allow McKey (P) to change her theory of recovery after the complaint was filed and answered. The trial court has broad discretion in the conduct of a trial, and this discretion was not abused in this case. A trial judge has broad discretion to exclude evidence supporting a theory of recovery not raised in the complaint, as a part of the conduct of the trial. Furthermore, since McKey's (P) decedent entered a room where she knew there was a slippery wet spot, her own negligence contributed to the accident. Affirmed.

DISSENT: (Fahy, J.) Modification at trial is to be permitted to prevent manifest injustice. We have previously held that a landlord's duty to a tenant is covered in some part by the housing regulations. Modification should be permitted to allow McKey (P) to include the regulations in the complaint as a basis for recovery. Furthermore, the issue of contributory negligence should be initially considered and answered by the district court, not by this court on appeal.

EDITOR'S ANALYSIS: Under Federal Rule of Civil Procedure 15, amendment of pleadings after responsive pleadings are served is permitted only by leave of the court or written consent of the adverse party. A party may proceed to trial of issues not raised by pleadings and later amend the pleadings to conform to the evidence, but trial of those unraised issues must be by "express or implied consent of the parties." McKey (P) was outside of all these possibilities in this case.

[For more information on amendments to pleadings, see Casenote Law Outline on Civil Procedure, Chapter 5, Pleading, § VII, Amendments to Pleadings.]

QUICKNOTES

DIRECTED VERDICT - A verdict ordered by the court in a jury trial.

FRCP 15(a) - Sets forth the rule that a party may amend its pleading once as a matter of course at any time before a responsive pleading is served, or within 20 days if no responsive pleading is permitted and the action has not been placed on the trial calendar; otherwise a party may amend its pleading only by leave of court or written consent of the opposing party; a party is required to plead in response to an amended pleading within the time remaining for response to the original pleading or within ten days of service of the amended pleading, whichever is longer, unless otherwise stated by court order.

AMENDMENT TO PLEADING - The modification of a pleading either as a matter of course upon motion to the court or by consent of both parties; a party is entitled to change its pleading once as a matter of course before a responsive pleading has been served.

NOTES:

BEACON THEATERS, INC. v. WESTOVER

Theater company (D) v. Owner of competing theater (P)

359 U.S. 500 (1959).

NATURE OF CASE: Petition for writ of mandamus to require a district judge to reverse his denial of Beacon's (D) request for a jury trial in a declaratory relief action wherein Beacon's (D) counterclaim asks for treble damages.

FACT SUMMARY: Beacon (D) threatened to bring an antitrust action against Fox (P) based on Fox's (P) contract granting it exclusive rights to show first-run movies. Fox (P) brought a declaratory relief action against Beacon (D). Beacon (D) counterclaimed, seeking treble damages, and demanding a jury trial.

CONCISE RULE OF LAW: Only under the most imperative circumstances can the right to a jury trial of legal issues be lost through prior determination of equitable claims, and in view of the flexible procedures of the federal rules, the Supreme Court cannot now anticipate such circumstances.

FACTS: According to its complaint, Fox (P) operated a movie theater in San Bernardino. Its contracts with movie distributors granted it the exclusive right to show first-run movies in the San Bernardino competitive area and provide for "clearance," a period of time during which no other theater can exhibit the same picture. Beacon (D) built a theater eleven miles away and notified Fox (P) that it considered Fox's (P) contracts to be in violation of the antitrust laws. Fox (P) alleged that this notification together with threats of lawsuits gave rise to duress and coercion and deprived Fox (P) of its right to negotiate for first-run contracts. Fox (P) prayed for a declaration that the clearances are not in violation of the antitrust laws and an injunction to prevent Beacon (D) from bringing an antitrust action against Fox (P). Beacon (D) filed a counterclaim asserting that there was no substantial competition between the two theaters and, hence, the clearances were unreasonable. It also alleged that a conspiracy existed between Fox (P) and its distributors to restrain trade and monopolize first-run movies in violation of the antitrust laws. Beacon (D) asked for treble damages. The district court found that Fox's (P) complaint for declaratory relief presented basically equitable issues. It directed that these issues be tried by the court without a jury before jury determination of the validity of Beacon's (D) charges of antitrust violations.

ISSUE: Where a complaint alleges circumstances which traditionally have justified equity to take jurisdiction, in light of the Declaratory Judgment Act and the Federal Rules of Civil Procedure, would a court be justified in denying defendant a trial by jury on all legal issues?

HOLDING AND DECISION: (Black, J.) No. In this case, the reasonableness of the clearances granted Fox (P) was an issue common to Fox's (P) action for declaratory relief and to Beacon's (D) counterclaim. Hence, the effect of the district court's action could be to limit Beacon's (D) opportunity to try before a jury every issue which has a bearing on its treble damage suit. The determination of the issues of the clearances by the judge might operate by way of res judicata or collateral estoppel so as to conclude both parties with respect to those issues at the subsequent trial of the treble damage claim. Since the right to trial by jury applies to treble damage suits under the antitrust laws, the antitrust issues were essentially jury questions. Assuming that Fox's (P) complaint supports a request for an injunction, and further alleges the kind of harassment by a multiplicity of lawsuits which traditionally have justified equity to take jurisdiction, in light of the Declaratory Judgment Act and the Federal Rules of Civil Procedure, a court would not be justified in denying a defendant a jury trial on all the legal issues. Only under the most imperative circumstances can the right to a jury trial of legal issues be lost through prior determination of equitable claims. In view of the flexible procedures of the federal rules, the court cannot now anticipate such circumstances. Under the federal rules, the same court may try both legal and equitable claims in the same action. Hence, any defenses, equitable or legal, Fox (P) may have to Beacon's (D) charges can be raised either in its declaratory relief suit or in its answer to Beacon's (D) counterclaim. Any permanent injunctive relief to which Fox (P) might be entitled could be given by the court after the jury renders its verdict. The judgment denying Beacon's (D) jury demand is reversed.

DISSENT: (Stewart, J.) The federal rules make possible the trial of legal and equitable claims in the same proceeding, but they expressly affirm the power of a trial judge to determine the order in which claims shall be heard. They did not expand the substantive law. In this case, Beacon's (D) counterclaim cannot be held to have transformed Fox's (P) original complaint into an action at law.

EDITOR'S ANALYSIS: The right to a jury trial depends not so much on the form of the action as the kind of relief sought. Hence, as long as the ultimate remedy is legal in nature, the right is recognized, even though the plaintiff has invoked an historically equitable procedural device, as demonstrated by this case. Here the effect of the declaration of its rights sought by Fox (P) would be to defeat (or establish) Beacon's (D) claim for money damages. Hence, the issues must be tried before a jury.

Continued on next page.

[For more information on jury trial right in cases of law and equity, see Casenote Law Outline on Civil Procedure, Chapter 9, Trial and Post-Trial Motions, § II, The Right to Jury Trial in Federal Court.]

QUICKNOTES

RES JUDICATA - The rule of law that a final judgment by a court precludes subsequent litigation between the parties regarding the same cause of action

COLLATERAL ESTOPPEL - A doctrine whereby issues litigated and determined in a prior proceeding are binding upon all subsequent litigation between the parties regarding that issue.

ACTION IN LAW - Lawsuit in a which a plaintiff seeks legal remedies such as damages.

ACTION IN EQUITY - Lawsuit in which a plaintiff seeks equitable remedies.

NOTES:

EDMONSON v. LEESVILLE CONCRETE CO.

Construction worker (P) v. Concrete company (D)

111 U.S. 2077 (1991).

NATURE OF CASE: Appeal of award of damages for negligence.

FACT SUMMARY: Edmonson (P) sought to overturn a low award of damages on the ground that Leesville (D) had used two peremptory challenges to strike African-Americans from the jury.

CONCISE RULE OF LAW: A civil litigant may not use peremptory challenges to strike jurors solely on the basis of race.

FACTS: Edmonson (P), an African-American construction worker, sought damages from Leesville (D) after he was injured in a job-site accident as the result of the alleged negligence of one of Leesville's (D) employees. During voir dire, Leesville (D) used two of its three peremptory challenges to strike African-Americans from the jury. The jury rendered a verdict for Edmonson (P) and determined that the value of his damages was $90,000. However, the jury also determined that 80% of the negligence which resulted in the accident and injury to Edmonson (P) was attributable to him, reducing his actual award to $18,000. Edmonson (P) appealed the reduced amount of the award, arguing that it was unconstitutional for the trial court to have permitted race-based peremptory challenges on the part of Leesville (D). The court of appeals held only criminal prosecutors, and not civil litigants, were barred from making race-based peremptory challenges. The U.S. Supreme Court granted certiorari.

ISSUE: May a civil litigant use peremptory challenges to strike jurors solely on the basis of race?

HOLDING AND DECISION: (Kennedy, J.) No. A civil litigant may not use peremptory challenges to strike jurors solely on the basis of race. In Batson v. Kentucky , 476 U.S. 79 (1986), the Court held that race-based peremptory challenges by criminal prosecutors are state action which violate the equal protection rights of excluded jurors. The requisite state action is also present where a private civil litigant uses race-based peremptory challenges. When private litigants participate in jury selection, they serve a government function and act with the substantial assistance of the judge, who ultimately must exclude the jurors. Automatic invocation of racial stereotypes is made even worse when the government allows it to occur in the courtroom, where the constitutional authority of the government is most expressed. Under established principles of third-party standing, a civil litigant may assert the rights of the excluded jurors. Applying Batson, Edmonson (P) must now make out a prima facie case of race-based peremptory challenges by establishing a pattern of strikes against a particular race. If he can, the burden will shift to Leesville (D) to present a race-neutral reason for its strikes. Reversed and remanded.

DISSENT: (O'Connor, J.) Not everything that happens in a courtroom is state action. A peremptory challenge by a civil litigant is fundamentally a private matter.

DISSENT: (Scalia, J.) Minority litigants will be harmed by the majority's decision because they will no longer be able to use race-based peremptory challenges to obtain racially diverse juries. If this ruling on state action is applied to race-based peremptory challenges by criminal defendants, which it logically must be, minorities will lose a valuable tool in preventing conviction by all-white juries. The majority's decision puts an unjustified, heavy burden on trial courts.

EDITOR'S ANALYSIS: In a concurrence in Batson, Justice Marshall argued that peremptory challenges should be completely eliminated because their use cannot be reconciled with the requirements of equal protection. Even under Batson, race-based peremptory challenges cannot be attacked unless their use is so flagrant as to establish a prima facie case. Even if a prima facie case can be made out, a prosecutor may easily fabricate non-discriminatory motives. The trial judge will have a difficult time determining the prosecutor's motives and the judge's decision may be based on his own conscious or unconscious racism. Justice Scalia's prediction in his Edmonson dissent proved correct when the Court extended Batson to prohibit race-based peremptory challenges by criminal defendants in Georgia v. McCollum, No. 91-372 (U.S. Supreme Court June 18, 1992). However, Justice Scalia's prediction in his dissent above that minorities will suffer by this decision seems to ignore the fact that prosecutors conversely, by not being able to strike minority jurors without legal cause, will no longer be assured of empaneling all-white juries when trying minority defendants.

[For more information on voir dire, see Casenote Law Outline on Civil Procedure, Chapter 9, Trial and Post-Trial Motions, § I, Overview of the Trial Process.]

QUICKNOTES

VOIR DIRE - Examination of potential jurors on a case.

PEREMPTORY CHALLENGE - The exclusion by a party to a lawsuit of a prospective juror without the need to specify a particular reason.

LILJEBERG v. HEALTH SERVICES ACQUISITION CORP.

Real property claimant (D) v. Health services company (P)

U.S. Sup. Ct., 108 S. Ct. 2194 (1980).

NATURE OF CASE: Review of order mandating judicial recusal and vacating a declaratory judgment.

FACT SUMMARY: A federal judge refused to recuse himself and vacate a judgment he had rendered before he became aware of a conflict which he should have known before making the judgment.

CONCISE RULE OF LAW: A court is under a duty to recuse itself and vacate a judgment rendered if it becomes aware of acts showing a conflict of interest which it should have known before making the judgment.

FACTS: A dispute arose between Liljeberg (D) and Health Services Acquisition Corp. (P) regarding certain real estate adjacent to Loyola University. The litigants had conflicting claims to the proper use of the property. Loyola University stood to benefit greatly if Liljeberg (D) prevailed. Health Services (P) filed a declaratory relief action. The case was tried before a federal judge, sitting without a jury. The judge was a trustee of Loyola. During the trial, Loyola's interest in the litigation was not discussed, although at Loyola board meetings the litigation had at times been mentioned. Eight days after entering judgment for Liljeberg (D), the judge became aware of Loyola's interest. Health Services (P) moved for recusal and a new trial. The judge refused, contending he was not aware of Loyola's interest before entering judgment. The court of appeals reversed, applying a "should have known" standard. The Supreme Court granted certiorari.

ISSUE: Is a court under a duty to recuse itself and vacate a judgment rendered if it becomes aware of facts showing a conflict of interest which it should have known before making the judgment?

HOLDING AND DECISION: (Stevens, J.) Yes. A court is under a duty to recuse itself and vacate a judgment rendered if it becomes aware of facts showing a conflict of interest which it should have known before making the judgment. 28 U.S.C. § 455 provides that a judge shall disqualify himself in any proceeding in which his impartiality might reasonably be questioned. This is a broad standard, and one necessary to preserve public confidence in the judiciary. The statute does not, by its terms, require that a judge have actual knowledge of the conflict to recuse himself. Granted, a judge cannot rule on such a matter until the conflict comes to his attention. However, if during a proceeding a judge should have known of a conflict, and after the proceeding the conflict is brought to the judge's attention, a refusal to recuse could lead to serious questions about the judge's impartiality. This is precisely what a § 455 was drafted to prevent. Here, the

court of appeals found that the judge should have been aware of the conflict, and it properly vacated the judgment. Affirmed.

DISSENT: (Rehnquist, C.J.) A judge considering recusal is necessarily limited to facts of which he has knowledge. To hold that a judge should be recused for knowing facts he does not know is to posit a conundrum not decipherable by ordinary mortals.

EDITOR'S ANALYSIS: There were necessarily two related problems here. The first was that cited above, the subjective vs. objective knowledge issue. The second was whether a § 455 violation based on constructive knowledge would warrant a post-judgment vacation. The Court held that it did.

QUICKNOTES

CONFLICT OF INTEREST - Refers to ethical problems that arise, or may be anticipated to arise, between an attorney and his client if the interests of the attorney, another client or a third party conflict with those of the present client.

RECUSAL - Procedure whereby a judge is disqualified from hearing a case either on his own behalf, or on the objection of a party, due to some bias or interest in the subject matter of the suit.

28 U.S.C. § 435 - Requires that a judge disqualify himself in a proceeding where he cannot discharge his duties impartially.

NOTES:

CHAPTER 11
APPEAL

QUICK REFERENCE RULES

1. **Appellate Jurisdiction and the Final Judgment Rule**. An interlocutory appeal under Rule 54(b) of the Federal Rules of Civil Procedure is limited expressly to multiple claims actions. (Liberty Mutal Insurance Co. v. Wetzel)

    [For more information on interlocutory appeals, see Casenote Law Outline on Criminal Procedure, Chapter 10, Appeal, § III, The Federal Courts and the Model of Finality.]

2. **Practical Finality.** Under the collateral order doctrine, a prejudgment order may be appealed only when it conclusively determines the disputed question, resolves an important issue completely separable from the merits of the action, and is effectively unreviewable on appeal from a final judgment. (Lauro Lines s.r.l. v. Chasser)

    [For more information on the collateral order doctrine, see Casenote Law Outline on Civil Procedure, Chapter 10, Appeal, § III, The Federal Courts and the Model of Finality.]

3. **Law and Fact.** Under Federal Rule of Civil Procedure 52(a), a finding is clearly erroneous only when, although there is evidence to support it, the reviewing court, on the entire evidence, is left with the definite and firm conviction that a mistake has been made. (Anderson v. Bessemer City)

    [For more information on errors of fact, see Casenote Law Outline on Criminal Procedure, Chapter 10, Appeal, § I, The Mechanics of Appeal.]

LIBERTY MUTUAL INS. CO. v. WETZEL
Insurer (D) v. Employer insured (P)
424 U.S. 737 (1976).

NATURE OF CASE: Appeal from finding of liability for violation of Title VII of the Civil Rights Act of 1964.

FACT SUMMARY: Wetzel (P) alleged that Liberty Mutual's (D) employee insurance benefits and maternity leave regulations discriminated against women in violation of Title VII of the Civil Rights Act of 1964.

CONCISE RULE OF LAW: An interlocutory appeal under Rule 54(b) of the Federal Rules of Civil Procedure is limited expressly to multiple claims actions.

FACTS: Wetzel (P) filed a complaint which asserted that Liberty Mutual's (D) employee insurance benefits and maternity leave regulations discriminated against women in violation of Title VII of the Civil Rights Act of 1964. Wetzel's (P) complaint sought several forms of relief, including monetary damages, attorney fees, and injunctive relief. On January 9, 1974, after finding no issues of material fact in dispute, the district court granted partial summary judgment for Wetzel (P) on the issue of liability only. On February 20, 1974, the district court issued an order of final judgment as to Liberty Mutual's (D) liability, but granted none of the relief requested in Wetzel's (P) complaint. The court of appeals held that it had jurisdiction over Liberty Mutual's (D) appeal under 28 U.S.C. § 1291 and affirmed the judgment of the district court.

ISSUE: Is an interlocutory appeal under Rule 54(b) of the Federal Rules of Civil Procedure limited expressly to multiple claims actions?

HOLDING AND DECISION: (Rehnquist, J.) Yes. Rule 54(b) is limited expressly to multiple claims actions in which one or more, but less than all, of the multiple claims have been finally decided and are found otherwise to be ready for appeal. Here, Wetzel's (P) complaint set forth a single claim, which advanced a single legal theory which was applied to only one set of facts. Even if the district court's order was a declaratory judgment on the issue of liability, it still left unresolved Wetzel's (P) requests for an injunction, for compensatory and exemplary damages, and for attorney fees. The district court's order is therefore not appealable pursuant to 28 U.S.C. § 1291. Reversed.

EDITOR'S ANALYSIS: The basic rationale for the policy in federal courts of requiring final judgments is one based upon a cost-benefit analysis. If the trial judge turns out to have been correct, the cost of allowing an interlocutory appeal is the cost of an unnecessary extra appeal. Conversely, if the trial judge turns out to have been wrong in his or her judgment, the cost of not allowing an interlocutory appeal is the sum expended for an unnecessary or an unnecessarily long trial. However, because trial judges are affirmed far more often than they are reversed, the federal policy seems to be logical.

[For more information on interlocutory appeals, see Casenote Law Outline on Criminal Procedure, Chapter 10, Appeal, § III, The Federal Courts and the Model of Finality.]

QUICKNOTES

INTERLOCUTORY APPEAL - The appeal of an issue that does not resolve the disposition of the case, but is essential to a determination of the parties' legal rights.

FRCP 54 - Sets forth the provisions regarding judgments and costs.

NOTES:

LAURO LINES S.R.L. v. CHASSER
Ship company (D) v. Passenger (P)
490 U.S. 495 (1989).

NATURE OF CASE: Interlocutory appeal of a denial of a motion to dismiss action for damages for personal injuries.

FACT SUMMARY: After the district court denied Lauro's (D) motion for dismissal based on a forum-selection clause which purportedly limited Chasser (P) to suing in Naples, Italy, Lauro (D) sought to overturn the denial on interlocutory appeal.

CONCISE RULE OF LAW: Under the collateral order doctrine, a prejudgment order may be appealed only when it conclusively determines the disputed question, resolves an important issue completely separable from the merits of the action, and is effectively unreviewable on appeal from a final judgment.

FACTS: Chasser (P) and the other plaintiffs were passengers aboard Lauro's (D) ship, the Achille Lauro, when it was hijacked in the Mediterranean Sea by terrorists. Lauro (D) moved to dismiss Chasser's (P) personal injury suit on the ground that a forum-selection clause printed on the passenger tickets limited any passenger to suing in Naples, Italy. The district court denied the motion, holding that the ticket did not give passengers reasonable notice that they were giving up the right to sue in the United States. The court of appeals dismissed Lauro's (D) appeal, finding that the district court's order was interlocutory and not appealable. Lauro (D) appealed to the U.S. Supreme Court.

ISSUE: Is a prejudgment order subject to interlocutory appeal when it can be effectively reviewed on appeal from a final judgment?

HOLDING AND DECISION: (Brennan, J.) No. Under the collateral order doctrine, a prejudgment order may be appealed only when it conclusively determines the disputed question, resolves an important issue completely separable from the merits of the action, and is effectively unreviewable on appeal from a final judgment. An order is "effectively" unreviewable on final judgment when the order involves an asserted right the practical value of which would be destroyed if it were not vindicated before trial. Thus, interlocutory appeal is allowed when the defendant asserts a right that is not an ultimate right upon which the suit is brought. Here, Lauro (D) only asserted a right not to be sued in a particular forum. This right was not lost. Lauro (D) could assert the forum-selection clause in appealing any unfavorable final judgment. If an appeals court agreed with Laurel's (D) position, it could vacate trial judgment and limit the refiling of the case in Naples. Affirmed.

CONCURRENCE: (Scalia, J.) Implicit in the Court's ruling is that

Lauro's (D) right of forum selection is not important enough to require vindication on interlocutory appeal.

EDITOR'S ANALYSIS: Where a criminal defendant asserts a right not to be tried, an order denying that right is reviewable on interlocutory appeal. In civil cases, a partial list of orders reviewable on interlocutory appeal includes denial of a motion to dismiss based on a claim of absolute or qualified official immunity, an order denying a party leave to proceed in forma pauperis, an order requiring class action defendants to bear the cost of notifying members of the plaintiff class, and an order vacating attachment of a vessel.

[For more information on the collateral order doctrine, see Casenote Law Outline on Civil Procedure, Chapter 10, Appeal, § III, The Federal Courts and the Model of Finality.]

QUICKNOTES

INTERLOCUTORY APPEAL - The appeal of an issue that does not resolve the disposition of the case, but is essential to a determination of the parties' legal rights.

COLLATERAL ORDER - Doctrine pursuant to which an appeal from an interlocutory order may be brought in order to hear and determine claims which are collateral to the merits of the case and which could not be granted adequate review on appeal.

IN FURMA PAUPERIS - Permission to proceed with litigation without incurring fees or costs.

JUDGMENT ON THE MERITS - A determination of the rights of the parties to litigation based on the presentation evidence, barring the party from initiating the same suit again.

NOTES:

ANDERSON v. BESSEMER CITY

Sex discrimination claimant v. Municipality (D)

470 U.S. 564 (1985).

NATURE OF CASE: Appeal of finding of discriminatory intent in action brought under Title VII of the Civil Rights Act of 1964.

FACT SUMMARY: In Anderson's (P) action against Bessemer City (D) for discrimination in an action brought under Title VII of the Civil Rights Act of 1964, Anderson (P), a woman applying for a job as a Recreation Director for Bessemer City (D), alleged that she had been denied the position because of her sex, and that the district court's finding of discriminatory intent in Anderson's (P) action was a factual finding that could be overturned on appeal only if it was clearly erroneous.

CONCISE RULE OF LAW: Under Federal Rule of Civil Procedure 52(a), a finding is clearly erroneous only when, although there is evidence to support it, the reviewing court, on the entire evidence, is left with the definite and firm conviction that a mistake has been made.

FACTS: In Anderson's (P) action against Bessemer City (D) for discrimination in an action brought under Title VII of the Civil Rights Act of 1964, Anderson (P), a woman, alleged that she had been denied a position as Recreation Director in a city athletic program because of her sex. After a two-day trial, the court issued a memorandum of decision setting forth its finding that Anderson (P) had been denied the position because of her sex and that male members of the Bessemer City (D) hiring commission for the position had been biased against Anderson (P) because she was a woman. The City (D) appealed and the Fourth Circuit reversed, holding that the lower court's findings were clearly erroneous. Anderson (P) appealed.

ISSUE: Under Federal Rule of Civil Procedure 52(a), is a finding clearly erroneous only when, although there is evidence to support it, the reviewing court, on the entire evidence, is left with the definite and firm conviction that a mistake has been made?

HOLDING AND DECISION: (White, J.) Yes. Under Federal Rule of Civil Procedure 52(a), a finding is clearly erroneous only when, although there is evidence to support it, the reviewing court, on the entire evidence, is left with the definite and firm conviction that a mistake has been made. Application of the foregoing principles to the facts of this case lays bare the errors committed. The Fourth Circuit improperly conducted what amounted to a de novo weighing of the evidence in the record. The district court's findings were based on essentially undisputed evidence and from the evidence, the court determined that Anderson's (P) more varied educational and employment background and her extensive experience in variety of civil activities left her better

qualified to implement such a rounded program than the other job applicants. Our determination that the findings of the district court regarding Anderson's (P) qualifications, the conduct of her interview, and the bias of the male committee members were not clearly erroneous leads this Court to conclude that the court's finding that Anderson (P) was discriminated against on account of her sex was also not clearly erroneous. Reversed and remanded.

EDITOR'S ANALYSIS: Anderson v. Bessemer City grows out of a practice that has its roots in the distinction between law and equity. Because cases in equity were considered only on a written record and the appellate court was able to read the record as the trial court, the rule evolved in equity that the appellate court reviewed equity decisions de novo. That standard came to dominate appellate review not just of decisions in equity, but of all decisions by a judge sitting without a jury.

[For more information on errors of fact, see Casenote Law Outline on Criminal Procedure, Chapter 10, Appeal, § I, The Mechanics of Appeal.]

QUICKNOTES

FED. R. CIV. P. 52(a) - Requires that findings of fact not be set aside unless clearly erroneous.

CHAPTER 12
RESPECT FOR JUDGMENTS

QUICK REFERENCE RULES

1. **Efficiency.** Claim preclusion bars a second suit where the first suit arose out of the same transaction. (Frier v. City of Vandalia)

    [For more information on res judicata, see Casenote Law Outline on Civil Procedure, Chapter 12, Preclusion Doctrines—Res Judicata and Collateral Estoppel, § I, Res Judicata Defined.]

2. **The Logical Implications of the Former Judgment.** Res judicata bars a counterclaim when its prosecution would nullify rights established by a prior action. (Martino v. McDonald's System, Inc.)

    [For more information on res judicata and counterclaims, see Casenote Law Outline on Criminal Procedure, Chapter 12, Preclusion Doctrines—Res Judicata and Collateral Estoppel, §, I, Res Judicata Defined.]

3. **Between the "Same" Parties.** A person is in privity with another if he is so identified in interest with the other that he represents the same legal right. (Searle Brothers v. Searle)

    [For more information on collateral estoppel, see Casenote Law Outline on Criminal Procedure, Chapter 12, Preclusion Doctrines—Res Judicata and Collateral Estoppel, § II, Collateral Estoppel or Issue Preclusion.]

4. **After a Judgment "On the Merits."** A dismissal of an action due to a plaintiff's failure to satisfy a technical prerequisite does not have res judicata effect upon a subsequent action by a different plaintiff against the same defendant on the basis of the same conduct or transactions. (Saylor v. Lindsley)

    [For more information on res judicata, see Casenote Law Outline on Criminal Procedure, Chapter 12, Preclusion Doctrines—Res Judicata and Collateral Estoppel, § I, Res Judicata Defined.]

5. **An Issue "Actually Litigated and Determined."** The doctrine of estoppel by verdict allows a judgment in a prior action to operate as a complete bar to those facts or issues actually litigated and determined in the prior action. (Illinois Central Gulf Railroad v. Parks)

    [For more information on doctrine of estoppel, see Casenote Law Outline on Criminal Procedure, Chapter 12, Preclusion Doctrines—Res Judicata and Collateral Estoppel, § II, Collateral Estoppel or Issue Preclusion.]

6. **An Issue "Essential to the Judgment."** When a prior judgment adjudicating one a bankrupt rests on two or more independent alternative grounds, the judgment is not conclusive as to issues which were necessary in order to establish only one of those grounds. (Halpern v. Schwartz)

    [For more information on doctrine of estoppel, see Casenote Law Outline on Criminal Procedure, Chapter 12, Preclusion Doctrines—Res Judicata and Collateral Estoppel, § II, Collateral Estoppel or Issue Preclusion.]

7. **An Issue "Essential to the Judgment."** The doctrine of collateral estoppel only bars the relitigation of issues which were not only actually litigated and determined in the original action but which were also "necessary" to the judgment entered in that suit. (Winters v. Lavine)

[For more information on collateral estoppel, see Casenote Law Outline on Criminal Procedure, Chapter 12, Preclusion Doctrines—Res Judicata and Collateral Estoppel, § II, Collateral Estoppel or Issue Preclusion.]

8. **The Precluder.** A trial judge has broad discretion to permit the offensive use of collateral estoppel to establish an element of a plaintiff's case where it is not unfair to the defendant. (Parklane Hosiery Co. v. Shore)

    [For more information on offensive use of collateral estoppel, see Casenote Law Outline on Criminal Procedure, Chapter 12, Preclusion Doctrines—Res Judicata and Collateral Estoppel, § II, Collateral Estoppel or Issue Preclusion.]

9. **The Precluder.** Where prior judicial determinations on a particular matter are inconsistent, the doctrine of collateral estoppel will not bar relitigation of that matter. (State Farm Fire & Casualty Co. v. Century Home Components)

    [For more information on doctrine of estoppel, see Casenote Law Outline on Criminal Procedure, Chapter 12, Preclusion Doctrines—Res Judicata and Collateral Estoppel, § II, Collateral Estoppel or Issue Preclusion.]

10. **Claim Preclusion.** Non-appealing parties may not benefit from a reversal when their position is closely interwoven with that of appealing parties. (Federated Department Stores v. Moitie)

    [For more information on principles of res judicata, see Casenote Law Outline on Criminal Procedure, Chapter 12, Preclusion Doctrines—Res Judicata and Collateral Estoppel, § I, Res Judicata Defined.]

11. **Full Faith and Credit as a Bar to Collateral Attack.** The principles of res judicata and full faith and credit preclude relitigation of judgments of a foreign state when the parties have appeared and have fully and fairly litigated the issues. (Durfee v. Duke)

    [For more information on doctrine of res judicata, see Casenote Law Outline on Criminal Procedure, Chapter 12, Preclusion Doctrines—Res Judicata and Collateral Estoppel, § I, Res Judicata Defined.]

12. **The Reopened Judgment as an Alternative to Collateral Attack.** When the wrongful conduct of one party prevents the other party from fully and fairly presenting her case, a new trial may be ordered. (Rozier v. Ford Motor Co.)

    [For more information on misconduct of adverse party, see Casenote Law Outline on Criminal Procedure, Chapter 9, Trial and Post-Trial Motions, § VII, Extraordinary Post-Judgment Relief in the Trial Court.]

FRIER v. CITY OF VANDALIA

Owner of towed car (P) v. Municipality (D)

770 F.d. 699 (7th Cir. 1985).

NATURE OF CASE: Appeal of dismissal of action for deprivation of property without due process under color of law.

FACT SUMMARY: After Frier (P) lost his state court suit against Vandalia (D) for replevin of his car, he then sued Vandalia (D) in federal court under 42 U.S.C. § 1983 for depriving him of his car without due process under color of law.

CONCISE RULE OF LAW: Claim preclusion bars a second suit where the first suit arose out of the same transaction.

FACTS: Vandalia (D) police had a garage tow Frier's (P) car because it was parked in traffic. Frier (P) did not receive a citation or a hearing either before the car was towed or after he refused to pay to retrieve it. Frier (P) sued Vandalia (D) and the garage in state court for replevin of his car. After a trial, the court decided that Vandalia (D) had the right to tow Frier's (P) car because it was obstructing traffic. Therefore, the court did not issue the writ of replevin. Frier (P) then filed a 42 U.S.C. § 1983 suit in federal court, seeking equitable relief and compensatory and punitive damages from Vandalia (D) for depriving him of his car without due process under color of law. The district court dismissed Frier's (P) suit for failure to state a claim, and Frier (P) appealed, arguing that he was not precluded from filing a federal suit under a different legal theory than the one he on which he based his state court action.

ISSUE: Does claim preclusion bar a second suit where the first suit arose out of the same transaction?

HOLDING AND DECISION: (Easterbrook, J.) Yes. Claim preclusion bars a second suit where the first suit arose out of the same transaction. Claim preclusion, also called res judicata, is designed to impel parties to consolidate all closely related matters in the same suit. First, this prevents oppression of defendants through multiple cases. Second, when the facts and issues of all theories of liability are closely related, there is no good reason to incur the cost of litigation more than once. Frier (P) could have sued in his state court action for both replevin, to get his car back, and under § 1983, for damages. Both theories alleged the same conduct: that Vandalia (D) towed and detained his cars without lawful process, i.e., without a determination of a parking violation. Thus, claim preclusion bars Frier's (P) federal suit. The district court, though it properly dismissed the case, should not have reached the merits. Affirmed.

CONCURRENCE: (Swygert, J.) Frier's (P) suit should properly have been dismissed on summary judgment, but not for claim preclusion. Illinois law, applicable in this case, follows the narrower, traditional rule of claim preclusion, not the broader Restatement rule applied by the majority. Under the traditional rule, one suit bars a second where the evidence necessary to sustain a second verdict would have sustained the first, i.e., where the causes of action are based on a common core of operative facts. To prevail on his replevin claim, Frier (P) would have had to prove a superior right to possession of the car, which turned on whether he had parked illegally. However, under § 1983, the legality of Frier's (P) parking was irrelevant. The issues as to § 1983 were whether Frier (P) had notice that he would be towed for parking where he did, and whether he had a fair hearing on the detaining of his car. The fact that Frier (P) could have brought the two causes of action in the same suit is irrelevant under the traditional rule of claim preclusion.

EDITOR'S ANALYSIS: Judge Easterbrook and Judge Swygert agree that under the "same transaction" rule Frier's (P) second suit was barred by claim preclusion or res judicata. However, Judge Swygert applied the narrower, traditional, "core of operative facts" rule to reach the opposite result on the claim preclusion issue. The federal courts and most states follow the "same transaction" rule, which is codified in the Restatement (Second) of Judgments § 24 (1982).

[For more information on res judicata, see Case note Law Outline on Civil Procedure, Chapter 12, Preclusion Doctrines — Res Judicata and Collateral Estoppel, § I, Res Judicata Defined.]

QUICKNOTES

42 U.S.C. § 1983 - The Civil Rights Act; usually invoked when a party commences suit based on the alleged state's violation of the party's civil rights.

RES JUDICATA - The rule of law that a final judgment by a court precludes subsequent litigation between the parties regarding the same cause of action.

CLAIM - The demand for a right to payment or equitable relief; the fact or facts giving rise to such demand.

MARTINO v. McDONALD'S SYSTEM, INC.

Franchise owner (P) v. Fast food company (D)

598 F.2d 1079 (7th Cir. 1979).

NATURE OF CASE: Appeal from summary judgment in antitrust action.

FACT SUMMARY: Martino (P) alleged that a franchise and lease agreement between Martino (P) and McDonald's (D) violated provisions of the Sherman Antitrust Act.

CONCISE RULE OF LAW: Res judicata bars a counterclaim when its prosecution would nullify rights established by a prior action.

FACTS: In 1962, Martino (P) entered into a franchise and lease agreement with McDonald's (D), which specified that neither Martino (P) nor a member of his immediate family would acquire a financial interest in a competing self-service food business without the written consent of McDonald's (D). In 1968, Martino's (P) son purchased a Burger Chef franchise in Pittsburg, Kansas. After McDonald's (D) brought suit for breach of contract, Martino (P) and McDonald's (D) entered into a consent agreement which provided for the sale of Martino's (P) franchise back to McDonald's (D). In 1975, Martino (P) brought this action, alleging that the enforcement of the restriction on acquisition in the franchise and lease agreements violated the Sherman Act. The district court held that both res judicata and the compulsory counterclaim rule of the Federal Rules of Civil Procedure barred Martino (P) from suing for antitrust violations.

ISSUE: Does res judicata bar a counterclaim when its prosecution would nullify rights established by a prior action?

HOLDING AND DECISION: (Pell, J.) Yes. Because the earlier action between Martino (P) and McDonald's (D) was terminated by a consent judgment before an answer was filed, Federal Rule of Civil Procedure 13(a), which bars compulsory counterclaims that are not raised at the proper time, is not applicable here. However, the res judicata effect of the earlier consent judgment is a bar to raising the antitrust claim in this action. The conclusion of the earlier contract lawsuit with a consent judgment does not prevent the earlier judgment from having a res judicata effect, because that judgment was accompanied by judicial findings of fact and conclusions of law that go to the merits of the controversy. It is an accepted general rule that when facts form the basis of both a defense and a counterclaim, the defendant's failure to allege these facts as a defense or a counterclaim does not preclude him from relying on those facts in an action subsequently brought by him against the plaintiff. However, an exception to this general rule provides that res judicata bars a counterclaim when its prosecution would nullify rights established by the prior action. In this case, the doctrine of res judicata bars Martino (P) from waging this direct attack on the rights established by the prior judgment. Affirmed.

EDITOR'S ANALYSIS: Because Martino (P) had not entered pleadings in the action which ended in the consent judgment, it was necessary here to consider the relationship between res judicata and counterclaims. The same process must be undertaken in jurisdictions which have no rule governing compulsory counterclaims.

[For more information on res judicata and counterclaims, see Casenote Law Outline on Criminal Procedure, Chapter 12, Preclusion Doctrines — Res Judicata and Collateral Estoppel, §, I, Res Judicata Defined.]

QUICKNOTES

RES JUDICATA - The rule of law that a final judgment by a court precludes subsequent litigation between the parties regarding the same cause of action.

COUNTERCLAIM - An independent cause of action brought by a defendant to a lawsuit in order to oppose or deduct from the plaintiff's claim.

COMPULSORY COUNTERCLAIM - An independent cause of action brought by a defendant to a lawsuit in order to oppose or deduct from the plaintiff's claim that arises out of the same transaction or occurrence that is the subject matter of the plaintiff's claim and does.

NOTES:

SEARLE BROS. v. SEARLE

Father-son partnership (P) v. Wife (D)

588 P.d. 689 (Utah 1978).

NATURE OF CASE: Appeal from decision barring claim of interest in real property.

FACT SUMMARY: Searle Bros. (P) claimed an undivided one-half interest in Slaugh House, which had been awarded to Searle (D) in a divorce proceeding.

CONCISE RULE OF LAW: A person is in privity with another if he is so identified in interest with the other that he represents the same legal right.

FACTS: Edlean Searle (D) sued Woodey Searle for divorce. During that proceeding, the court determined that a piece of property known as the "Slaugh House," which was recorded in Woodey's name, was part of the marital property and subsequently awarded the entire property to Edlean Searle (D). Woodey had argued that he had a half interest in the property and that the other half was owned by a partnership with his sons as partners. Searle Bros. (P), the partnership, then sued Edlean Searle (D), claiming an undivided one-half interest in Slaugh House. The trial court held that res judicata and collateral estoppel barred the action by Searle Bros. (P).

ISSUE: Is a person in privity with another if he is so identified in interest with the other that he represents the same legal right?

HOLDING AND DECISION: (Ellett, C.J.) Yes. A divorce decree, like other final judgments, is conclusive as to parties and their privies and operates as a bar to any subsequent action. The legal definition of a person in privity with another is a person so identified in interest with another that he represents the same legal right. This includes a mutual or successive relationship to rights in property. Here, Searle Bros.' (P) interest was neither mutual nor successive. Searle Bros. (P) claims no part of the interest owned by Woodey Searle, but asserts its own, independent, and separate partnership interest in 50% of the property involved. Collateral estoppel may not be applied against Searle Bros. (P) because it was not a partner to the first suit, and there is insufficient evidence in the record to show that the interest of the partnership in the Slaugh House was ever litigated. Reversed.

DISSENT: (Crockett, J.) The doctrine of collateral estoppel should bar the suit by Searle Bros. (P). It is plain that the members of the family were actively involved in the divorce action, which involved whatever interest any of them had in the family assets. Further, Searle Bros. (P) was fully aware of the adverse claims being asserted to the Slaugh House.

EDITOR'S ANALYSIS: It is possible for both res judicata and collateral estoppel to apply here. Res judicata requires that the causes of action be identical, and it is generally assumed that different parties automatically have different causes of action. However, if Searle Bros. (P) were in privity with the parties to the earlier divorce action, the requirements for res judicata are met.

[For more information on collateral estoppel, see Case note Law Outline on Criminal Procedure, Chapter 12, Preclusion Doctrines — Res Judicata and Collateral Estoppel, § II, Collateral Estoppel or Issue Preclusion.]

QUICKNOTES

RES JUDICATA - The rule of law that a final judgment by a court precludes subsequent litigation between the parties regarding the same cause of action.

COLLATERAL ESTOPPEL - A doctrine whereby issues litigated and determined in a prior proceeding are binding upon all subsequent litigation between the parties regarding that issue.

ISSUE - A fact or question that is disputed between two or more parties.

CLAIM - The demand for a right to payment or equitable relief; the fact or facts giving rise to such demand.

NOTES:

SAYLOR v. LINDSLEY
Shareholder (P) v. Officer of corporation (D)
391 F.2d 965 (1968).

NATURE OF CASE: Appeal from dismissal of shareholders' derivative suit.

FACT SUMMARY: Saylor's (P) shareholders' derivative action was dismissed on the ground of res judicata because of the dismissal of a prior action by a different plaintiff on the basis of the same transactions and against the same defendant, Lindsley (D).

CONCISE RULE OF LAW: A dismissal of an action due to a plaintiff's failure to satisfy a technical prerequisite does not have res judicata effect upon a subsequent action by a different plaintiff against the same defendant on the basis of the same conduct or transactions.

FACTS: Hawkins brought a shareholder's derivative action alleging securities law violations and breaches of fiduciary duties which was dismissed "with prejudice" upon Hawkins' failure to post a bond for security as required by statute. On the basis of the same transactions as alleged in Hawkins' action, Saylor (P) brought this action. Lindsley (D) moved for summary judgment on the ground that the Hawkins' action's dismissal operated as res judicata barring Saylor's (P). The district court granted the motion and Saylor (P) appealed.

ISSUE: Does a dismissal of an action due to a plaintiff's failure to satisfy a technical prerequisite have res judicata effect upon a subsequent action by a different plaintiff against the same defendant on the basis of the same conduct or transactions?

HOLDING AND DECISION: (Anderson, J.) No. The inquiry here is whether the dismissal of the Hawkins action was "on the merits." At common law, a dismissal upon a ground which did not resolve the substantive merit of the complaint was not a bar to a subsequent action. One of the exceptions to that general rule is that a dismissal for failure to prosecute the claim will be deemed "on the merits." However, the reason for such failure in this case, noted as the basis for the dismissal of Saylor's (P) claim by the district court, was the inability to pay the bond as required. The failure then is the real reason. A dismissal of an action due to a plaintiff's failure to satisfy a technical prerequisite does not have res judicata effect upon a subsequent action by a different plaintiff against the same defendant on the basis of the same conduct or transactions. Reversed and remanded.

EDITOR'S ANALYSIS: In a shareholders' derivative action, the rights of many are determined by the plaintiff bringing the action. Those others should not be prejudiced by the failure of the one who acted first. The shareholders are entitled to their "day in court." Technical failures unrelated to the merits of the case are an unfair basis for a bar to suit.

[For more information on res judicata, see Casenote Law Outline on Criminal Procedure, Chapter 12, Preclusion Doctrines — Res Judicata and Collateral Estoppel, § I, Res Judicata Defined.]

QUICKNOTES

SHAREHOLDER'S DERIVATIVE ACTION - Action asserted by a shareholder in order to enforce a cause of action on behalf of the corporation.

RES JUDICATA - The rule of law that a final judgment by a court precludes subsequent litigation between the parties regarding the same cause of action.

NOTES:

ILLINOIS CENTRAL GULF R.R. v. PARKS
Railroad company (D) v. Injured car occupants (P)
181 Ind. App. 141, 390 N.E.2d 1078 (1979).

NATURE OF CASE: Interlocutory appeal from denial of motion for summary judgment.

FACT SUMMARY: Parks (P) was injured when his car collided with an Illinois Central (D) train.

CONCISE RULE OF LAW: The doctrine of estoppel by verdict allows a judgment in a prior action to operate as a complete bar to those facts or issues actually litigated and determined in the prior action.

FACTS: Parks (P) and his wife were injured when their car collided with an Illinois Central (D) train. Parks' (P) wife recovered $30,000 on her claim for damages for personal injuries, but judgment was rendered for Illinois Central (D) on Parks' (P) own claim for damages for loss of services and loss of consortium. Parks (P) then sued Illinois Central (D) to recover damages for his own injuries. On Illinois Central's (D) motion for summary judgment, the trial court held that Parks' (P) claim was not barred by res judicata, and that the prior action did not collaterally estop Parks (P) on the issue of contributory negligence.

ISSUE: Does the doctrine of estoppel by verdict allow a judgment in a prior action to operate as a complete bar to those facts or issues actually litigated and determined in the prior action?

HOLDING AND DECISION: (Lybrook, J.) Yes. The doctrine of estoppel by verdict allows the judgment in a prior action to operate as an estoppel as to those facts or questions actually litigated and determined in the prior action. Where a prior judgment may have been based upon either or any of two or more distinct facts, a party desiring to plead the judgment as an estoppel by verdict must show the actual basis for the prior judgment. Here, the basis for the prior judgment against Parks (P) could have been predicated on a finding by the jury that either Parks (P) had sustained no damages, or that his own negligence was a proximate cause of his damages. Illinois Central (D) failed to show that the judgment against Parks (P) in the prior action was based upon a finding that Parks (P) was contributorily negligent in the accident. Affirmed.

EDITOR'S ANALYSIS: The doctrine of collateral estoppel is reflective of a policy that the needs of judicial finality and efficiency outweigh the possible gains of fairness or accuracy which would result from the continued litigation of an issue that had been decided in prior judicial proceedings. There is a strong policy favoring consistency of judicial rulings in both state and federal courts.

[For more information on doctrine of estoppel, see Casenote Law Outline on Criminal Procedure, Chapter 12, Preclusion Doctrines — Res Judicata and Collateral Estoppel, § II, Collateral Estoppel or Issue Preclusion.]

QUICKNOTES

COLLATERAL ESTOPPEL - A doctrine whereby issues litigated and determined in a prior proceeding are binding upon all subsequent litigation between the parties regarding that issue.

NOTES:

HALPERN v. SCHWARTZ

Bankrupt debtor (D) v. Trustee in bankruptcy (P)

426 F.2d 102 (2d Cir. 1970).

NATURE OF CASE: Appeal from summary judgment denying a discharge in bankruptcy.

FACT SUMMARY: Schwartz (P) sought to deny Halpern (D) a discharge in bankruptcy.

CONCISE RULE OF LAW: When a prior judgment adjudicating one a bankrupt rests on two or more independent alternative grounds, the judgment is not conclusive as to issues which were necessary in order to establish only one of those grounds.

FACTS: At a previous proceeding, after a trial court had found that she had committed each of three acts of bankruptcy, Halpern (D) was determined to be legally bankrupt. One of the three acts of bankruptcy was a transfer with the intent to hinder and delay creditors. Schwartz (P), a trustee in bankruptcy, then brought suit to deny Halpern (D) a discharge in bankruptcy, because she had caused a transfer of debts with the intent to hinder, delay, or defraud creditors. Schwartz's (P) motion for summary judgment denying Halpern (D) a discharge and alleging that the issue of intent to hinder, delay, or defraud creditors was estopped by the decision adjudicating Halpern (D) a bankrupt was granted by the bankruptcy judge.

ISSUE: When a prior judgment adjudicating one a bankrupt rests on two or more independent alternative grounds, is the judgment conclusive as to issues which were necessary in order to establish only one of those grounds?

HOLDING AND DECISION: (Smith, J.) No. Although an issue was fully litigated in a prior action, the prior judgment will not foreclose reconsideration of the same issue if that issue was not necessary to the rendering of the prior judgment. A decision on an issue not essential to the prior judgment may not have been afforded the careful deliberation and analysis normally applied to essential issues. Further, an appeal of a nonessential issue might be deemed frivolous by an appellate court, thereby denying a losing litigant the opportunity to obtain a conclusive judgment on that issue. Because the earlier proceeding's determination of Halpern's (D) actual intent to hinder and delay her creditors was only one of three independent grounds establishing an act of bankruptcy, the prior judgment cannot be given conclusive effect in the second action for a discharge in bankruptcy. Reversed.

EDITOR'S ANALYSIS: This case, which limits the doctrine of collateral estoppel, represents the minority view in this area. In a later case decided by the same court, the holding in this case was specifically limited to the specific context of bankruptcy proceedings. See Winters v. Lavine, 574 F. 2d 46 (2d Cir. 1978),

where collateral estoppel was involved in an action under the federal civil rights statutes.

[For more information on doctrine of estoppel, see Casenote Law Outline on Criminal Procedure, Chapter 12, Preclusion Doctrines — Res Judicata and Collateral Estoppel, § II, Collateral Estoppel or Issue Preclusion.]

QUICKNOTES

COLLATERAL ESTOPPEL - A doctrine whereby issues litigated and determined in a prior proceeding are binding upon all subsequent litigation between the parties regarding that issue.

ISSUE - A fact or question that is disputed between two or more parties.

NOTES:

WINTERS v. LAVINE
Medicaid corporation claimant (P) v. State (D)
574 F.2d 46 (2d Cir. 1978).

NATURE OF CASE: Action for Medicaid compensation for the services of a Christian Science practitioner.

FACT SUMMARY: In Winters' (P) action for Medicaid compensation for the services of a Christian Science practitioner against Lavine (D) as representative of the State of New York, Lavine (D) alleged that Winters (P) had no right to compensation under the statute and that her proof of illness and treatment was inadequate.

CONCISE RULE OF LAW: The doctrine of collateral estoppel only bars the relitigation of issues which were not only actually litigated and determined in the original action but which were also "necessary" to the judgment entered in that suit.

FACTS: Winters (P) sought Medicaid compensation for the services of a Christian Science practitioner. Lavine (D), representing the State of New York, refused to pay, alleging that Winters (P) had no right to compensation under the statute and that her proof of illness and treatment was inadequate. Winters (P) sued in New York State court, where the claim was rejected on alternative grounds: (1) Winters (P) had no right to compensation under the statute, and failure of the statute to cover her claim did not violate the first amendment; and (2) her proof of illness and treatment was inadequate. Winters (P) subsequently brought suit on the same issues in federal court.

ISSUE: Does the doctrine of collateral estoppel only bar the relitigation of issues which were not only actually litigated and determined in the original action, but which were also "necessary" to the judgment entered in that suit?

HOLDING AND DECISION: (Waterman, J.) Yes. The doctrine of collateral estoppel only bars the relitigation of issues which were not only actually litigated and determined in the original action but which were also "necessary" to the judgment in that suit. Also, where the judgment is based on alternative grounds, as here, the judgment is determinative on both grounds, although either alone would have been sufficient to support the judgment. Here, Winters (P) was prosecuting both actions at once, and there is, therefore, no reason to depart from the rule that a decision based on alternative grounds bars relitigation of any of these grounds in an instance where the plaintiff was pursuing the two actions simultaneously and thus could fully anticipate the potential barring effect of the earlier judgment in deciding not to appeal from that decision. In summary, it is held that the appellate division's decision bars Winters (P) from relitigating here, in the context of a § 1983 suit, the issue of the constitutionality of the denial of Medicaid benefits for the services of a Christian Science

nurse. That issue was determined adversely to her by the appellate division as well as was the issue of whether there was an independent ground, peculiar to Winter's (P) case, relative to whether she should have the state pay the specific benefits she sought to have the state pay. Affirmed.

EDITOR'S ANALYSIS: In a trial to the bench, Federal Rule of Civil Procedure 52(a) requires the judge to set forth findings of fact and conclusions of law. Where there are alternative grounds for decision, the First Restatement of Judgments took the position that both grounds should be precluded in subsequent litigation. Comment 1 of the Restatement (Second) of Judgments § 27 states that neither determination should be binding in subsequent litigation.

[For more information on collateral estoppel, see Casenote Law Outline on Criminal Procedure, Chapter 12, Preclusion Doctrines — Res Judicata and Collateral Estoppel, § II, Collateral Estoppel or Issue Preclusion.]

QUICKNOTES

COLLATERAL ESTOPPEL - A doctrine whereby issues litigated and determined in a prior proceeding are binding upon all subsequent litigation between the parties regarding that issue.

ISSUE - A fact or question that is disputed between two or more parties.

FED. R. CIV. P. 52(a) - Requires that findings of fact not be set aside unless clearly erroneous.

NOTES:

PARKLANE HOSIERY CO., INC. v. SHORE
Hosiery company (D) v. Shareholder (P)
439 U.S. 322 (1979).

NATURE OF CASE: Review of denial of relitigation of issue determined in a separate case.

FACT SUMMARY: Shore (P) sought rescission of a merger on the ground that Parklane (D), a party to the merger, had issued a false and misleading proxy statement, and in a separate action filed by the Securities Exchange Commission (SEC), the district court found the proxy statement to be false, so Shore (P) moved for partial summary judgment in this action on that issue, alleging that Parklane (D) was collaterally estopped from relitigating the issue.

CONCISE RULE OF LAW: A trial judge has broad discretion to permit the offensive use of collateral estoppel to establish an element of a plaintiff's case where it is not unfair to the defendant.

FACTS: Shore (P) brought a shareholder's class action against Parklane (D) alleging that Parklane (D) had issued a materially false and misleading proxy statement in violation of §§ 14(a), 10(b), and 20(a) of the Securities Exchange Act. Shore (P) sought rescission of merger to which Parklane (D) was a party because of the proxy statement, which related to the merger. Before trial, however, the Securities Exchange Commission filed suit on the same basis seeking injunctive relief. The court in that suit found the statement false and misleading and entered a declaratory judgment to that effect. Shore (P) then moved for partial summary judgment on the issue of falsity, alleging that Parklane (D) was collaterally estopped from relitigating the issue. The district court denied the motion, but the court of appeals reversed. The United States Supreme Court granted certiorari.

ISSUE: Has a trial judge broad discretion to permit the offensive use of collateral estoppel to establish an element of a plaintiff's case where it is not unfair to the defendant?

HOLDING AND DECISION: (Stewart, J.) Yes. The defensive use of collateral estoppel to prevent relitigation of issues previously litigated and lost by a plaintiff against another defendant has been upheld by this court. But the present case involves the offensive use of collateral estoppel to prevent relitigation of issues by a defendant against whom a different plaintiff has obtained a ruling. It is argued that such offensive use will not promote judicial economy because plaintiffs can await a ruling in another matter without intervening, and then be relieved of making proofs if the issue is resolved to their satisfaction, but not be foreclosed from raising it again if it is not. Here, however, it is doubtful that Shore (P) could have joined in the SEC injunction suit, so that this argument is inapplicable. Another argument is that a defendant may have little incentive to defend in an action for

small or nominal damages, and should not be subjected to unforeseeable future suits against which he will not be adequately able to defend. But here, Parklane (D) had as strong an incentive to defend against the SEC as it would have to defend against Shore (P). A trial judge has broad discretion to permit the offensive use of collateral estoppel to establish an element of a plaintiff's case where it is not unfair to the defendant. Under these circumstances, it is not unfair to use collateral estoppel against Parklane (D), who had a full and fair opportunity to litigate its claims.

EDITOR'S ANALYSIS: In a separate part of the opinion, the Court found that the offensive use of collateral estoppel in this case would violate Parklane's (D) right to a jury trial in the legal action as opposed to the SEC's equitable suit. This Seventh Amendment right did not, however, affect the propriety of use of collateral estoppel offensively where not unfair to the defendant if the jury trial right was not at issue.

[For more information on offensive use of collateral estoppel, see Casenote Law Outline on Criminal Procedure, Chapter 12, Preclusion Doctrines — Res Judicata and Collateral Estoppel, § II, Collateral Estoppel or Issue Preclusion.]

QUICKNOTES

OFFENSIVE COLLATERAL ESTOPPEL - A doctrine that may be invoked by a plaintiff whereby a defendant is prohibited from relitigating issues litigated and determined in a prior proceeding against another plaintiff.

JOINDER OF PARTIES - The joining of parties in one lawsuit.

NOTES:

STATE FARM FIRE & CASUALTY CO. v. CENTURY HOME COMPONENTS, INC.

Insurance company (P) v. Builder of prefab housing (D)

275 Or. 97, 550 P.2d 1185 (1976).

NATURE OF CASE: Appeal from award of damages for negligence.

FACT SUMMARY: State Farm (P) and many others claimed that Century Home (D) had been negligent by allowing a fire to erupt and spread, causing damage to property.

CONCISE RULE OF LAW: Where prior judicial determinations on a particular matter are inconsistent, the doctrine of collateral estoppel will not bar relitigation of that matter.

FACTS: Over 50 separate actions for damages were filed against Century Home (D) to recover losses from a fire. Three of the actions proceeded separately through trial to final judgment. One judgment was awarded in favor of Century Home (D), and judgment was twice awarded to separate claimants. State Farm (P), who was not a party to any of the previous actions, sought to utilize the prior claimants' judgments to establish conclusively Century Home's (D) negligence and its responsibility for any losses caused by the fire. The trial court held that Century Home (D) was collaterally estopped from any further contesting its liability.

ISSUE: Where prior judicial determinations on a particular matter are inconsistent, does the doctrine of collateral estoppel bar relitigation of that matter?

HOLDING AND DECISION: (Holman, J.) No. In every situation where collateral estoppel is asserted by a person who was neither a party nor in privity with a party to the prior case, it is essential to determine that no unfairness will result to the prior litigant if the estoppel is applied. Where outstanding judicial determinations are inconsistent on the matter sought to be precluded, it would be patently unfair to estop a party by the judgment it lost. The question of whether preclusion would be fair under all the circumstances is independent of, and in addition to, whether a party had a full and fair opportunity to present its case in the action resulting in the adverse judgment. Here, because the prior determinations are basically inconsistent, it would be unfair to preclude Century Home (D) from relitigating the issue of liability. Reversed and remanded.

EDITOR'S ANALYSIS: The Restatement position regarding mutuality of estoppel is consistent with the view taken in this case. It allows relitigation of an issue when "the determination relied on as preclusive was itself inconsistent with another determination of the same issue." Restatement of the Law (Second) Judgments (Tent. Draft No. 2 1975). The Restatement would also allow relitigation of an issue in cases where preclusion would complicate the determination of issues in subsequent actions, prejudice the interests of another party, or where the person seeking preclusion could have joined in the initial action.

[For more information on doctrine of estoppel, see Casenote Law Outline on Criminal Procedure, Chapter 12, Preclusion Doctrines — Res Judicata and Collateral Estoppel, § II, Collateral Estoppel or Issue Preclusion.]

QUICKNOTES

COLLATERAL ESTOPPEL - A doctrine whereby issues litigated and determined in a prior proceeding are binding upon all subsequent litigation between the parties regarding that issue.

MUTUALITY OF ESTOPPEL - Doctrine pursuant to which a court may not consider a judgment final as to one party to a cause of action if it is not final as to the other.

NOTES:

FEDERATED DEPARTMENT STORES, INC. v. MOITIE

Department store owner (D) v. Federal government (P)

452 U.S. 394 (1981).

NATURE OF CASE: Appeal from denial of application of res judicata.

FACT SUMMARY: Moitie (P) contended that he should not be barred by principles of res judicata from relitigating an action in federal court.

CONCISE RULE OF LAW: Non-appealing parties may not benefit from a reversal when their position is closely interwoven with that of appealing parties.

FACTS: In 1976, the United States (P) brought an antitrust action against Federated (D), owners of various department stores, alleging that they had violated § 1 of the Sherman Antitrust Act by agreeing to fix the retail price of women's clothing sold in Northern California. Seven parallel civil actions were subsequently filed by private plaintiffs seeking treble damages on behalf of proposed classes of retail purchasers, including that of Moitie (P) in state court (Moitie I) and Brown (P) in federal court (Brown I). Each of these complaints tracked almost verbatim the allegations of the Government's (P) complaint, though Moitie I referred solely to state law. The district court dismissed all of the actions on the ground that Moitie (P) had not alleged an injury to their business or property within the meaning of § 4 of the Clayton Act. The plaintiffs in five of the suits appealed that judgment to the Ninth Circuit Court of Appeals. The single counsel representing Moitie (P) and Brown (P), however, chose not to appeal and instead refiled the two actions in state court. Although Moitie II and Brown II purported to raise only state law claims, they made allegations similar to those made in prior complaints. After those cases were removed to federal court, the district court concluded that because Moitie II and Brown II involved the same parties, the same alleged offenses, and the same time periods as Moitie I and Brown I, the doctrine of res judicata required that the subsequent actions be dismissed. The court of appeals reversed, holding that non-appealing parties may benefit from a reversal when their position is closely interwoven with that of appealing parties. Federated (D) then appealed.

ISSUE: May non-appealing parties benefit from a reversal when their position is closely interwoven with that of appealing parties?

HOLDING AND DECISION: (Rehnquist, J.) No. Non-appealing parties may not benefit from a reversal when their position is closely interwoven with that of appealing parties. A judgment merely voidable because based upon an erroneous view of the law is not open to collateral attack, but can be corrected only by a direct review and not by bringing another action upon the same cause of action. There is no general equitable doctrine which countenances an exception to the finality of a party's failure to

appeal merely because his rights are closely interwoven with those of another party. Public policy dictates that there be an end to litigation, that those who have contested an issue shall be bound by the result of the contest, and that matters once tried shall be considered forever settled as between the parties. Accordingly, Moitie I and Brown I are res judicata as to the subsequent claims. Reversed.

CONCURRENCE: (Blackmun, J.) There may be cases in which the doctrine of res judicata must give way to overriding concerns of public policy and simple justice. However, this is not a case where the rights of appealing and non-appealing parties are so interwoven or dependent upon each other as to require a reversal of the whole judgment when a part of the action is reversed.

DISSENT: (Brennan, J.) The Court justifies removal of this claim, stated solely in terms of state law, on the vague and confusing ground that the claim is somehow "federal in character." This state law claim was not properly removable. The Court then further errs in failing to reach the "res judicata" issue, and decide the claim.

EDITOR'S ANALYSIS: The principles of res judicata state that a final judgment on the merits of an action preclude the parties or their privies from relitigating issues that were or could have been raised in that action. The res judicata principles of a final, unappealed judgment on the merits are not altered by the fact that the judgment may have been wrong or rested on a legal principle subsequently overruled in another case. An erroneous conclusion reached by a court in the first suit does not deprive the defendants in the second action of their right to rely on a plea of res judicata.

[For more information on principles of res judicata, see Casenote Law Outline on Criminal Procedure, Chapter 12, Preclusion Doctrines — Res Judicata and Collateral Estoppel, § I, Res Judicata Defined.]

QUICKNOTES

RES JUDICATA - The rule of law that a final judgment by a court precludes subsequent litigation between the parties regarding the same cause of action.

JUDGMENT ON THE MERITS - A determination of the rights of the parties to litigation based on the presentation evidence, barring the party from initiating the same suit again.

DURFEE v. DUKE
Landowner (D) v. Title claimant (P)
375 U.S. 106 (1963).

NATURE OF CASE: On writ of certiorari in action to quiet title to land.

FACT SUMMARY: Duke (P), having lost a quiet title action brought in the Nebraska court by Durfee (D), brought an additional quiet title action regarding the same land in a Missouri court.

CONCISE RULE OF LAW: The principles of res judicata and full faith and credit preclude relitigation of judgments of a foreign state when the parties have appeared and have fully and fairly litigated the issues.

FACTS: Durfee (D) brought an action against Duke (P) in a Nebraska court to quiet title to land situated on the Missouri River at the Missouri-Nebraska boundary line. The Nebraska court had subject matter jurisdiction only if the land was in Nebraska. Duke (P) appeared in the Nebraska court and finally litigated the issues, including the court's jurisdiction. Both the Nebraska trial and appellate courts found for Durfee (D) and held that the Nebraska court had subject matter jurisdiction based on their finding that the land was in Nebraska. Duke (P) then brought this action in a Missouri court to quiet title on the same land. Because of diversity of citizenship, the action was removed to the federal district court. That court held that, although the disputed land was in Missouri, since the Nebraska litigation had adjudicated and determined all the issues, the judgment of the Nebraska court was res judicata and binding. Duke (P) argued that the Nebraska judgment was not conclusive on the merits in the Missouri court since Nebraska had no jurisdiction over Missouri land. The appellate court reversed, holding that the court was not obliged to give full faith and credit to the Nebraska judgment and that res judicata was inapplicable because the controversy involved land and the Missouri court was therefore free to retry the issue of the Nebraska court's jurisdiction over the subject matter.

ISSUE: Once a matter has been fully and fairly litigated and judicially determined, does the principle of res judicata preclude the same issue being retried by the same parties in another state?

HOLDING AND DECISION: (Stewart, J.) Yes. The constitutional command of full faith and credit requires that judicial proceedings shall have the same full faith and credit in every court with the United States as they have by law or usage in the courts of the state from which they are taken. Full faith and credit as well as the principle of res judicata therefore preclude relitigation of judgments of a foreign state when the parties have appeared and have fully and fairly litigated the issues. Here, it is not questioned that the Nebraska courts would give full res judicata effect to the Nebraska judgment quieting title in Durfee (D) and therefore the

Missouri court was limited to inquiring only whether the jurisdictional issues had been fully and fairly litigated by the parties and finally determined in the Nebraska courts. The underlying rationale is the doctrine of jurisdictional finality which holds that one trial of an issue is enough. The principles of res judicata apply to questions of jurisdiction of the subject matter as well as to other issues. Also public policy demands that there be an end to litigations, that those who have voluntarily, fully, and fairly contested an issue should be bound by the result. This rule applies to real as well as personal property. While there are the exceptions of federal preemption and sovereign immunity, these overriding considerations are not present here. The judgment of the court of appeals is reversed and that of the district court is affirmed.

CONCURRENCE: (Black, J.) The dispute in this case is as to whether the tract of land in question is in Nebraska or in Missouri. The Nebraska Supreme Court has held that it is in that state and the majority today has agreed that the determination in that suit bars a second suit brought in Missouri. I concur in the holding, but with the understanding that the Nebraska decision would be binding in the event of an authoritative determination by an original suit between the two states or by state compact.

EDITOR'S ANALYSIS: Following the principle of collateral attack, a judgment may always be attacked either in the state where rendered, or in any other state or forum, on the basis of lack of jurisdiction. Lack of subject matter jurisdiction is never waived and hence a collateral attack may be made for the first time when the judgment is accorded res judicata effect in some other action. However, collateral attack is available only to a party who did not appear in the original action. No such attack is permitted by a party who raised and litigated the jurisdictional defect in the original action (or merely appeared and therefore could have raised it). In such a case, the first court's findings as to its jurisdiction — no matter how erroneous — are themselves entitled to res judicata and cannot be relitigated.

[For more information on doctrine of res judicata, see Casenote Law Outline on Criminal Procedure, Chapter 12, Preclusion Doctrines — Res Judicata and Collateral Estoppel, § I, Res Judicata Defined.]

QUICKNOTES

FULL FAITH AND CREDIT - Doctrine that a judgment by a court of one state shall be given the same effect in another state.

RES JUDICATA - The rule of law that a final judgment by a court precludes subsequent litigation between the parties regarding the same cause of action.

ISSUE - A fact or question that is disputed between two or more parties.

ROZIER v. FORD MOTOR CO.
Wife of decedent driver (P) v. Car company (D)
573 F.2d 1332 (5th Cir. 1978).

NATURE OF CASE: Appeal from denial of motion for a new trial.

FACT SUMMARY: Rozier's (P) husband died when his 1969 Ford Galaxy 500 was struck from behind by another car and the fuel tank exploded, and after a trial judgment for Ford (D), Rozier (P) sought a new trial on the ground that Ford (D) failed to produce a document requested during discovery.

CONCISE RULE OF LAW: When the wrongful conduct of one party prevents the other party from fully and fairly presenting her case, a new trial may be ordered.

FACTS: Rozier's (P) husband died when his 1969 Ford Galaxy 500 was struck from behind and the fuel tank exploded. Ten months after a jury had held in favor of Ford (D) in a wrongful death action, Rozier (P) moved for a new trial on the ground that Ford (D) had failed to disclose a document covered by Rozier's (P) interrogatories. On January 6, 1976, the trial court had ordered Ford (D) to produce "cost/benefit analyses, and written reports or analyses which are applicable to the 1969 Ford Galaxy 500." Although Ford (D) denied that any such documents existed, it was later ascertained that a relevant document, the 1971 Trend Cost Estimate, had been located by Ford (D) one week prior to trial but had never been acknowledged or produced. The motion for new trial was denied, and Rozier (P) appealed.

ISSUE: Is a new trial mandated when the wrongful conduct of one party prevents the other party from fully and fairly presenting her case?

HOLDING AND DECISION: (Simpson, J.) Yes. By any fair reading, the trial court's discovery order of January 6, 1976, called for production of the Trend Cost Estimate, which was a safety report covering rear end collisions and proposed alternative fuel tank designs for full-size Ford (D) automobiles. If Ford (D) had in good faith believed that the trial court's order was not intended to compel production of the Trend Cost Estimate, the appropriate remedy was to seek a ruling on this issue at that point of the litigation. Rozier (P) has proved by clear and convincing evidence that Ford (D) engaged in misrepresentation and other misconduct. Because disclosure of the Trend Cost Estimate would have made a difference in the way that Rozier's (P) counsel approached the case or prepared for trial, Rozier (P) has been prevented from fully and fairly presenting her case. Through its misconduct, Ford (D) completely sabotaged the federal trial machinery, precluding the fair contest which the Federal Rules of Civil Procedure are intended to assure. Motion granted.

EDITOR'S ANALYSIS: The remedy given to a trial court under the Federal Rules of Civil Procedure to grant relief from judgments previously entered is rarely available. The usual post-trial remedies for litigants are posttrial motions in the trial court and in the courts of appeal. Rule 60(b), discussed in this case, is not a substitute for the usual appeals process.

[For more information on misconduct of adverse party, see Casenote Law Outline on Criminal Procedure, Chapter 9, Trial and Post-Trial Motions, § VII, Extraordinary Post-Judgment Relief in the Trial Court.]

QUICKNOTES

FED. R. CIV. P. 60 (b) - Authorizes relief from judgment based on certain specified grounds.

INTERROGATORY - A method of pretrial discovery in which written questions are provided by one party to another who must respond in writing under oath.

NOTES:

CHAPTER 13
JOINDER

QUICK REFERENCE RULES

1. **Claims by the Defendant.** A claim for the amount of a debt owed pursuant to a transaction which is the subject of a truth-in-lending suit brought in federal court is a compulsory counterclaim of such suit. (Plant v. Blazer Financial Services)

    [For more information on joinder of counterclaims, see Casenote Law Outline on Civil Procedure, Chapter 6, Joinder of Claims and Parties, § I, Joinder of Claims.]

2. **By Plaintiffs.** Permissive joinder of parties is to be broadly granted under F.R.C.P. 20 where each party seeks relief arising out of the same transaction or series of transactions and a common question of fact or law will arise in the action. (Mosley v. General Motor Corp.)

    [For more information on class actions, see Casenote Law Outline on Civil Procedure, Chapter 6, Joinder of Claims and Parties, § IV, Additional Procedural Devices for Joinder of Parties.]

3. **Third-Party Claims.** A third-party claim cannot be maintained unless the liability asserted against the third-party is derivative of the main claim. (Watergate Landmark Condominium Unit Owners' Association v. Wiss, Janey, Elstner Associates)

4. **More Complex Litigation.** In a diversity case, the federal court does not have ancillary jurisdiction over the plaintiff's claims against a third-party defendant who is a citizen of the same state. (Owen Equipment & Erection)

    [For more information on ancillary jurisdiction, see Casenote Law Outline on Civil Procedure, Chapter 6, Joinder of Claims and Parties, § V, Supplemental Jurisdictions.]

5. **Compulsory Joinder.** A tenant under a lease which violates a clause in another tenant's lease from a common landlord is not an indispensable party under F.R.C.P. 19 to a suit by such other tenant against that landlord. (Helzberg's Diamond Shops v. Valley West Des Moines Shopping Center)

    [For more information on indespensable parties, see Casenote Law Outline on Civil Procedure, Chapter 6, Joinder of Chairs and Parties, § II, Joinder of Parties.]

6. **Intervention.** A party may intervene in an action under F.R.C.P. 24(a)(2) it he has an interest upon which the disposition of that action will have a significant legal effect. (Natural Resources Defense Council v. United States Nuclear Regulatory Commission)

    [For more information on intervention, see Casenote Law Outline on Civil Procedure, Chapter 6, Joinder of Claims and Parties, § IV, Additional Procedural Devices for Joinder of Parties.]

7. **Intervention.** A party may not be bound by a judgment rendered in an action in which he was not a party, even If he had had knowledge of the action. (Martin v. Wilks)

    [For more information on res judicata, see Casenote Law Outline on Civil Procedure, Chapter 12, Preclusion Doctrines—Res Judicata and Collateral Estoppel, § I, Res Judicata Defined. For more information on joinder of parties, see also Casenote Law Outline on Civil Procedure, Chapter 6, Joinder of Claims and Parties, § III, Joinder of Additional Parties.]

8. **Interpleader.** A party has an unconditional right to intervene if the party can prove a risk of practical impairment of a relevant interest, timely application, and lack of adequate representation. (Cohen v. The Republic of the Phillipines)

   [For more information on interpleader, see Casenote Law Outline on Civil Procedure, Chapter 6, § IV, Additional Procedural Devices for Joinder of Parties.]

9. **Statutory Requirements.** A class-action suit must meet criteria for numerosity, commonality, adequacy, and typicality. (In re Alco International Group, Inc. Securities Litigation)

   [For more information on class actions, see Casenote Law Outline on Civil Procedure, Chapter 6, § IV, Additional Procedural Devices for Joinder of Parties.]

10. **Statutory Requirements.** A judge may issue a writ of mandamus directing a lower judge to decertify class action if allowing the class action would cause irreparable harm to the defendants and the certification far exceeded the bounds of judicial discretion. (In the Matter of Rhone-Poulenc Rorer, Inc.)

11. **Representative Adequacy.** There must be adequate representation of the members of a class action or the judgment is not binding on the parties not adequately represented. (Hansberry v. Lee)

    [For more information on class action, see Casenote Law Outline on Civil Procedure, Chapter 6, Joinder of Claims and Parties, § IV, Additional Procedural Devices for Joinder of Parties.]

12. **Jurisdiction.** A state may exercise jurisdiction over absent plaintiffs in a classification suit even if the plaintiffs have no contacts with that state. (Phillips Petroleum v. Shutts)

    [For more information on class actions and minimum contacts with forum state, see Casenote Law Outline on Civil Procedure, Chapter 6, Joinder of Claims and Parties, § IV, Additional Procedural Devices for Joinder of Parties.]

13. **Settlement and Dismissal**. A class settlement agreement may be approved by the court if it is fair, adequate, and reasonable. (Georgine v. Achem Products)

    [For more information on class actions, see Casenote Law Outline on Civil Procedure, Chapter 6, § IV, Additional Procedural Devices for Joinder of Parties.]

PLANT v. BLAZER FINANCIAL SERVICES, INC.
Borrower (P) v. Lender (D)
598 F.2d 1357 (1979).

NATURE OF CASE: Appeal from ruling finding a counterclaim compulsory.

FACT SUMMARY: Plant (P) was a debtor of Blazer (D) who sued Blazer (D) for violations of the Truth-In-Lending Act, and Blazer (D) asserted a counterclaim on the debt owing which Plant (P) sought to dismiss.

CONCISE RULE OF LAW: A claim for the amount of a debt owed pursuant to a transaction which is the subject of a truth-in-lending suit brought in federal court is a compulsory counterclaim of such suit.

FACTS: Plant (P) executed a note for $2,520 to be paid to Blazer (D) in monthly installments. No payments were made. Plant (P) brought suit in federal court alleging violations of the Truth-In-Lending Act by Blazer (D) for failure to disclose a limitation on an after-acquired security interest. Blazer (D) sought to interpose a counterclaim for the amount of the note which Plant (P) challenged as not compulsory and an improper permissive counterclaim, as no diversity or federal question existed. The district court ruled the counterclaim compulsory, and Plant (P) appealed.

ISSUE: Is a claim for the amount of debt owed pursuant to a transaction which is the subject of a truth-in-lending suit brought in federal court a compulsory counterclaim?

HOLDING AND DECISION: (Roney, J.) Yes. Rule 13(a) of the Federal Rules of Civil Procedure provides that a counterclaim is compulsory if it "arises out of the transaction or occurrence" which is the subject matter of the plaintiff's claim. Four inquiries are designed to provide an answer: (1) Are the issues of fact and law the same? (2) Would res judicata bar a subsequent suit on the counterclaim? (3) Is the same evidence involved? (4) Is the counterclaim logically related to the main claim? All need not be satisfied. Under the last, or logical relation test, it is clear that the same operative facts give rise to both claims here. A claim for the amount of a debt owed pursuant to a transaction which is the subject of a truth-in-lending suit brought in federal court is a compulsory counterclaim of such suit. Other district courts are in accord. Had Congress intended to insulate truth-in-lending recoveries from counterclaims of creditors, it could have done so. Affirmed.

EDITOR'S ANALYSIS: A compulsory counterclaim falls under a federal court's ancillary jurisdiction. Unlike a permissive counterclaim, it needs no independent basis for jurisdiction. The policy of avoiding multiple litigation is served by allowing courts to resolve all matters which are substantially enough related to an action properly brought.

[For more information on joinder of counterclaims, see Casenote Law Outline on Civil Procedure, Chapter 6, Joinder of Claims and Parties, § I, Joinder of Claims.]

QUICKNOTES

FED. R. CIV. P. 13 (a) - Lays out the requirements for a compulsory counterclaim.

RES JUDICATA - The rule of law that a final judgment by a court precludes subsequent litigation between the parties regarding the same cause of action.

COMPULSORY COUNTERCLAIM - An independent cause of action brought by a defendant to a lawsuit in order to oppose or deduct from the plaintiff's claim that arises out of the same transaction or occurrence that is the subject matter of the plaintiff's claim and does.

ANCILLARY JURISDICTION - Authority of a federal court to hear and determine issues related to a case over which it has jurisdiction, but over which it would not have jurisdiction if such claims were brought independently.

NOTES:

MOSLEY v. GENERAL MOTORS CORP.
Class action plaintiffs (P) v. Car company (D)
497 F.d. 1330 (1974).

NATURE OF CASE: Appeal from order requiring severance of joint action.

FACT SUMMARY: Mosley (P) and nine others brought this class action against GM (D) for various acts of race and sex discrimination, and the district court ordered the 10 plaintiffs to bring 10 separate actions due to the wide variety of the claims and the unmanageability of the joint proceeding.

CONCISE RULE OF LAW: Permissive joinder of parties is to be broadly granted under F.R.C.P. 20 where each party seeks relief arising out of the same transaction or series of transactions and a common question of fact or law will arise in the action.

FACTS: Mosley (P) and nine other plaintiffs brought this class action against GM (D) alleging various different acts which in some cases they contended constituted racial discrimination and in others sex discrimination. They filed complaints individually with the Equal Employment Opportunity Commission (EEOC), and the EEOC notified each of their right to bring a civil action in federal court. At that point the plaintiffs joined in bringing the class action. The district court ordered that each plaintiff bring a separate action, separately filed, due to the differing types of claims alleged and the unmanageability of the joint proceeding. The judge found that there was no right to relief arising out of the same transaction or series of transactions or a common question of fact or law as required by F.R.C.P. 20. Mosley (P) appealed.

ISSUE: Is permissive joinder to be broadly granted under F.R.C.P. 20 where each party seeks relief arising out of the same transaction or series of transactions and a common question of fact or law will arise in the action?

HOLDING AND DECISION: (Ross, J.) Yes. The purpose of F.R.C.P. 20 is to promote trial convenience and expedite the final determination of disputes. The Rules permit the trial judge, however, to order separate trials within his discretion if such an order will prevent delay or prejudice. Reversal of such an order depends upon an abuse of that discretion. In this case, a series of "logically related" events occurred, which has been held to constitute a single series of transactions as required. Furthermore, the rights asserted depend on a common question of law. The district court abused its discretion, therefore, in ordering the separate trials. Permissive joinder is to be broadly granted under F.R.C.P. 20 where each party seeks relief arising out of the same transaction or series of transactions and a common question of fact or law will arise in the action. Reversed.

EDITOR'S ANALYSIS: It is not often easy to determine what is

a single series of transactions when distinct events have taken place. However, a series of employment or advancement decisions together appearing like a policy of discrimination is the kind of matter that F.R.C.P. 20 seeks to have determined in one action. It is when the rights of the parties suffer at the expense of judicial economy that F.R.C.P. 20(b) can be involved to require separate trials, rather than when the judge finds the case "unmanageable."

[For more information on class actions, see Case note Law Outline on Civil Procedure, Chapter 6, Joinder of Claims and Parties, § IV, Additional Procedural Devices for Joinder of Parties.]

QUICKNOTES

FRCP 20 - Provides that parties requesting relief for injuries arising from the same transaction or common question of law or fact be permitted to consolidate their actions into a single one

PERMISSIVE JOINDER - The joining of parties or claims in a single suit if the claims against the parties arise from the same transaction or occurrence or involve common issues of law or fact; such joinder is not mandatory.

NOTES:

WATERGATE LANDMARK CONDOMINIUM UNIT OWNERS' ASS'N v. WISS, JANEY, ELSTNER ASSOCIATES

Condominium owners association (P) v.
Management company (D)

117 F.R.D. 576 (E.D. Va. 1987).

NATURE OF CASE: Motion to dismiss third-party complaint in action for negligent design.

FACT SUMMARY: The Watergate Landmark Condominium manager Legum (D), who was sued by Association (P) because repairs, designed by Wiss (D), to the condominium complex were unsatisfactory, cross-complained against Wiss (D) and filed a third-party complaint against Brisk (D), who had faithfully done the repairs designed by Wiss (D).

CONCISE RULE OF LAW: A third-party claim cannot be maintained unless the liability asserted against the third-party is derivative of the main claim.

FACTS: Watergate Landmark Condominium Unit Owners' Ass'n (P) notified Legum & Norman (D), its management company, that the balconies of the units required repair. Legum (D) hired Wiss (D), an engineering firm, to design the repairs. Legum (D) hired Brisk (D) to make the repairs designed by Wiss (D). However, the repairs were unsatisfactory to Association (P), which in turn brought suit against Legum (D) and Wiss (D) in federal court, invoking diversity jurisdiction. The pleadings filed by Association (P) conceded that Brisk (D) did the repairs per the Wiss (D) specifications. Legum (D) filed a cross-complaint against Wiss (D) and a third-party claim against Brisk (D) alleging Brisk (D) performed the repairs negligently. Brisk (D) moved for dismissal of the third-party complaint, arguing that the claim against it was derivative of the main claim.

ISSUE: Can a third-party claim be maintained if the liability asserted against the third party is not derivative of the main claim?

HOLDING AND DECISION: (Ellis, J.) No. A third-party claim can only be maintained if the liability asserted against the third-party is derivative of the main claim. A third-party claim may be maintained only if the third party would be either secondarily or derivatively liable to the defendant if the defendant were found liable. Typically, third-party claims result when one tortfeasor impleads another, an indemnitee impleads an indemnitor, or a secondarily liable party impleads one who is primarily liable. Without such derivative liability, the claim must fail. Here, the claim asserted by Legum (D) was that the work done by Brisk (D) was negligent. However, in its papers, Association (P) noted that the work done by Brisk (D) was not done negligently and that it was done according to the specifications designed by Wiss (D). An analysis of the evidence required to prove each case demonstrated the inappropriateness of the claim against Brisk

(D) by Legum (D). In the suit by Association (P) against Legum (D), the focus would be on the adequacy of the specifications provided by Wiss (D). In the Legum (D) action against Brisk (D), the focus would be on the quality of work done by Brisk (D). This evidence is irrelevant to the Association's (P) claim against Legum (D). Therefore, the claim asserted against Brisk (D) by Legum (D) is separate from and not derivative of the claim asserted against Legum (D) by the Association (P), and the outcome of the action asserted against Legum (D) by Association (P) is independent of the action asserted by Legum (D) against Brisk (D). For these reasons, the third-party action brought against Brisk (D) was inappropriate. Motion granted.

EDITOR'S ANALYSIS: To be valid, the third party impleaded into the action must be liable to the defendant if the defendant is found liable to the plaintiff. This is really saying, "If I am found liable, then my liability is secondary because I am going to be reimbursed by someone else." The third-party action is disallowed if the defense can state, "It was he, not I," because the third party's liability runs directly to the plaintiff.

QUICKNOTES

CROSS-CLAIM - A claim asserted by a plaintiff or defendant to an action against a co-plaintiff or co-defendant, and not against an opposing party, arising out of the same transaction or occurrence as the subject matter of the action.

IMPLEADER - Procedure by which a third party, who may be liable for all or part of liability, is joined to an action so that all issues may be resolved in a single suit.

NOTES:

OWEN EQUIPMENT & ERECTION v. KROGER

Crane company (D) v. Wife of electrocuted decedent (P)

437 U.S. 365 (1978).

NATURE OF CASE: Action for damages for wrongful death.

FACT SUMMARY: Kroger (P) brought a wrongful death action in federal court against a defendant of diverse citizenship and then amended her complaint to include an impleaded third-party defendant, Owen (D), even though they were citizens of the same state.

CONCISE RULE OF LAW: In a diversity case, the federal court does not have ancillary jurisdiction over the plaintiff's claims against a third-party defendant who is a citizen of the same state.

FACTS: Kroger's (P) husband was electrocuted when the boom of a steel crane owned and operated by Owen (D), and next to which he was walking, came too close to a high tension electric power line of the Omaha Public Power District (OPPD). Kroger (P) brought a wrongful death action against OPPD in federal court in Nebraska, she being a resident of Iowa. However, OPPD filed a third-party complaint against Owen (D), alleging its negligence had caused the electrocution. Eventually, OPPD's motion for summary judgment was granted, and Owen (D) was the only defendant left in the case. During trial, it was discovered that Owen (D), a Nebraska corporation, had its principal place of business in Iowa and was therefore a citizen of the same state as Kroger (P). The district court denied Owen's (D) motion to dismiss the complaint for lack of jurisdiction, and the jury returned a verdict in favor of Kroger (P). The court of appeals affirmed.

ISSUE: Can a federal court exercise ancillary jurisdiction over a plaintiff's claims against a third-party defendant who is a citizen of the same state in a diversity case?

HOLDING AND DECISION: (Stewart, J.) No. The concept of ancillary jurisdiction is not so broad as to permit a federal court in a diversity case to exercise jurisdiction over the plaintiff's claims against a third-party defendant who is a citizen of the same state. 28 U.S.C. § 1332(a)(1) requires complete diversity of citizenship. To allow ancillary jurisdiction in a case like this would be to allow circumvention of that requirement by the simple expedient of suing only those defendants who were of diverse citizenship and waiting for them to implead nondiverse defendants. Reversed.

DISSENT: (White, J.) Section 1332 requires complete diversity only between the plaintiff and those parties he actually brings into the suit, which would not include Owen (D) in this case. Beyond that, I would hold the district court has the power to entertain all claims among the parties arising from the same nucleus of operative fact as the plaintiff's original, jurisdiction-conferring claim against the original defendant. Thus, ancillary jurisdiction existed in this case.

EDITOR'S ANALYSIS: Rule 14 of the F.R.C.P. is the one which permits ancillary jurisdiction. In amending it, the Advisory Committee stated that any attempt by a plaintiff to amend his complaint to assert a claim against an impleaded third party would be unavailing, by majority view, where the third party could not have been joined by the plaintiff originally due to jurisdictional limitations. Congress reenacted § 1332 without relevant change and with knowledge of the aforementioned view. The majority opinion took this as evidence of congressional approval of that view.

[For more information on ancillary jurisdiction, see Casenote Law Outline on Civil Procedure, Chapter 6, Joinder of Claims and Parties, § V, Supplemental Jurisdictions.]

QUICKNOTES

ANCILLARY JURISDICTION - Authority of a federal court to hear and determine issues related to a case over which it has jurisdiction, but over which it would not have jurisdiction if such claims were brought independently.

28 U.S.C. § 1332 - Governs the requirements for diversity jurisdiction.

FED. R. CIV. P. 14 - Permits the impleader of a party who is or may be liable in order to determine the rights of All parties in one proceeding.

NOTES:

HELZBERG'S DIAMOND SHOPS, INC. v. VALLEY WEST DES MOINES SHOPPING CENTER, INC.

Jewelry stores (P) v. Shopping center (D)

564 F.2d 816 (1977).

NATURE OF CASE: Appeal from denial of motion to dismiss for failure to join an indispensable party.

FACT SUMMARY: Helzberg's (P) brought this suit to enjoin Valley West (D), Helzberg's (P) commercial landlord, from breaching their lease agreement by leasing more than two full-line jewelry stores in the mall where Helzberg's (P) leasehold was located, and Valley West (D) unsuccessfully moved to dismiss on the ground that Helzberg's (P) failed to join the full-line jewelry store tenant, Lord's.

CONCISE RULE OF LAW: A tenant under a lease which violates a clause in another tenant's lease from a common landlord is not an indispensable party under F.R.C.P. 19 to a suit by such other tenant against that landlord.

FACTS: Helzberg's (P), a full-line jewelry store, leased space in Valley West's (D) shopping center to operate their store. The lease agreement provided that no more than two such stores would be allowed to rent space other than Helzberg's (P) in the mall. Valley West (D), however, leased space to a third such store, Lord's. Helzberg's (P) brought this action to enjoin such a lease, and Valley West (D) moved to dismiss on the ground that Lord's was not joined and was an indispensable party. Helzberg's (P) brought suit in district court in Missouri and could not obtain personal jurisdiction over Lord's, which had no Missouri contacts. The district court denied Valley West's (D) motion, and Valley West (D) appealed.

ISSUE: Is a tenant under a lease which violates a clause in another tenant's lease from a common landlord an indispensable party under F.R.C.P. 19 to a suit brought by such other tenant against that landlord?

HOLDING AND DECISION: (Alsop, J.) No. F.R.C.P. 19 defines an indispensable party as one in whose absence complete relief cannot be accorded, or claims an interest related to the subject of the action and whose absence will impair or impede his ability to protect that interest or force him to risk multiple or inconsistent obligations. Valley West (D) contends that Lord's and Valley West's (D) rights under their contract cannot be adjudicated in Lord's absence. However, the determination that may result in this action is that Valley West (D) may be forced to terminate that contract, in which case Lord's will still be empowered to assert its rights under the contract for that eventuality. The claim that Valley West (D) may be subjected then to inconsistent obligations following another contract action also fails. Valley West's (D) inconsistent obligations will result from their voluntary execution of two lease agreements with inconsistent obligations required

under them. The litigation here can proceed without Lord's, which is not an indispensable party under these circumstances. A tenant under a lease which violates a clause in another tenant's lease is not an indispensable party under F.R.C.P. 19 to a suit by such other tenant against their common landlord. Affirmed.

EDITOR'S ANALYSIS: In federal practice, the court will balance the prejudice to an absent party against the desirability of ruling on a meritorious claim. The judge can shape the relief granted under his equitable powers so as to avoid any such prejudice so long as he renders an effective judgment.

[For more information on indispensable parties, see Casenote Law Outline on Civil Procedure, Chapter 6, Joinder of Chairs and Parties, § II, Joinder of Parties.]

QUICKNOTES

FED. R. CIV. P. 19 - Governs compulsory party joinder.

COMPULSORY JOINDER - The joining of parties to a lawsuit that is mandatory if complete relief cannot be afforded to the parties in his absence or his absence will result in injustice.

INDISPENSABLE PARTY - Parties whose joining in a lawsuit is essential for the adequate disposition of the action and without whom the action cannot proceed.

NOTES:

NATURAL RESOURCES DEFENSE COUNCIL, INC. v. UNITED STATES NUCLEAR REGULATORY COMMISSION

Federal regulatory agency (D) v. Federal commission (P)

578 F.2d 1341 (1978).

NATURE OF CASE: Appeal of denial of motion to intervene.

FACT SUMMARY: The American Mining Congress (AMC) and Kerr-McGee (KM) appealed the denial of their motion to intervene in an action brought by the Natural Resources Defense Council (NRDC) (P) against the Nuclear Regulatory Commission (NRC) (D) seeking a declaration that state-granted nuclear power operation licenses are subject to the requirement of filing an environmental impact statement and seeking an injunction of the grant of one such license by the New Mexico Environmental Improvement Agency (NMEIA).

CONCISE RULE OF LAW: A party may intervene in an action under F.R.C.P. 24(a)(2) it he has an interest upon which the disposition of that action will have a significant legal effect.

FACTS: The NRC (D) is permitted by federal law to give the several states the power to grant licenses to operate nuclear power facilities. The NRC (D) is empowered to grant such licenses subject to a requirement that such "major federal action" be preceded by the preparation of an environmental impact statement. The NRC (D) entered into an agreement with NMEIA permitting it to issue a license, which it did, to United Nuclear without preparing an impact statement. NRDC (P) brought this action seeking a declaration that state-granted licenses are the product of "major federal action" and subject to the statement requirement and seeking an injunction against the issuance of the license. United Nuclear intervened without objection. KM, a potential recipient of a NMEIA license, and AMC, a public interest group, sought to intervene, but their motions were denied. Both appealed.

ISSUE: May a party intervene in an action under F.R.C.P. 24(a)(2) if he has an interest upon which the disposition of that action will have a significant legal effect?

HOLDING AND DECISION: (Doyle, J.) Yes. F.R.C.P. 24(a) gives a party the right to intervene when he has a sufficiently protectable interest related to the property or transaction which is the subject of the action and the disposition will "as a practical matter, impair or impede his ability to protect that interest." The argument that the effect upon the movant's right must be a res judicata effect is unpersuasive. The effect must "as a practical matter" impair or impede the ability to protect the right. A party may thus intervene in an action under F.R.C.P. 24(a)(2) if he has an interest upon which the disposition of that action will have a significant legal effect. It need not be a strictly legal effect. KM and AMC each have rights, not protected by other parties to the litigation, which will be thus effected, and they must be allowed to intervene. Reversed and remanded.

EDITOR'S ANALYSIS: F.R.C.P. 24(a) covers the intervention of right, while Rule 24(b) sets forth criteria for permissive intervention. Intervention is permissive if there is a common question of law or fact or if a statute gives a conditional right to intervene. In either case, an intervenor has the same status in the litigation as an original party, but he cannot raise any new issues. Ancillary jurisdiction attaches over the intervenor.

_____

[For more information on intervention, see Casenote Law Outline on Civil Procedure, Chapter 6, Joinder of Claims and Parties, § IV, Additional Procedural Devices for Joinder of Parties.]

QUICKNOTES

FED. R. CIV. P. 24 - Governs permissive intervention and intervention as a matter of right.

NOTES:

MARTIN v. WILKS
Firefighters (P) v. Court (D)
490 U.S. 755 (1989).

NATURE OF CASE: Review of reversal of dismissal of reverse discrimination action.

FACT SUMMARY: Several white firefighters challenged affirmative action plans mandated by a consent decree which was entered in an action of which they had knowledge but had not intervened.

CONCISE RULE OF LAW: A party may not be bound by a judgment rendered in an action in which he was not a party, even If he had knowledge of the action.

FACTS: As part of a discrimination action, a consent decree was rendered between the City of Birmingham, Alabama, and a class of black firefighters. As part of the decree, the City instituted an affirmative action program. Subsequent to this, a group of white firefighters filed a reverse discrimination action. The district court dismissed, holding that because the white firefighters had notice of the prior action but had elected not to intervene, the matter was res judicata as to them. The Eleventh Circuit reversed, and the Supreme Court granted review.

ISSUE: May a party be bound by a judgment rendered in an action in which he was not a party, if he had knowledge of the action?

HOLDING AND DECISION: (Rehnquist, C.J.) No. A party may not be bound by a judgment rendered in an action in which he was not a party, even if he had knowledge of the action. It is a principle of general application that one is not bound by an in personam judgment in a litigation in which he is not designated as a party or has not been made a party by service of process. The argument asserted by those defending the consent decree is that by knowing about the underlying action and failing to intervene, the plaintiffs herein waived that objection to being bound. This is incorrect. A party seeking a judgment binding on another cannot obligate that person to intervene; he must be joined. This was the position taken by the Eleventh Circuit, and it was correct in so doing. Affirmed.

DISSENT: (Stevens, J.) In no sense were the white firefighters herein "bound" by the consent decree; rather it was the City that was so bound. The district court properly dismissed the action because the City was fulfilling its legal obligations, not because the white firefighters were somehow bound by the consent decree.

EDITOR'S ANALYSIS: Joinder is governed by F.R.C.P. 19. The rule distinguishes between parties that should be joined and parties that must be joined. Parties may be joined either as defendants or as involuntary plaintiffs.

[For more information on res judicata, see Casenote Law Outline on Civil Procedure, Chapter 12, Preclusion Doctrines — Res Judicata and Collateral Estoppel, § I, Res Judicata Defined. For more information on joinder of parties, see also Casenote Law Outline on Civil Procedure, Chapter 6, Joinder of Claims and Parties, § III, Joinder of Additional Parties.]

QUICKNOTES

FED. R. CIV. P. 19 - Governs compulsory party joinder.

PERMISSIVE JOINDER - The joining of parties or claims in a single suit if the claims against the parties arise from the same transaction or occurrence or involve common issues of law or fact; such joinder is not mandatory.

COMPULSORY JOINDER - The joining of parties to a lawsuit that is mandatory if complete relief cannot be afforded to the parties in his absence or his absence will result in injustice.

RES JUDICATA - The rule of law that a final judgment by a court precludes subsequent litigation between the parties regarding the same cause of action.

INTERVENTION - The method by which a party, not an initial party to the action, is admitted to the action in order to assert an interest in the subject matter of a lawsuit.

NOTES:

COHEN v. THE REPUBLIC OF THE PHILIPPINES
Painting consignee (P) v. Sovereign country (D)
146 F.R.D. 90 (S.D.N.Y. 1993).

NATURE OF CASE: Motion to intervene in ownership dispute.

FACT SUMMARY: Imelda Marcos (D) sought to intervene in an interpleader action before the court to determine who legally owned several paintings.

CONCISE RULE OF LAW: A party has an unconditional right to intervene if the party can prove a risk of practical impairment of a relevant interest, timely application, and lack of adequate representation.

FACTS: Cohen (P) had in his possession four paintings valued at approximately five million dollars which were received on consignment from Braemer (D), Marcos's agent, whom she had entrusted to run her New York home. Braemer (D) demanded return of the paintings, but Cohen (P) refused and brought an interpleader action to determine the ownership of the paintings, naming the Republic of the Philippines (D) and Braemer (D) as defendants. Marcos sought leave to intervene in the interpleader action to assert her claim to the paintings. The Philippine government (D) objected and asserted that existing parties would be prejudiced.

ISSUE: Does a party have an unconditional right to intervene if the party can prove a risk of practical impairment of a relevant interest, timely application, and lack of adequate representation?

HOLDING AND DECISION: (Conner, J.) Yes. A party has an unconditional right to intervene if the party can prove a risk of practical impairment of a relevant interest, timely application, and lack of adequate representation pursuant to Fed. R. Civ. P. 24(a)(2). Here, Marcos made her claim before the proceedings reached an advanced stage; thus, her claim is timely. Marcos's affidavit indicates that her interests will be impaired if she is not permitted to intervene as she risks losing her interest in the paintings. Marcos's interest is not being represented by either existing party; thus, it is not presently protected. Motion to intervene is granted.

EDITOR'S ANALYSIS: A party who possesses property that is the subject of multiple claims may bring an interpleader action in federal court. There are two types of federal interpleader actions: statutory interpleader and rule interpleader. Statutory interpleader actions have more generous subject matter jurisdiction and venue provisions.

[For more information on interpleader, see Casenote Law Outline on Civil Procedure, Chapter 6, § IV, Additional Procedural Devices for Joinder of Parties.]

QUICKNOTES

INTERVENTION - The method by which a party, not an initial party to the action, is admitted to the action in order to assert an interest in the subject matter of a lawsuit.

INTERPLEADER - An equitable proceeding whereby a person holding property, which is subject to the claims of multiple parties, may require such parties to resolve the matter through litigation.

FED. R. CIV. P. 24 - Governs permissive intervention and intervention as a matter of right.

NOTES:

IN RE ALCO INTERNATIONAL GROUP, INC. SECURITIES LITIGATION

Investment company/investor (P) v. Corporation (D)

158 F.R.D. 152 (S.D. Calif. 1994).

NATURE OF CASE: Motion to certify a class action suit.

FACT SUMMARY: Investment Corporation of America, Inc. (P) and Marks (P) sought a class-action suit against Alcoa International Group, Inc. (D) for securities fraud.

CONCISE RULE OF LAW: A class-action suit must meet criteria for numerosity, commonality, adequacy, and typicality.

FACTS: Investment Corporation of America, Inc. (P) and Marks (P) consolidated their individual claims against Alcoa (D) and its officers and directors for securities fraud. They then sought to certify a class action which included all persons who purchased Alcoa stock between June 1, 1992 and March 29, 1993. Plaintiffs alleged that Alcoa (D) engaged in a scheme of issuing a series of false and misleading statements which artificially inflated Alcoa (D) stock. Alcoa (D) objected that plaintiffs failed to meet criteria to establish a class action.

ISSUE: Is a class-action suit established when the criteria for numerosity, commonality, adequacy, and typicality are met?

HOLDING AND DECISION: (Turrentine, J.) Yes. A class action suit which meets criteria for numerosity, commonality, adequacy, and typicality satisfies Fed. R. Civ. P. 23. This action meets each of the criteria: (1) the class is so numerous that joinder of all members is impractical because they exceed 4,000 members; (2) questions of law or fact are common to the class as defendants issued a series of press releases and public statements; (3) claims of the representative parties are typical of the claims of the class since plaintiffs allege they are victims of a common course of conduct by defendants; (4) representative parties fairly and adequately represent the interests of the class because plaintiffs' attorneys are experienced in securities litigation and no antagonistic interests are present; and (5) Rule 23(b)(3) is satisfied as plaintiffs have demonstrated that common questions predominate as each plaintiff is united in its desire to prove defendants' complicity. Motion ordered.

EDITOR'S ANALYSIS: Class actions seeking damages based upon diversity of citizenship are very rare in the federal court because each plaintiff must present a claim which exceeds the jurisdictional limit of $50,000 as plaintiffs may not aggregate their claims. Damage claims and injunctive relief claims based upon federal law are far more common.

[For more information on class actions, see Casenote Law Outline on Civil Procedure, Chapter 6, § IV, Additional Procedural Devices for Joinder of Parties.]

QUICKNOTES

CLASS ACTION SUIT - A suit commenced by a representative on behalf of an ascertainable group that is too large to appear in court, who shares a commonality of interests and who will benefit from a successful result.

FRCP 23 - Sets forth the requirements in order to maintain a class action suit.

NOTES:

IN RE RHONE-POULENC RORER, INC.

AID's infected hemophiliac (P) v. Drug companies (D)

51 F.3d 1293 (7th Cir. 1995).

NATURE OF CASE: Petition for a writ of mandamus by defendant drug companies asking the court of appeals to direct the district court judge to rescind his order certifying a mass tort case as a class action.

FACT SUMMARY: A plaintiff class of hemophiliacs infected by the AIDS virus brought a class action against the drug companies (D) that manufactured blood solids to treat hemophilia. The drug companies (D) sought a writ of mandamus directing the district judge to decertify the plaintiff class.

CONCISE RULE OF LAW: A judge may issue a writ of mandamus directing a lower judge to decertify class action if allowing the class action would cause irreparable harm to the defendants and the certification far exceeded the bounds of judicial discretion.

FACTS: The plaintiff class (P) was a group of hemophiliacs who were infected with the AIDS virus through blood transfusions. They brought a class action in tort against the drug companies (D) who manufactured the blood solids that carried the virus. The drug companies (D) filed a petition for mandamus asking the court of appeals to direct the district judge to rescind his order certifying the case as a class action.

ISSUE: When a judge's certification of a class action would cause irreparable harm to defendants and the order far exceeds the proper bounds of judicial discretion, may a superior judge issue a writ of mandamus directing that judge to rescind his order?

HOLDING AND DECISION: (Posner, J.) Yes. When the certification of a case as a class action would cause irreparable harm to the defendants and the certification is a clear abuse of judicial discretion, a superior judge may issue a writ of mandamus directing the district judge to rescind his certification order. First, the potential harm to the drug companies (D) in this class action is enormous, even if a vast majority of the causes of action are nonmeritorious. The drug companies (D) could be forced to settle with the entire plaintiff class (P) to avoid exorbitant litigation fees or the possibility of one jury decision wiping out their entire industry. Second, the district court judge abused his discretion by joining this hodgepodge of claims as a class action. The judge is forcing the drug companies (D) to stake their livelihood on the outcome of a single jury trial. The fear of bankruptcy might force the drug companies (D) to settle, even if they are not in the wrong. Also, the district judge's plan forces the merging of fifty different state negligence standards. This application of a general common law violates the holding of Erie v. Tompkins, 304 U.S. 64 (1938). Lastly, the judge exceeded his authority by dividing the

trial to resolve certain issues in the class action and others in individual suits. The likelihood that many of the same issues will be tried by different juries violates the Seventh Amendment right of defendants to have juriable issues decided by the first jury empaneled to hear them. Petition for mandamus is granted, and the district court judge is directed to decertify the plaintiff class.

DISSENT: (Rovner, J.) The majority overstepped its bounds by issuing a writ of mandamus because there is not sufficient evidence to show that the defendants will suffer irreparable harm. Also, although there are many criticisms of class actions, the district judge's plan does not violate Fed. R. Civ. P. 23.

EDITOR'S ANALYSIS: Ordinarily, the decision of a district court judge to certify a class is a nonappealable interlocutory order. However, Judge Posner used his mandamus power to circumvent this rule, claiming that the potential of a large damage award could force a settlement and cause irreparable harm to the defendants. This decision sets a dangerous precedent since most class actions involve the possibility of large damage awards. Courts must determine the point at which potential damages become too coercive to allow the defendants a fair trial.

QUICKNOTES

CLASS ACTION - A suit commenced by a representative on behalf of an ascertainable group that is too large to appear in court, who shares a commonality of interests and who will benefit from a successful result.

INTERLOCUTORY (ORDER) - An order entered by the court determining an issue that does not resolve the disposition of the case, but is essential to a proper adjudication of the action.

FRCP 23 - Sets forth the requirements in order to maintain a class action suit.

NOTES:

HANSBERRY v. LEE
Black land purchaser (D) v. Party to covenant (P)
311 U.S. 32 (1940).

NATURE OF CASE: A class action to enforce a racially restrictive covenant.

FACT SUMMARY: Lee (P) sought to enjoin a sale of land to Hansberry (D) on the grounds that the sale violated a racially restrictive covenant.

CONCISE RULE OF LAW: There must be adequate representation of the members of a class action or the judgment is not binding on the parties not adequately represented.

FACTS: Hansberry (D), a black, purchased land from a party who had signed a restrictive covenant forbidding the sale of the land to blacks. Lee (P), one of the parties who signed the covenant, sought to have the sale enjoined because it breached the covenant. Lee (P) contended that the validity of the covenant was established in a prior case in which one of the parties was a class of landowners involved with the covenant. To be valid, 95% of the landowners had to sign the covenant, and the trial court in the prior case held that 95% of the landowners had signed the covenant. That case was appealed, and the Illinois Supreme Court upheld the decision, even though they found that 95% of the landowners had not signed the covenant, but they held that since it was a class action, all members of the class would be bound by the decision of the court. Hansberry (D) claimed that he and the party selling him the house were not bound by the res judicata effect of the prior decision, as they were not parties to the litigation. The lower court held that the decision of the Illinois Supreme Court would have to be challenged directly in order that it be set aside or reversed. Otherwise, their decision was still binding. The case was appealed to the United States Supreme Court.

ISSUE: For a judgment in a class action to be binding, must all of the members of the class be adequately represented by parties with similar interests?

HOLDING AND DECISION: (Stone, J.) Yes. It is not necessary that all members of a class be present as parties to the litigation to be bound by the judgment if they are adequately represented by parties who are present. In regular cases, to be bound by the judgment the party must receive notice and an opportunity to be heard. If due process is not afforded the individual, then the judgment is not binding. The class action is an exception to the general rule. Because of the numbers involved in class actions, it is enough if the party is adequately represented by a member of the class with a similar interest. Hansberry (D) was not adequately represented by the class of landowners. Their interests were not similar enough to even be considered members of the same class. Lee (P) and the landowners were trying to restrict blacks from buying any of the land, and Hansberry (D) was a black attempting to purchase land. When there is such a conflicting interest between members of a class, there is most likely not adequate representation of one of the members of the class. There must be a similarity of interest before there can even be a class. Since there was no similarity of interests between Lee (P) and Hansberry (D), Hansberry (D) could not be considered a member of the class and so the prior judgment was not binding on Hansberry (D). Hansberry (D) was not afforded due process because of the lack of adequate representation. The judgment is reversed.

EDITOR'S ANALYSIS: Rule 23(c)(3) requires that the court describe those whom the court finds to be members of the class. The court is to note those to whom notice was provided and also those who had not requested exclusion. These members are considered members of the class and are bound by the decision of the court whether it is in their favor or not. The federal rules allow a member of the class to request exclusion from the class, and that party will not be bound by the decision of the court. Since a party must receive notice of the class action before he can request exclusion from the class, the court must determine if a party received sufficient notice of the action or if sufficient effort was made to notify him of the action. The rules state if the court finds that the party did have sufficient notice and was considered a member of the class, he is bound by the decision.

[For more information on class action, see Casenote Law Outline on Civil Procedure, Chapter 6, Joinder of Claims and Parties, § IV, Additional Procedural Devices for Joinder of Parties.]

QUICKNOTES

CLASS ACTION - A suit commenced by a representative on behalf of an ascertainable group that is too large to appear in court, who shares a commonality of interests and who will benefit from a successful result.

FRCP 23 - Sets forth the requirements in order to maintain a class action suit.

COVENANT - A written promise to do, or to refrain from doing, a particular activity.

PHILLIPS PETROLEUM v. SHUTTS
Gas and oil company (D) v. Class of lessees (P)
472 U.S. 797 (1985).

NATURE OF CASE: Appeal of a judgment in a class action suit.

FACT SUMMARY: Shutts (P) filed a class action suit against Phillips Petroleum (D) for allegedly underpaying royalties on gas leases.

CONCISE RULE OF LAW: A state may exercise jurisdiction over absent plaintiffs in a classification suit even if the plaintiffs have no contacts with that state.

FACTS: Phillips Petroleum (D) had gas and mineral leases with numerous individuals. Royalties were based on the selling price of the final product. When prices were raised, Phillips (D) would often pay royalties at a lower price. Shutts (P) filed a class action suit on behalf of over 33,000 individuals, seeking damages. A Kansas court certified the class. Letters were sent to all members of the plaintiff class. A plaintiff had the right to opt out of the class or be bound by the judgment. About 3,000 opted out. A judgment for the plaintiffs was entered. The Kansas Supreme Court rejected an appeal by Phillips (D) claiming that Kansas could not exercise jurisdiction over plaintiffs not residents of Kansas. Phillips (D) appealed to the U.S. Supreme Court.

ISSUE: May a state exercise jurisdiction over absent plaintiffs in a class action suit, if the plaintiffs have no contacts with that state?

HOLDING AND DECISION: (Rehnquist, J.) Yes. A state may exercise jurisdiction over absent plaintiffs in a class action suit even if the plaintiffs have no contacts with that state. The "minimum contacts" rule is a matter of personal liberty, not state sovereignty. It exists to protect defendants from being hauled into a distant forum unfairly. A plaintiff in a class action suit is in a much different position. He is in no danger of a loss of freedom or assets and, in fact, can sit back and let others do the work for him. His ability to opt out of the class further protects him; he is not forced to enter a class unwillingly. Affirmed.

EDITOR'S ANALYSIS: The Court stated in this opinion that minimum contacts is an issue of liberty, not sovereignty. This issue has been touched upon since Pennoyer v. Neff. The Court here held that the opt out procedure was a sufficient protection of personal liberty.

[For more information on class actions and minimum contacts with forum state, see Casenote Law Outline on Civil Procedure, Chapter 6, Joinder of Claims and Parties, § IV, Additional Procedural Devices for Joinder of Parties.]

QUICKNOTES

MINIMUM CONTACTS - The minimum degree of contact necessary in order to sustain a cause of action within a particular forum, consistent with the requirements of due process.

CLASS ACTION - A suit commenced by a representative on behalf of an ascertainable group that is too large to appear in court, who shares a commonality of interests and who will benefit from a successful result.

NOTES:

GEORGINE v. ACHEM PRODUCTS

Court (P) v. Consolidated asbestos companies (D)

157 F.R.D. 246 (E.D. Penn. 1994).

NATURE OF CASE: Motion for class certification and court approval of settlement agreement in mass tort action.

FACT SUMMARY: The district court was asked to approve a global settlement that would settle both existing claims of asbestos victims and those which had not been filed.

CONCISE RULE OF LAW: A class settlement agreement may be approved by the court if it is fair, adequate, and reasonable.

FACTS: Several cases were consolidated which involved asbestos-related injuries or deaths against twenty defendant companies represented by the Center for Claims Resolution (D) (CCR). CCR (D) indicated it was unwilling to settle the present claims unless the plaintiffs formed a class action suit and agreed to a settlement agreement that encompassed the presently injured plaintiffs as well as a class of potential claimants. Notice was personally given to future claimants who could be so identified, and a mass media campaign was used to provide notice to all others that they could opt out of the class. Approximately 201,654 of a potential class of possibly twenty million claimants chose to opt out of the class. Those objecting to the settlement asserted that plaintiffs' counsel was not adequately representing future claimants and that the settlement agreement was unfair to future claimants.

ISSUE: May a class settlement agreement that is fair, adequate and reasonable be approved by the court?

HOLDING AND DECISION: (Reed, J.) Yes. A class settlement agreement that is fair, adequate, and reasonable may be approved by the court. In deciding fairness, the court balances the strength of the claims of the class against benefits to be provided by settlement. Present asbestos-tort victims are subjected to a long court process, and there is uncertainty as to verdict results and funds received. Under the settlement agreement, asbestos claimants need only prove injury to receive prompt cash compensation. Another subsidiary factor the court may consider in deciding fairness is the experience of those that negotiated the agreement and how the negotiations proceeded. Here, counsel is experienced and the negotiation process was long and deliberative. Motion granted.

EDITOR'S ANALYSIS: This case demonstrates that many defendants prefer certainty over risk of the unknown. The trial court plays an important role in managing a class action suit and approving the settlement agreement. The court may divide a class into subclasses to overcome a potential conflict of interest. If a class action is certified under Fed. R. Civ. P. 23(b)(3), members of the class must be given notice of their right to opt out of the class.

[For more information on class actions, see Casenote Law Outline on Civil Procedure, Chapter 6, § IV, Additional Procedural Devices for Joinder of Parties.]

QUICKNOTES

FED. R. CIV. P. 23 (b) (3) - Type of class action when common questions of law or fact predominate and class action procedure is superior to other means of adjucating the controversy.

CLASS ACTION - A suit commenced by a representative on behalf of an ascertainable group that is too large to appear in court, who shares a commonality of interests and who will benefit from a successful result.

SETTLEMENT - An agreement entered into by the parties to a civil lawsuit agreeing upon the determination of rights and issues between them, thus disposing of the need for judicial determination.

NOTES:

NOTES

NOTES

ABBREVIATIONS FOR BRIEFING

The following list of abbreviations will assist you in the process of briefing and provide an illustration of the technique of formulating functional personal abbreviations for commonly encountered words, phrases, and concepts.

acceptance	acp	offer	O
affirmed	aff	offeree	OE
answer	ans	offeror	OR
assumption of risk	a/r	ordinance	ord
attorney	atty	pain and suffering	p/s
beyond a reasonable doubt	b/r/d	parol evidence	p/e
bona fide purchaser	BFP	plaintiff	P
breach of contract	br/k	prima facie	p/f
cause of action	c/a	probable cause	p/c
common law	c/l	proximate cause	px/c
Constitution	Con	real property	r/p
constitutional	con	reasonable doubt	r/d
contract	K	reasonable man	r/m
contributory negligence	c/n	rebuttable presumption	rb/p
cross	x	remanded	rem
cross-complaint	x/c	res ipsa loquitur	RIL
cross-examination	x/ex	respondent superior	r/s
cruel and unusual punishment	c/u/p	Restatement	RS
defendant	D	reversed	rev
dismissed	dis	Rule Against Perpetuities	RAP
double jeopardy	d/j	search and seizure	s/s
due process	d/p	search warrant	s/w
equal protection	e/p	self-defense	s/d
equity	eq	specific performance	s/p
evidence	ev	statute of limitations	S/L
exclude	exc	statute of frauds	S/F
exclusionary rule	exc/r	statute	S
felony	f/m	summary judgment	s/j
freedom of speech	f/s	tenancy in common	t/c
good faith	g/f	tenancy at will	t/w
habeas corpus	h/c	tenant	t
hearsay	hr	third party	TP
husband	H	third party beneficiary	TPB
in loco parentis	ILP	transferred intent	TI
injunction	inj	unconscionable	uncon
inter vivos	I/v	unconstitutional	unconst
joint tenancy	j/t	undue influence	u/e
judgment	judgt	Uniform Commercial Code	UCC
jurisdiction	jur	unilateral	uni
last clear chance	LCC	vendee	VE
long-arm statute	LAS	vendor	VR
majority view	maj	versus	v
meeting of minds	MOM	void for vagueness	VFV
minority view	min	weight of the evidence	w/e
Miranda warnings	Mir/w	weight of authority	w/a
Miranda rule	Mir/r	wife	W
negligence	neg	with	w/
notice	mtc	within	w/I
nuisance	nus	without prejudice	w/o/p
obligation	ob	without	w/o
obscene	obs	wrongful death	wr/d